STILL ON RECORD

The Return of the Archivist

by

Berwick Coates

Published by Paragon Publishing, Rothersthorpe
First published 2018

© Berwick Coates 2018

The rights of Berwick Coates to be identified as the author of this work have been asserted by him in accordance with the Copyright, Designs and Patents Act of 1988.

All rights reserved; no part of this publication may be reproduced, stored in a retrieval system, or transmitted in any form or by any means, electronic, mechanical, photocopying, recording or otherwise without the prior written consent of the publisher or a licence permitting copying in the UK issued by the Copyright Licensing Agency Ltd. www.cla.co.uk

ISBN 978-1-78222-596-6

CONTENTS

	Introduction	4
1	2000	6
2	2001	18
3	2002	40
4	2003	66
5	2004	85
6	2005	104
7	2006	127
8	2007	141
9	2008	157
10	2009	174
11	2010	189
12	2011	209
13	2012	222
14	2013	246
15	2014	257
16	2015	264
	Acknowledgements	279

1. Introduction

THOSE OF YOU WHO were lucky enough to make the acquaintance of the previous book of this series (of two) – *Nearly off the Record* – will know what to expect with this one, given the closeness of the two titles to each other.

To those poor souls who are languishing in the darkest limbo of ignorance, I must explain that, when the teaching dried up in my part-time, post-retirement employment, the Headmaster offered me the chance to set up a school archive. The school did not have an archive, and I did not have any professional archivist's experience or qualifications, so it was going to be a 'seat-of-the-pants' job. But I was a historian, and I had published books, so I was off to some kind of start. Better, I was given complete freedom to tackle it any way I liked.

One of the first things I discovered was that a large part of my work was to be taken up with solving the problem of making people simply aware that a school archive existed, and might have some kind of relevance or use. To that end, in the course of the next decade or so, I wrote articles for the press and local magazines; I provided ammunition for the Head's speeches on formal occasions when some reference to the school's history was required; I gave talks to groups and parties connected with the school; I spoke at various formal occasions – to old boys' dinners and lunches, parents' gatherings, the school's masonic lodge, and local history clubs; I took school assemblies.

I published books about the school – three of them. A fourth book dealt with making public much of the work described in the previous paragraph. Hence the title: *Nearly off the Record*. And the subtitle: *The Archives of an Archivist*.

An idea persisted. It occurred to me that there was one more book left to be written. Over the years, in my campaign to make the work of the Archive known to the Common Room, and maybe generate interest, I had, regularly, put up on the notice board inconsequential one-page items, jokes, squibs, scraps, odds and ends which purveyed titbits of gossip, scandal, sadness, humour, and, often, generally useless information – anything to make colleagues pause before them just for a few seconds, in the hope that they might generate interest, offer an insight, suggest a line of thought, or perhaps just crack a smile.

Once published, the book, I hoped, would still have a sort of shelf-life, with some attraction to anyone connected with the school – say, colleagues sitting back with a cup of coffee during the morning break. Brief, to the point, and, I hope, undemanding. But nevertheless worth a glance.

And here it is. Start anywhere you like.

The year printed under the chapter headings simply refers to the year in which I put those entries on the Common Room notice board. It seemed as good a system as any for dividing up the book. The length of the chapters is not uniform, because some material had outlived its point, had become irrelevant, or reflected an 'in' joke which would lose its force if one had to explain it at length . So it could not be used.

1. 2000

You win some, you lose some

IN OCTOBER, 1913, THE school magazine reported that the long, hot summer had made the wickets extremely dry and hard. (They must have broken bowlers' hearts. Scores were up in the stratosphere for boys' cricket.) Some games took several days to finish. The total number of runs scored in only five inter-house matches was 2,451.

In the fourth, between Brereton and Fortescue houses, the total numbers of runs scored was 770. And Brereton won by 2 runs.

[A near-unbelievable nail-biter. If a writer had put that in a story, no editor would have accepted it.]

And Brereton still weren't finished: in their junior match with Courtenay house, they dismissed their opponents for 0. That is, zero, nought, nothing, all eleven – nobody scored. Not even extras.

[In the early days of the school, there were no boundaries to the cricket fields. Every single run had to be physically run. Think of 2,451 runs – all run. Somebody in an Old Boys' match in 1885 hit a five – *all run*. It must have been a fearsome wallop.

[The school authorities were clearly very lenient in allowing these matches to go on as long as they did. But this was the high-water-mark of the British Empire, which, we all know, was built on the Trivium of Classics, Cricket, and Christianity. And for developing a boy's character, there was no doubt as to which of the three was the greatest agent.]

Here's to the School

TWENTY-EIGHT YEARS AFTER THE school was founded, a very public-spirited old boy called Richard Pearse Chope (more of him later) organised the very first Old Boys' Dinner.

They did it in style – London (of course). On Monday, 20th December, 1886. (Odd how many of the early dinners were held on a Monday.) In the Holborn Restaurant, with 'entrances in High Holborn and Little Queen Street', as the programme helpfully mentioned. In the 'Prince of Wales' Salon', too. Notice the apostrophe. Without it, it would mean simply a room named *after* the Prince of Wales. *With* the apostrophe, it seems as if His Royal Highness had kindly lent his own personal accommodation for the occasion. A nice touch.

Old Boys' dinners continued to be held in the Holborn Restaurant right up to the First World War, and in the Archive are several huge photographs of the members, resplendent in boiled shirts and white ties, with moustaches, wine bottles, and cigars all over the place. There even survive covers in tracing paper over the print, with the numbers marked of every man present, and a key of names provided. Chope's work, almost without a doubt.

It must have been some evening. The Chairman was Rev. J.H. Thompson, M.A. – the first headmaster. Appointed aged 21 in 1858. With no degree and no dog collar – which was a bit *avant-garde* for headmasters in those days. However, he did later take both holy orders and a degree, which showed that he was swung by tradition in the end. He was still in office in 1886. Though he did go two years later.

Among the committee was Mr. Michael Bowden Snell, the first winner of the Fortescue Medal, presented and named after Earl Fortescue, the school's adjacent aristocrat (about two miles up the road) and regular benefactor. It was, and remains, the highest award in the school's gift.

Secretary was the industrious Mr. Chope, who, later, during his term of office as President, raised the membership of the Association from 100 to 320. At other dinners, he used to give recitations in the Devon dialect, on which he was an acknowledged authority. He was a formidable and unstoppable presence for years at every big school function. Considering that he lived in Hartland, and that Hartland had no railway station (not even in the halcyon days of ubiquitous line construction in the late nineteenth century), it speaks volumes for his energy and resilience. Oh – and he regularly commuted to London, to the Patent Office, where he worked all his life. It is impossible in this small context to do him justice, but I have attempted it elsewhere. (See *The Natural History of a Country School*, published in 2005 by Woodfield Publishing.)

Well, now – the dinner. It had seven courses.

Soup – two on offer – 'Calf's tail à la Regent' and 'Spring à la Royale'. They put an accent over the 'a' but not over the 'e' in 'Régent'. Nowadays we don't have 'calf's tail' (well not that I know of); we have vulgar oxtail. And what is 'Spring' – 'à la Royale'?

Fish – 'Cod and Shrimp Sauce', and, *underneath*, 'Whitebait'. Not whitebait with cod and shrimp sauce; but cod and shrimp sauce on whitebait. Ah, well. . .

Entrées – now we are getting down to the serious business. 'Lamb Cutlets and Peas' (when did you last see humble peas awarded a capital letter?), accompanied (or followed – it is not clear) with 'Pigeons Sauté and Mushrooms'. (It sounds a mite pedantic, but, if they had managed to put the accent in 'Sauté', they might have put the 's' on the end to make the adjective agree, don't you think?) Tut, tut.

Then came the 'Removes'. Well, that's what it says – 'Removes'. 'Ribs of Beef and Horseradish.' Now we're in a comfort zone. But why 'Removes'? I've never heard of it on a menu, but that may simply show my ignorance, or my proletarian upbringing. The Oxford Dictionary says a 'remove' was/is 'the act of taking away a dish or course in order to bring on another in its place'; especially a 'dish taken away or brought on in this way'.

But surely every dish is taken away and replaced by another. Unless they used the same plates for soup and entrées. Which sounds rather off for a posh place like the Holborn Restaurant – Prince of Wales' salon and all.

There was another 'Remove' too – 'Boiled Turkey and Celery Sauce', and 'Ham and Madeira'.

VEGETABLES got a different paragraph to themselves, and a title in capital letters too – 'Plain Potatoes'. Plain – slumming it a bit after the 'pigeons sauté' and the 'spring à la Royale'. But they did offer 'Potatoes Sauté' too. They did like their 'sauté'. Finally, 'Brussels Sprouts'. Predictable enough.

'SWEETS' offered 'Mince Pies, Plum Pudding, Macédoine Jelly, Ice Pudding, and Cheese, and Celery'.

Finally, there was a section entitled 'DESSERTS', but, after the 'SWEETS', what did they have to offer by way of tantalising novelty, especially after the 'Removes' and 'Calf's Tail' and the 'Ice Pudding'?

And that, as they say, was only the half of it. There were the toasts – to the Queen and Royal Family, and the Old Boys, both proposed by the Chairman and replied to by Dr. G.W. Hill and Mr. J. Waldon (one of the first three pupils of the school in 1858). Mr. Snell proposed the school, and two teachers replied. Finally, there was the usual admin. about the next meeting and so on.

It must have been interminable. Yet, at the bottom of the menu page, there is a crisp note to the effect the 'Service of Wine closes at 12 o'clock, and the whole Building at 12.30. On Saturdays, thirty minutes earlier'. Perhaps that was why they had the dinner on a Monday. But – forgive the pun – how did they pack it all in?

Making the punishment fit the crime

THE *REGISTER* (THE SCHOOL magazine) of March, 1925 printed a report of the previous term's production of *The Mikado*. The Headmaster, the Revd. E.C. Harries ('Ernie" to one and all), was crackers about Gilbert and Sullivan, and inspired a production of one of their comic operas every year from 19i5 to 1934. When one considers the school's modest finances, the near-total absence of females on the campus, the fact that the musical contribution stemmed almost exclusively from the pianistic talent of the music master, Mr. Watson (who was to become the longest-serving teacher in the school's history – 42 years), and the modest dramatic gifts of the average philistine boarding schoolboy, it remains a remarkable achievement.

The *Register* claimed that there was a 'large audience' for each performance, which says a lot too for the sales technique of the school's publicity department, who persuaded so many parents to make the nine-mile journey from Barnstaple to the edge of Exmoor, when the average family did not possess a motor car. An added attraction may have been the 'recent installation of electric light', which 'enabled us to produce a number of stage effects'. Up to 1923, the school had employed a special servant whose sole job was to go round and trim all the oil lamps.

It is difficult for us now, inured to and *blasé* about endless 'special effects', Cinerama, three-D, Panavision, lasers, Bluetooth, quadrophonic sound, and I don't know what, to appreciate the appetite for this modest entertainment that existed in a rural environment like North Devon between the wars (even more so, of course, in the nineteenth century).

The productions were hardly the Old Vic, but that was not the point. For a start, and obviously, fond parents were prepared to tackle a long journey, and a creaky performance, in order to witness the performances of their offspring. For those boarding parents who lived a long way away, perhaps it was a rare opportunity to see their sons at all. Secondly, apart from an occasional visit to the cinema, perhaps a Christmas pantomime, the annual fair, and of course the County Show, there wasn't much else. But, such was the face-to-face intimacy of a rural community, and sense of local identity, that, like domestic servants from Edwardian London licking ice cream on Southend Pier on their annual half-day off, everybody went determined to have a good time – with perhaps just the occasional wince.

For once the Headmaster did not play the lead. He did do it but not in 1924. We have group photographs of many of the casts over the years, and there, in the middle, is 'Ernie', as Major-General Stanley, the Lord Chancellor, or the captain of the *Pinafore*. But it is hard to deny such a busy, dedicated man the chance of a modest ego trip; after all, he had inspired all these ambitious projects, he worked tirelessly on them, and he was clearly passionate about them. And he expected everybody to commit themselves in the same way. They usually did. Nobody was allowed to slide out of a rehearsal, much less a performance, on the grounds of ill health, for instance. Apparently, if the weather showed signs of becoming threatening, all the *young* cast at least had to report to the Headmaster's house, where his wife ('Ellie' to everybody – a good pair, eh? – Ernie and Ellie) doled out some hideously unpalatable concoction which prevented or cured everything from chills and ills to pains and sprains.

However, as I said, this time the leading part, the Mikado, the Emperor of Japan, was played by a French teacher, Mr. T.C. Bellot. He enjoyed the enigmatic nickname of 'Inky'. This puzzled me for a long time, until one day I realised that there were two ways of pronouncing his name – either as '*Bell*ot', with the stress on the first syllable, or as 'Bell*ot*', with the stress on the second. So think about it – Bell*ot* – Blot – Inky. QED.

Chorus parts were relatively straightforward. It didn't matter much if there were a lot of near-tone-deaf boys; their approximate unison got close enough to the score, and some heavy left-hand octaves from Mr. Watson no doubt produced some useful camouflage.

For female chorus parts, there was no shortage of pre-pubertal treble voices; boys tended to mature later in those days. And Ellie's firewater ensured that the vocal chords were in good shape on the night.

For principal parts, it was members of staff, a few wives (there was one female teacher at the time, and she had no choice in the matter), and the occasional musical old boy, who was brought back to the boards by sentiment, nostalgia, and the chance of local, albeit short-lived, celebrity.

One of the 'three little maids from school' was Charles Penny, who wrote to me about this performance, which had taken place at Christmas, 1924. Mr. Penny was still alive 76 years later.

Another young chorus member recalled that he had to do duty as a fairy in a production (*Iolanthe?*). During one performance, his costume caught fire. He tried to save himself by wrapping himself in the front curtain. In his urgency, he overbalanced, and fell out of the wings on to the keys of the piano (poor Mr. Watson). 'Up dashed. . . the French master,' he said, 'who lifted me up, put his arms round me, kissed me on both cheeks, said "Oh, pouf!" and extinguished the flames.'

Could it have been our dear Inky? Oh, one does hope so.

The total cost of staging *The Mikado* was 121 pounds, 2 shillings, and ninepence. This was met by six pounds, fourteen shillings, and eightpence balance in hand, and ninety-six pounds, eight shillings and a penny receipts at the door. (Why that odd penny?)

If you are quick with your sums, you will note that there was a shortfall of eighteen pounds. This was met by the balance from a whist drive and dance. A whist drive and dance – isn't that lovely?

Worthy of his hire

EXPECTEDLY, TEACHERS DISCUSS SALARIES from time to time. This usually happens when union negotiations with the government are in the news. There are the usual righteous huffing and puffing on one side, and bland platitudes about difficult times for the Treasury on the other. So, just for a bit of fun (or mischief?), I put on the board details of what an assistant teacher was paid in a school like this early in the twentieth century.

There is in the Archive a hefty book, recording the particulars of the staff. It was begun by Ernie Harries (who began quite a lot of things when he arrived in 1907).

From that date, till about the 1950's, each teacher's particulars were set there, in handwritten ink, if not in stone. For each member of staff, one can see obvious things like date of birth, date of appointment (as opposed to 'date of *definitive* appointment' – to do with salaries and contracts, I should guess), special subjects, duties assigned, and so on. It can also be revealing to read how very often the teacher's formal qualifications did not match up with the subjects he was called upon to teach. This was a regular phenomenon among the education profession right through the twentieth century, and, for all I know, still is.

I have taken at random the record of Mr. Herbert Powell. The Christian name Herbert dates it at once. Boys don't get christened 'Herbert' now. And the dates bear this out. Herbert was born on 11th June, 1891. He was appointed on 19th September, 1914, and 'definitively' appointed on 18th October of the same year.

So he was young, barely out of university. His record supports this. He had only one previous appointment recorded, at the High School for Boys in Norwich, from 1913 to 1914. One wonders what on earth induced him to apply to a school right across the entire breadth of the country?

He had been educated at Caterham School in Surrey, which placed him firmly in the south-east quarter of England. Yet he took his degree at University College of Wales, from 1909 to 1913. So he had already crossed the country once to go to university, and again to work in Norfolk. Perhaps he liked change.

He was certainly going to get challenge. The record says that he had to teach Science right through the whole school, with Set A Maths for good measure. (There hadn't been a Science teacher at all till the first decade of the century.) The school wasn't very big then – a whisker away from 120 up to the First World War. He had to live in too.

The boarding part of the school – over ninety per cent of it – needed resident staff, and young graduates were the obvious candidates. They couldn't get anywhere anyway. Nobody then had motor cars – well, certainly not teachers. There were no bus services from Barnstaple to places like West Buckland. (Nor are there today to a host of outlying villages in Devon.) They would have to be iron-limbed cyclists to reach South Molton (six miles one way) or Barnstaple (nine the other) – every day. Thank God there was a railway, but the station was two miles away at Filleigh. These young men were almost as imprisoned as the boarders. Of course they involved themselves with the boys; there wasn't much else to do.

So the school got its money's worth. The last entries at the bottom of the page tell us that Herbert's annual salary was £140. To put this in perspective, the old age pension, awarded for the first time in 1908, was five shillings a week (25p.). Even the Headmaster was getting no more than £210 p.a., in 1922. This was *after* the First World War, and eight years after Herbert was appointed. And Harries had just been given a rise.

Herbert could expect an increment of £10 p.a. at the end of the first year, and £5 per year thereafter. Five pounds – as an increment for a whole year. It is true that he was given board and lodging, and this was displayed as being worth £50 a year. So, if he was willing to cycle every day to and from digs in Barnstaple, or any village in between, and buy and cook his own meals, he would get another fifty quid. Herbert joined the Army in 1915.

What governs the governors?

When the school was founded, it was a limited company, with shareholders and directors and dividends (there weren't many of those in the event). Until 1912, the school was known as the Devon County School (long story – see elsewhere), and in 1893, it published a set of 'Qualifications and Disqualifications of Governors' – just to make sure, as you might say. This section is an extract from the 'Articles of Association of the Devon County School'.

41. Every Governor shall hold at least two shares in the School. [Not exactly breaking the bank, is it?]

42. The office of Governor shall be vacated –

If he hold any office other than of Trustee or any place of profit under the School;

If he become bankrupt or put his affairs or estate in liquidation, or make an assignment for the benefit of or composition with his creditors whether under the bankruptcy law for the time being or otherwise;

If he be concerned in or participates in the profits of any contract with the School;

If he become lunatic [one hopes that the contingency would have been remote];

If he be absent from Meetings of the Governors for 12 months (except for causes to be approved by the Board);

If he resign his office;

If he cease to be a registered holder of two shares in the School;

If he become incapable to act, such incapacity to be determined by the unanimous vote of such of the other Governors as may be present at a Meeting to be convened for the purpose. [This looks decidedly dodgy. If you wanted to get rid of a governor, all you had to do was get a couple of the lads together quickly without telling anyone else, and get them to vote 'unanimously', and bingo – he's gone. To repeat, very dodgy.]

It would be interesting to know if a school governor has even been dismissed for 'lunacy'.

The Bard at West Buckland

FOR A WHILE, I conducted a sort of running joke based on the spurious theory that William Shakespeare had attended the school – if only for a short while before or after his sojourn at Stratford Grammar School. From time to time I posted little squibs to 'prove' that our William had actually been a pupil here.

Like these:

He was once in a school play, as evidenced by his line: 'Let me not play a woman; I have a beard coming.'

Or his appearance at the cricket nets: 'Good words are better than bad strokes.'

As a prize for identifying the quotations, I offered a free visit to the West Buckland Archive Theme Park Experience.

Your past will catch up with you

GOVERNORS' MINUTES CAN BE a fruitful, enlightening, and often entertaining source of information.

One might expect Governors' meetings to be pretty ponderous occasions, with 'matters of great moment' being debated with suitable pomp and circumstance – lofty themes, world-affecting problems, mighty controversies, which could cause members' reactions to rise to the level of noble rhetoric.

Not so. It is remarkable how many entries are concerned with dormitories and kitchens and coal supplies and infectious diseases and drains – even 'cesspits'. (For years the school relied on springs for water; it used gas for lighting till 1923; and it still does not have access to mains sewerage.)

Other items can throw sharp light on social attitudes of the day. For instance, it was recorded that the caretaker was to get a salary rise. OK. But he was referred to as 'Hobbs'. Not as 'Jim Hobbs' or 'Mr. Hobbs', but plain 'Hobbs'. That produces several trains of thought.

Then again, skeletons can peep out of cupboards. We had a teacher who enjoyed a very long association with the school. His father, his grandfather, his great-uncles, and his sons all attended. But the association could not have been without incident. An entry from as far back as 1907 ruthlessly exposed the detail that this teacher's great-grandfather had got his name into the minutes because he had been dilatory in paying his sons' fees. Very dilatory. So much so that Minute 12 of the meeting of 23rd February declared that 'unless payment was made within a fortnight, it was decided to put the matter in the hands of' the school's solicitors'. That was good for a spot of ribbing.

The Minutes could be frustrating too.

One day, the Governors received a complaint about a head teacher who had several years of successful and popular leadership behind him. They investigated. At the end of the investigation, it was announced in the Minutes that no evidence could be found to substantiate the charges. Nevertheless, it said, the Governors had no option but to ask the Headmaster for his resignation.

Which they got. He left. And took half the school with him, to set up a school somewhere else. When the next headmaster took over, the number of remaining pupils had dropped to 31.

And we still don't know what he was supposed to have done.

2. 2001

Inflation and discrimination

MINUTE 14 OF THE Governors' Meeting of 23rd February, 1907 said, 'It was decided that £300 should be the maximum amount to be allowed for the salaries of Assistant Masters, excluding the Science Master.'

It was set out in the unfailingly fluent and handsome handwriting of the Secretary to the Governors', Mr. Adelbert Taylor, so there is no question as to its accuracy and reliability. Mr. Taylor was one of the most assiduous, conscientious, loyal, versatile, and long-serving masters in the school's history. He was a teacher from 1895 to 1929, when ill health forced his retirement. During that time, he did practically everything, including being the Choirmaster and the Secretary to the Governors. He was an institution, part of the furniture. His nickname was 'Judy' because, so it was said, he had a voice like that of Mr. Punch.

I labour the point about accuracy because of an entry in the previous chapter, which recorded that Mr. Herbert Powell, was awarded only £140 per annum, and that was seven years later, in 1914. How come?

How was it that assistant masters could expect to be paid up to £300 per annum, when they got less than half that only seven years before? And the Headmaster himself was getting barely more than £200. And why should the Science Master be so specially favoured? And, if that were so, how was it that Mr. Powell, who had been a science teacher, hadn't received anything like that? More inconsistency. Clearly something is not right.

Unless – unless – the £300 referred not to the individual salaries of assistant masters but *to the total*? We know that the staff was small, but was it that small? All right, so the Headmaster and the Second Master – and maybe the Chaplain (and perhaps some others) – did not count as 'assistants', and were paid at a different rate. But, if you had only £300 to play with for the rest, it would have been a bit of a squeeze get two salaries out of it. If the Governors had to extract *three* salaries from it, it speaks of belt-tightening and austerity and thrift on a truly Carthusian scale. These were men with degrees and diplomas. It shows how over-filled the profession seems to have been at that time, that these teachers were prepared to work for such a sum. And if Mr. Powell received £140 (bearing in mind what the Minute said), it puts a very different slant on it.

It was not the teacher who was under pressure; it was the school; Science teachers must have been very thin on the ground.

Indeed, Science teaching must have been pretty sparse, because there were no purpose-built laboratories till 1904, and Mr. Spicer, who was appointed in that year, was the first proper Science teacher the school had ever had.

Career Development

ELEANOR BENDALL WAS BORN on 27th May, 1886. She attended Redland High School, Bristol, from 1902 to 1903. (There is no mention of her education before that.) Unusually, the next entry on her career record states that she was a 'pensioner' at 'Les Lilas, Berne' and at the 'University of Berne'. The dates say she was there from 1905 to 1914, so it would seem that, after her time there as a student, she joined the staff (perhaps that was what 'Pensioner' meant). It certainly makes sense that she taught French, as the record shows.

In between these duties, she secured a Froebel certificate in 1912 and an English Diploma in 1913. Plus a kindergarten certificate.

Then she came home, served in Lindisfarne College, Westcliff-on-Sea from 1914 to 1915, and Dowers School, Colwall (wherever that was) for a year after that. In 1917 she turned up at a place called Stancliff Hall, Matlock. So our Eleanor got around.

On 8th May, 1918, she was appointed ('on probation') to the staff of West Buckland School – one of the very few female members of staff at that time. Hardly surprising, in an all-boys boarding school. The record also mentions that she was 'non-resident'. Concern for her virtue? One wonders. Her 'definitive' appointment was confirmed in July, 1920.

Which seems rather a long time. However, there were extenuating circumstances, of a most unusual kind: she got married. All right, nothing special about that. But it was *who* (or whom) she married. The Headmaster, no less – the Revd. Ernest Charles Harries. And they were married only three months after she joined the staff. The date was recorded, understandably, in the *Register*. So Ernie had not wasted much time. Perhaps he felt that, at fifty, he had better snap up a chance while the going was still good. Incidentally, she was thirty-two (jolly near the shelf in 1918), so perhaps the same comment could be applied to her.

It is possible, however, that the courtship had not been as whirlwind as it might seem. Eleanor had four brothers, who all had attended the school. So – though we don't know how intimately – Ernie had been acquainted with the family for a long time.

If he had in fact known them that well, and the darts of Cupid had already been flying for a while, it is not beyond the bounds of possibility that he had engineered her appointment in the first place. After all, a diploma from a Swiss university and a kindergarten certificate were not the normal credentials for a French teacher in a boys' boarding school.

That was not the end of the intriguing dimensions to this story. Eleanor ('Ellie', as she became to generations of boys) had a sister. And Ernie had a brother. Guess what. That's right: the *Register* of 1918 recorded a double marriage. Finally, both brothers were clergymen, so guess what again. They married each other.

Ellie's career was a long one; she died in December, 1985, five months short of her hundredth birthday.

Time Span

In 1930, the school had its first and (mercifully so far), its only fire.

Some classrooms were destroyed, the library, a few prefects' studies, and various other rooms and offices. By good luck, nobody was hurt. Well, perhaps it was not all luck; Headmaster Harries' dog, Bob, gave the alarm by barking. Very sensible of him.

It razed a large chunk of the frontage at the right end of the school as you look at it. Which was a pity, and not only for the obvious reasons. The façade had been constructed in the heyday of Victorian taste (if there is such a thing), which embraced massive stonework (Devon was not short of stones), hints of Gothic, and the inevitable pointy windows. It mellowed well with age, and displayed to the world a monument of solidity, tradition, confidence, and the certainty of being right.

To the next century, which was well disposed to venerate such permanence and age (particularly when so much of value in England had been destroyed in the wartime bombing), it represented so much that people thought was valuable – sound education, a country setting, beautifully pointed stone walls – with just a touch of Greyfriars. Nowadays, of course one can add to Greyfriars a veneer of Hogwarts.

From the road, the effect was sensational. It was everyone's pipe dream of what a traditional country school ought to look like. (It didn't pay to look too deeply round the back.)

So some restoration had to be done, and quickly, preferably in the traditional stonework of the original, if only to harmonise with it. And they certainly got on with it. There were to be more classrooms, some laboratories, and, at the end, to match the great Karslake dining hall at the *other* end, a pretty massive Memorial Hall, with a great big bow window. Did the word 'Memorial' spring from the idea of the rising of the school from the ashes, or did it take its inspiration from the First World War memorial cross right the across the drive barely twenty yards away? Or was it a neat way of encapsulating both? Whatever it was, it became, and remains, the Memorial Hall.

The foundation stone was laid by the fourth Earl Fortescue on the 12th October, 1932. Among the witnesses was a little girl of eight. She was the Earl's granddaughter, Margaret. In his speech, Lord Fortescue mentioned that he, when *he* was small, had witnessed the laying of the original foundation stone, in 1860, by *his* grandfather.

Lady Margaret Fortescue went on to be head of the family, a governor for 38 years, and a lifelong benefactor.

So, as a little girl of eight, this lady, who did not die till 2013, once sat on the knee of a gentleman who had witnessed the beginning of the school in 1860 – a span of 153 years. It brings history together wonderfully.

There were two tailpieces to this.

One concerned the stocking of the new library. West Buckland has never been what you might call flush with cash, so a smart device was found for re-filling the library shelves. For years afterwards, whenever a boy came up at later Speech Days to receive his prize (always a book), he was allowed to bask in a brief moment of glory as he descended the steps from the stage. When he reached the bottom, he was brought down to earth with a bump, when the 'prize' was promptly taken off him, and found its way immediately to the library.

The second appeared in the novel about the school by R.F. Delderfield, an old boy of the school – *To Serve Them All My Days*. It covered the years of the school's history between the wars. The fire happened in 1930, almost exactly midway. Of course it went in. What novelist could resist a tailor-made drama like that?

Keeping it in the family

ON 19TH JUNE, 2001, I put on the notice board a photostat copy of a share certificate pertaining to West Buckland School, or the Devon County School, as it was then. Pertaining, I should say, to the Devon County School Association, which was registered as a limited company. The school's finances were initially (well, till 1912) based on the contributions of those investors who thought it was worth buying shares in this new venture of middle-class education.

The shares cost five pounds apiece. This particular certificate, representing forty shares, recorded that it had been bought by Francis Lloyd Brereton, M.A. It was dated 7th July, 1890. So – forty shares at £5 a throw, in 1890, was a pretty sizeable sum.

Who was Francis Lloyd Brereton, and why did he buy them?

The co-founder of the school was the Revd. Joseph Lloyd Brereton. The other was the Fortescue family. Brereton was a lifelong friend of the third Earl. It was, in many ways, an ideal partnership: Brereton had the imagination and the vision; Fortescue had the money, the connections, and the general clout. The relationship was far from peaceful, but it was sincere, and it lasted all their lives.

Their contributions to the start, and the survival, of the school were indivisible, though different. It couldn't have been done without Fortescue's patience, persistence, and loyalty – and money; but, ultimately it was Brereton who produced the inspiration, the spark. He was the one touched by the muse.

There is an arguable comparison with the career of Joan of Arc. It was Dunois who did the solid campaigning and won the battles, but the magic came from Joan. Without it, they wouldn't have won.

So with Brereton. For all Fortescue's dedication and hard work and solid common sense (and appreciation of the value of money), it was Brereton who lit up the venture. If the second and third earl were the Father and Son of the West Buckland trinity, Brereton was the Holy Spirit.

And, as with the Holy Spirit, his spell continued to influence the school long after he had gone – influence it, sway it, inspire it, possibly, sometimes, be a burden to it. One of his grandsons said later that, even from the grave, the family could feel his influence.

And much of this influence came through the family, and the idea of family. It was an inescapable feature of the Victorian scene. We are all familiar with the clichés of the small phalanx of offspring grouped, high collared and obedient, round the table for grace, which was intoned by the awesome *paterfamilias*, whose authority was unquestioned, by his children, his servants, and, with few exceptions, by his wife.

Brereton's whole ancestry, upbringing, education, career, and philosophy threaded into this background with perfect smoothness and ease. He was born for it. He himself was one of eleven children. He (and his long-suffering wife) had sixteen. His father was a clergyman; so was he, once he had got over the disappointment of failing to secure an academic career (ill health prevented him from doing justice to himself in the university exams). Once established as Rector at West Buckland, he threw himself into noble enterprises and good causes everywhere – boys' education, girls' education, new farming methods, setting up a national system of county schools all over the country, travelling, writing, publicising, lobbying – he was unstoppable. All the more remarkable considering his early poor health; he had come down to Devon in the first place because of his weak lungs. The mind boggles at how many children he might have had if they had been strong.

It may be no coincidence that nineteenth-century clergymen had large families. Obviously the general level of understanding of the mechanics, and wariness of rhe morals, of birth control were pitiful by today's standards. So that accounted for a lot. But it is possible to make a case for clergymen in particular. They tended to live in large, gaunt, lofty rectories, where heating in the tall rooms must have been a permanent problem. So what did you do when it got too cold on a winter's evening? You went to bed. The will of the Lord, and biology, did the rest.

It would be an interesting project to work out how many clergymen's children were born between August and February.

Be that as it may, Brereton stitched his family into this life of effort and pioneering; they were all swept up into his campaigns. When Joseph Thompson, the first headmaster, came courting Brereton's eldest daughter Anna, he was told sharply by her father that it was not possible, because she was needed 'for the work'.

Brereton had seven surviving daughters, and only two made it to the altar. The other five spent their lives sitting round his table, stitching endless table mats, cutting endless cucumber sandwiches for church fetes, bestowing thousands of well-meaning favours round the village, and doing 'the work' – West Buckland till 1867, and thereafter at Little

Massingham in Norfolk, whither Brereton went to succeed his late father in the church. He, and they, spent the rest of his life there.

Many of his sons found themselves consumed in a similar way. Two became clergymen. Others became teachers. Some gained (or were pushed into) headships in various of his new county schools. It went on beyond the first generation. One grandson became Head of Gordonstoun.

Which bring us back to Francis, from the second paragraph.

One thing you had to say for Brereton. He was not one those reformers who thought his new revolutionary ideas were all right for 'the people' (while he quietly had his own children educated privately somewhere else). He put his own sons into his new school. If it was a good idea, it was a good idea for his own family. When he set up a new college at Cambridge, he saw to it that his second son Francis was one of the early students. Difficult to argue with that.

Francis had a strikingly successful career; he became a headmaster at an absurdly young age, at the North-East County School (later Barnard Castle). But once again, the influence of Brereton was blindingly evident. After all, he had set up the system; it would have been surprising if he had not taken a hand in appointing 'suitable' men to fill headships in his prize venture. We don't know if Francis felt himself just a little inadequate in his premature post.

But we do know that the Headmaster of another of Brereton's new county schools was having trouble. This was the Revd. William Watson, formerly deputy head of the Devon County School, and one of Brereton's earliest appointments. Watson had improved his prospects by taking a degree, holy orders, and a wife. All in two or three years. He now had impeccable credentials, and Brereton had no hesitation in having him installed in the new Norfolk County School.

Well, he did at least one of the usual things that nineteenth-century clergymen did: he had a large family – eleven, to be precise. But the school was not prospering, and Watson's health was failing. In fact he died, barely fifty. Brereton realised that Something Had to be Done.

So he induced (persuaded, cajoled, shamed, nagged) Francis to give up his post at the North East County School (where he was doing very well), and go to do a rescue job on the Norfolk County School. Francis did his best to make the cup pass from him, but in the end there was no gainsaying the old man's force. Sick at heart, Francis resigned, and went to Norfolk.

He was not able to save it, and was reduced to giving private lessons for a while.

Then he had the most extraordinary piece of luck. His successor at the North East County School died suddenly. Francis applied a second time, was appointed a second time, and stayed till he retired.

The whole episode is a vindication of the enormous power Brereton exerted, and continued to exert, over his family. The wonder is that they remained loyal – all of them. The only example of possible rebellion is that of the eldest son William (with the odd second name of 'Munster'); he joined the Army. And died young – which is ironic, to say the least.

That power a grandson hinted at continued to be felt; the family took fifty years to pay off his debts.

And finally – look at that share certificate again. Forty shares at five pounds each – two hundred pounds. Other instances in this book show that schoolmasters had to get by on barely £150 – a year. Thompson, the first head, got only £100 when he was first appointed.

To repeat – over a year's salary for young Francis. How did his father persuade him to part with such a sum? How indeed?

Not a good year

1952 WAS A SOMBRE one for the Governors, and, in the first instance below, for the whole nation.

In February, King George VI died. As the Queen enters her 66th year on the throne, the number of citizens who recall King George remorselessly dwindles. But those who *do* remember 1952 don't forget him.

We now know, because we watch TV documentaries about the Royal Family, that George was appalled when it became clear that his elder brother, King Edward, was going to abdicate. Quite apart from the awe with which he, George, regarded the manifold duties that were stretching before like a colossal minefield of ceremony, protocol, and intrusion into privacy, his overpowering emotion was one of dread.

He had a speech impediment. Any formal gathering caused him agonies of strain and embarrassment; public speaking was agony. People understood this; they all knew somebody who stammered; some of course stammered themselves. Anybody who saw a film of the King making a speech strained and suffered with him, because his struggle was so obvious. It made everybody want to help him, prompt him, encourage him, do *something* to ease his anguish. It was all the worse because everybody knew that this was not possible; we had to sit and watch.

It was this, coupled with the dedication with which he and his wife, Queen Elizabeth, took on the thankless role of majesty and leadership at the worst possible time in the century – the Second World War – that caused nearly everybody to conceive great sympathy and respect for him.

So that was the blow for the country.

The blow for the Governors came because one of their number died – Mr. D.N. Purchase. Before the business of the meeting of 12th February, 1952 began, the Chairman invited all members to stand in silence for a minute. Losing a member of a whole club is not good; losing a member of a small committee with whom you have worked, possibly for years, is both sad and disturbing; it is so close.

Finally (forgive the unavoidable pun) another minute recorded the Chairman's announcement that the Headmaster, Mr S.E. Howells, had informed him that, on doctor's orders, he would be able to do no more work that term.

In the event, he did no more work at all. He died of lung cancer. He is the only headmaster to die when he was officially still the head of the school.

Sam (all the boys knew him as 'Sam' – though of course not to his face), had this much in common with King George; he had not applied for the job.

He was one of that rare and precious brigade of men in their middle years, who, after half a lifetime of unspectacular dedication, were invited to take on the headship of a school like West Buckland, because the incumbent had left to join the Forces, resigned, given up owing to bad health and strain, or whatever. Calling on their fathomless resources of experience, hard-learned patience and persistence, and determination to 'see it through', they kept the ship afloat, often in the roughest of seas. They did the unspectacular stuff while their younger ex-colleagues were busy winning the war.

After the War, they handed over to some new young lion, glittering with degrees and distinctions (and, often, a chestful of medal ribbons), and faded into the background again. Some stayed on; a grateful board of governors decided that their unavoidable stop-gap was in fact quite a good head, and made his appointment official, substantive, permanent – no more of the 'for the duration'.

Sam was one of them. He stayed on, through post-war austerity and shortages (a lot of people do not realise that food rationing, for instance, did not disappear till eight years *after* the War), and general re-building and recovery. If he had been a force before, he now became a legend – with his nicotine-stained fingers in evidence as he upbraided boys for smoking, and his pungent ''Gold Flake' suit. Very old boys, who once trembled before him and swore about him behind his back, now get misty-eyed as they launch into well-honed reminiscences.

Sadly, the weed got him in the end.

Belts will not be worn in the Mess

WHEN I DID MY National Service, I was put on an officer-training course. Nothing particularly glorious about that. Regular Army cadets spent two solid years training at Sandhurst; National Service cadets were put through their paces, and reckoned to be fit to lead men in battle, with a course lasting four months. It was just a touch frantic.

We didn't see it like that, of course. We did not know the full picture. As far as we were concerned, those four months were just like another dose of basic training, only ten times worse.

What surprised us was that the Army still thought it was necessary to squeeze in a lesson or two by way of preparation for life *after* being commissioned. How was an officer (and, we hoped, a gentleman) supposed to behave?

There were many more regiments in the Army then than there are now. And they were all very touchily different. Different names, of course. Different cap badges. Different histories. Different traditions, special privileges, battle honours, all jealously guarded. Even different headgear. You would have thought that a tightly-disciplined organisation like the Army would (obviously) allow very little leeway in anything. It is a fighting machine, and efficiency demanded uniformity.

But, to take just one example, look at what they wore on their heads. Peaked caps, forage caps, berets, busbies, bonnets, tam 'o' shanters, bedizened with badges, plumes, bobbles, tabs, and many more that I forget. And you daren't laugh.

If you think that was sacred, you should have heard about the officers' traditions and regulations that abounded with every regiment, and with which we were regaled as part of our preparation for becoming, as I said, officers and gentlemen. It was bewildering, overpowering.

One regiment took off Sam Browne belts when entering the Officers' Mess; another didn't. In one you addressed the Commanding Officer as 'Sir'; in another you had to say 'Colonel'. There was one, I believe, where you had to say 'Colonel' first thing in the morning, but 'Sir' thereafter. Nearly all insisted on officers wearing a hat when in civilian dress. The Guards were said to forbid an officer to be seen carrying a parcel in the street *regardless* of what he was wearing. And so on and so on.

You thought, 'I'll never remember all that. And that is for my own regiment. Suppose I go into another regiment's mess and drop a clanger.

I shall be unfrocked at the very least. Dawn parade and buttons snipped off.'

I was reminded of this when I caught sight of this entry in the *Register* for November, 1922. (The Headmaster, Harries, took a keen interest in whatever went into the magazine. Indeed, one is tempted to suspect that he wrote a good deal of it himself.)

School Colours

THE HEADMASTER THINKS IT is necessary to put down clearly the various Colours allowed for Sports, the conditions under which they may be awarded, and to call attention to a few alterations.

1. Members of the 1st Eleven at Cricket and Football, the Shooting Eight and the Running Team are entitled to caps and blazers with a badge on each. (Running Colours do not wear the badge on the cap.)
2. Members of the 2nd Eleven at Cricket and Football may wear a distinctive cap with a badge.
3. Any boy who represents the School on public occasions such as Inter-School Sports, or similar contests, may, provided he has been selected by the School Authorities, trim his vest with the School red and wear the ordinary cap badge on it. This does not confer on him the privilege of being reckoned a Colour.
4. A boy who, not having obtained his Running Colours, wins the Open Championship at the Sports, is entitled to wear the running blazer and the cap, the latter without the cross whips.
5. Sergeants in the O.T.C. rank as First Caps; Corporals as Second Caps, but Lance-Corporals are not counted as Colours.

NOTES

Certain Military decorations are permitted by the War Office to be worn on uniform only. These cannot be counted as Colours.

The Head Master expects that the 1st Eleven at Cricket and Football will all receive their colours by the end of July and December respectively. In the event of a boy being incapacitated through illness, a complimentary cap may be awarded to him as the discretion of the Captain. In the same way such caps may be awarded in the Lent term for Football.

The Shooting Colours need not be given on the Ashburton only.

The Old Boys' blazer has a distinctive badge; the blazer and badge may be worn by members of the Club only. School tailors have strict orders not to supply Colours to Old Boys without reference to the School

The Badges can be obtained only from the School.

The following Military decorations are allowed: –
1. An efficiency badge.
2. A badge for Certificate "A".
3. A single rifle to those who obtain a First Class either on the Miniature or Long Range.
4. Cross Silver Rifles to those who represent the School in the Ashburton, Cadets Trophy, the Rapid Fire Competition, or the "Country Life" Competition.

Speedy settlement would be appreciated

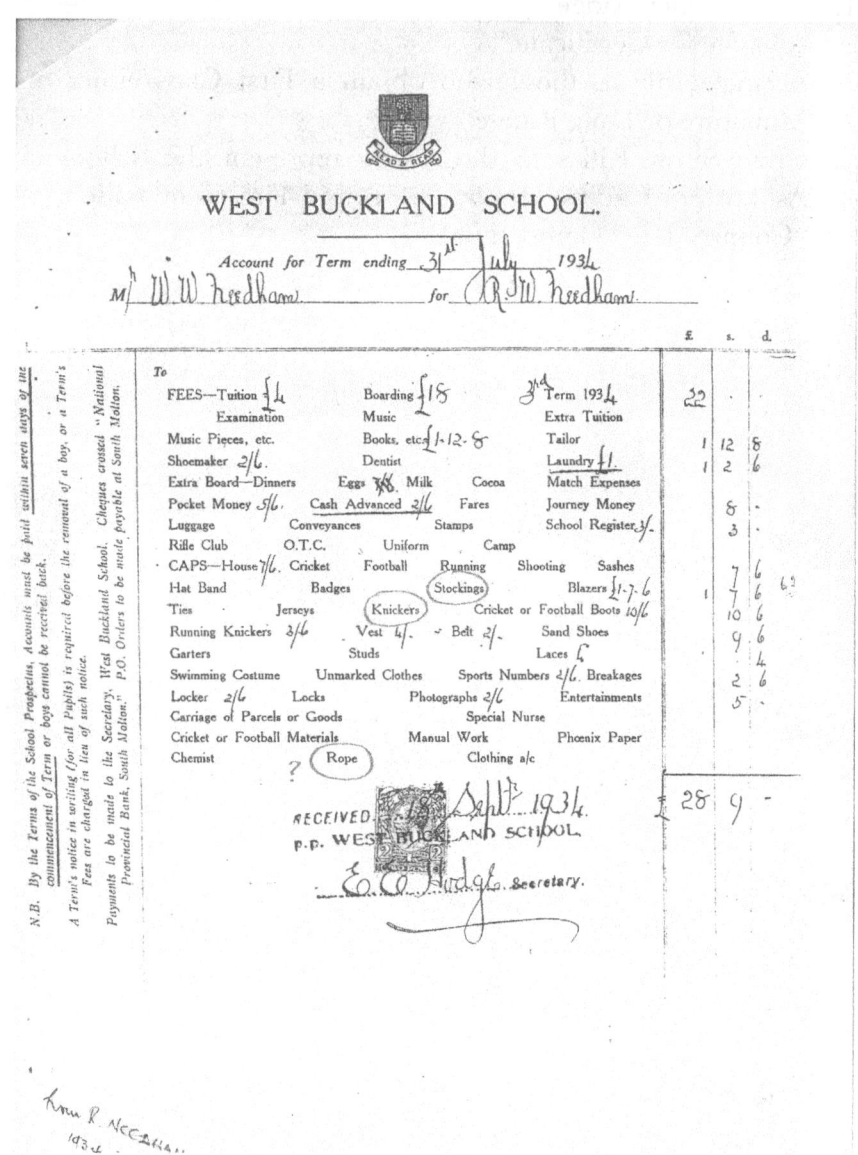

As always, one shakes one's head in amazement at the modesty of the costs – even allowing for inflation over the years. Did our society really run on funds as small as this? Yes, it clearly did. Well, West Buckland certainly did. No doubt the fashionable schools had a much more impressive budget.

A term's tuition for £4. Do a simple sum. Fewer than 300 boys in the school – at the very most £1,200. And all the staff salaries had to come out of that. To say nothing of school rates and taxes, maintenance of buildings and equipment, water and electricity supply, and a host of other charges which any reader can easily think of. Even if you add in the gargantuan fee of £18 for boarding, it is still an incredible sum – £22 And look at all the other things that were laid on for an additional six pounds and nine shillings.

It takes a great deal of believing. But there it is, in black and white. It must be genuine; nobody would ever dream of concocting a document like this; he would know that it would be immediately rejected as fantasy.

What also gives the game away is the vocabulary, which dates it beautifully, and rather endearingly. 'Conveyances', for example. I like that. Not 'transport'. 'Cricket and Football materials'. Not 'kit' – 'materials'. I don't know how many schools these days offer the services of a 'Tailor' or a 'Shoemaker'. How many pupils today would consider a 'Hatband' as part of everyday costume? Even a hat, for that matter? Four different types of cap. How many pupils in the 21st century would avail themselves of house-supplied cocoa? And what, they would wonder, are 'Sand Shoes'? How near is West Buckland to a beach? And even if they were, how often would a humble boarder have been able to get to one? (As late as the 1970's, West Buckland boarders were allowed out twice a term, on sharply-supervised excursions to Barnstaple.)

Pocket money – barely more than 25p. – for a term. All carefully doled out like gruel in Oliver Twist's workhouse. That works out at barely more than 2p. a week. God save us!

The 'School Register' entry did not mean that they had to pay for having their attendance recorded; the *Register* was the school magazine, and it was published three times a year. So – a shilling a go. For the times, not unreasonable.

Finally, one little, rather cheeky, speculation. Note the entries about 'Stockings' and 'Knickers' and 'Rope'. In these days when all sorts of near-unmentionable practices are commonplace on the TV news, the tabloid press, and in counsellors' briefs, the appearance on the same page of three incongruous items like stockings, knickers, and rope could easily set a fevered imagination off on a pretty eccentric course.

The Lord's Prayer – Home Counties Version

EVERY SO OFTEN, I would put up on the notice board something that had nothing to do with the Archive – well, not much. It might be a rare coincidence, a piece of useless information, a corny joke, a titbit of outside-school scandal. It wouldn't do to put up any inside-school scandal – though you would be surprised to find out how much there had and has been over the years. No doubt it continues. One very old boy told me stories from his time in the school, which were outrageous, and hilarious, but which were quite unprintable.

Where did I find these gems? Oh, anywhere – the newspaper, anthologies of humour, emails from chatty friends, remembered jokes from childhood (suitably updated – or cleaned up), conversations with compulsive raconteurs, an evening with old friends – anywhere.

Why put them up? Well, sometimes you come across something which cries out to be communicated to other people, regardless of its relevance or use.

More to the point, all these squibs have been, I hope, entertaining, and will therefore – again I hope – encourage colleagues to take a look at the 'Archive' spot from time to time, in the hope of some light relief. They would not always find something wildly entertaining; they might find, perhaps to their chagrin, that the item was not a joke; it was about school history. But they would get in the habit of looking, and some of this would sink in; they would learn something about West Buckland without having set out to do so. And it would be quite painless. It was all part of my crusade to raise the profile of the Archive, which I very soon discovered, after taking over the job, would turn out to be one of the most important functions of the post.

Many years ago, a Latin teacher (who also peddled useless information, which was welcomed as light relief to tenses and conjugations) told us this. I later forgot it, but came across it many years later – in fact when I was going through some near-rubbish documents which had found their way to the bottom of a storage box.

It was the Lord's Prayer based entirely on English railway stations. It went like this:

'Our Farnham, which art in Hendon, Harrow be thy Lane, thy Kingston come, thy Wimbledon in Erith as it is in Heston; give us this Bray our Maidenhead, and forgive us our by-passes, as we forgive them that by-pass against us And lead us not into Thames Ditton, but deliver us from Ewell. For thine is the Kingston, the Purley and the Crawley, for Iver and Iver, Crouch End.'

I agree, not exactly knee-slapping, falling-off-the-chair humour, but worth a spot on the notice board for a day or two, as alternative reading to detention lists and early lunch rosters.

Profit and Loss

THE SCHOOL – THE Devon County School, as it was to remain till 1912 – was a limited company, and it seems was about to give its shareholders a dividend. Such affluence was not to last; the agricultural depression of the 1870's and 80's was soon to bite.

REPORT OF THE DIRECTORS
OF THE
DEVON COUNTY SCHOOL ASSOCIATION
(LIMITED)
FOR THE YEAR 1871.

THE average number of Boarders for the year was 117, being six more than last year and 13 more than the year before. The buildings will hold about 130, and there is reason to expect that they will soon be filled.

The Shareholders will notice that a considerable addition has been made to the salaries. This is the result of a scheme adopted by the Directors, which they hope will give the Masters a permanent interest in the welfare and progress of the School.

There has been a slight loss on the Garden Account owing to the failure of a potato crop, and the charge for the New Buildings has increased the expenditure of capital; so that the dividend available will not be so large as last year.

The Board Account shows that the Matron has efficiently superintended the food and service, and in all respects the Directors have reason to be satisfied with the progress and state of the School. They recommend a dividend of 3½ per cent after making all the usual deductions for interest, repairs, depreciation, preliminary expenses and doubtful debts.

BALANCE SHEET
MADE UP TO DECEMBER 31ST, 1871.

Dr.	£	s.	d.	Cr.	£	s.	d.	£	s.	d.
178 Shares of £25 each	4450	0	0	Cost of Land				466	5	0
100 Trust ditto	2500	0	0							
Due on Mortgage	1466	5	0	Buildings, &c.	6108	4	2			
Due to Tradesmen, &c.	1321	12	4	additional 1871	141	18	6	6250	2	8
Due to National Provincial Bank	1695	16	3							
Unclaimed Dividends	31	16	5	Furniture	1902	4	11			
Building Fund	60	4	2	additional 1871	199	5	8			
Reserve Fund (amount set apart for Doubtful Debts)	181	11	1					2101	10	7
Due to Scholarship Fund	84	19	6	less total depreciation	1138	13	11	962	16	8
Profit and Loss Account	243	7	1	Preliminary Expenses being the cost of starting and carrying on the School to December 1863				1770	17	5
				Due from Parents, &c.				2409	12	0
				Garden Stock, Stationery and Books				124	4	2
				In Secretary's hands				19	13	2
	£11985	11	10					£11985	11	10

This represents the School's TOTAL ASSETS — land, buildings, everything.

REVENUE ACCOUNT

For the Year ending December 31st, 1871.

Dr.	£	s.	d.	Cr.	£	s.	d.
Salaries (including Extra Tuition and Examination Fees)	881	4	11	Charged for Board and Tuition	3219	16	0
Board	2025	0	0	,, Extra Tuition	383	10	1
Books, Stationery, Printing and Postage	294	1	4	,, Examination Fees	97	0	0
Prizes	32	12	6	,, Books, Stationery and use of Library	277	5	2
Advertisements	31	4	1	Donations for Prizes	19	11	4
Sundries	21	13	7	Received from Land, Garden and Pigs	177	12	10
Rates, Taxes, Rent, Insurance and Registration Fees	40	15	0	Doubtful Debts recovered	47	16	8
Expended on Land, Garden and Pigs	200	2	11				
Auditor's Fee	5	0	0				
Balance	690	17	9				
	£4222	12	1		£4222	12	1

PROFIT AND LOSS ACCOUNT.

Dr.	£	s.	d.	Cr.	£	s.	d.	£	s.	d.
Expended on House Repairs	90	6	2	Balance from 1870	325	12	9			
Furniture Depreciation	106	19	7	less Dividend declared and paid March 1871	310	17	10	14	14	11
Interest on Mortgage	55	2	10	Balance of Revenue Account				690	17	9
Interest to Bank	82	18	3	Taken from Building Fund				90	0	2
Set apart for Doubtful Debts	60	5	0							
,, ,, ,, Preliminary Expenses	63	4	11							
,, ,, ,, Building Depreciation	93	15	0							
Balance	243	7	1							
	£795	12	10					£795	12	10

I certify that I have examined the foregoing Balance Sheet and Accounts with the Books of the Association, also the Vouchers relating thereto, and find the same to be correct.

EDW. WALES JOHNSON, *Auditor.*

Morris Bros., Printers, Barnstaple.

3. 2002

Some are more equal than others

LIFE SEEMED MUCH MORE, sort of, flexible in the 'old days'. Well, in schools anyway.

Take public exams. The oldest generation alive today remember the great 'sixteen-plus'. It was called 'School Certificate'. But it had a predecessor. The very first sixteen-plus public exam for the whole country was set up in 1858, the very year in which West Buckland was founded, incidentally. And the four men who were the inspiration of that exam – the Revd. Joseph Lloyd Brereton, Earl Fortescue, Bishop (later Archbishop) Frederick Temple, and Sir Thomas Dyke Acland, a prominent Devon landowner – were all closely associated with West Buckland.

These tests were called the Oxford and Cambridge Local Examinations (each university ran its own), but were known, naturally, simply as 'the Locals'. (See Chapter 20 of my *The Natural History of a Country School* [Woodfield, 2005], pp. 118-134.)

By the same token, School Certificate, which replaced it in the second decade of the twentieth century, was truncated to 'School Cert'.

However, it was not so much the exam itself that I wanted to talk about as the regulations pertaining to it. As I said, it was expected that boys (and girls) would take this exam when they had passed their sixteenth birthday. And this was normally the case. But it happened quite regularly that pupils would be coming along who had started their primary school early, and so were several months, maybe even a year, in advance of their peers.

Nobody seemed to mind. I took School Cert. at fifteen, and, in our school at any rate, there had been plenty of instances of boys taking it at 14, even 13. (Reminiscent of the fifteenth century, when we are told that the young Thomas Wolsey entered Oxford University and took a degree, at fifteen.)

However, the reformers got to work on that, when they 'modernised' School Cert. shortly after the War. Round about 1950. They decreed that 'sixteen-plus' was going to *mean* 'sixteen-plus', and no pupil, however bright, was to be allowed to take it beforehand.

So we had log-jams of bright boys and girls who had reached the required level, mastered the material, and were required to cool their heels going through the same syllabus again while they waited for their sixteenth birthday to come round.

So much for flexibility, which wilted in the reforming sun of uniformity and modernity.

West Buckland kept its flexibility, however, but not in the way other schools had done. They did it the other way. If a boy was backward, for any reason, he was put in the class which corresponded to his academic progress so far. Fifty, sixty, seventy years ago, it was common to have boys in classes where the average age could be two years below their own.

This situation lasted remarkably late. There are plenty of active old boys today who remember friends who did not leave the sixth form till their twentieth birthday. Perhaps themselves.

A striking example of this reached the Archive when I came across a report of a boy in Class III. The old Third Form. Nowadays Year 9. In plain English, thirteen-to-fourteen-year-olds.

I have omitted his name for obvious reasons. But frankly, apart from what is written on the report, we know next to nothing about him, beyond the fact that his age was recorded at the end of the Christmas term, 1970, as seventeen years and three months. The average age of the class was thirteen years and ten months.

And he wasn't exactly setting the Thames on fire there. Twenty-first in Chemistry, and twenty-second in Geography – out of a class of twenty-three. His best effort was eighth in History, and he managed a creditable tenth in Physics, not an easy subject. He registered fifth in pottery, though. Quite what could be inferred from those results is anybody's guess.

His teachers did what they could to put a good shine on it. Five said he worked hard; one thought he 'takes his work seriously', and somebody else said he was 'neat'. The word 'progress' was employed a few times, possibly *faute de mieux*.

To his credit, he had an artistic bent. He clearly liked Art, Pottery (came fifth, as I said), and Technical Drawing, and showed a 'strong enthusiasm'.

Somebody referred to his 'obvious difficulties' – .whatever they were.

But nothing in the report gave a clue about what his life must have been like in a room full of thirteen-year-olds. Young people, particularly teenagers, change rapidly, at times almost from month to month. One gasps at the chasm that must have opened up here.

What company did he have? Not just sitting there – proper company, in and out of the classroom. Could he gossip with any of them? Moan and suffer with them? Simply knock around with them?

Young people also can be unkind to any of their number who are unusual. Was he laughed at? Picked on? Obviously they couldn't bully him, but there are plenty of ways one can make another person's life miserable without knocking him about.

Or was the boot on the other foot? Did they all go in fear and trembling of him? Was there a class creep who sucked up to him, and fed him secrets about the others, so that he could pick on them more easily?

It is a fine problem for the historian. What do we infer from what is there, and what do we infer from what is not there?

Coming along nicely

THE DEVON COUNTY SCHOOL
The EIGHTH ANNUAL REPORT of the DIRECTORS for the Year 1867

The Directors have again a favourable Report to make to the Shareholders of the state, progress, and prospects of the School.

The number of Boarders has been more than maintained as compared with the previous year; and the character of the Instruction given in the School has again most satisfactorily stood the test of the Cambridge and Oxford Examinations.

At the Cambridge Examinations held at Christmas, 1866, thirty-six boys passed; being for the third year in succession the largest number from any school in England. Thirteen obtained Honours; and the two boys who held Scholarships in the School were declared to be in English Subjects First and Second in order of Merit in England.

At the Oxford Examinations, held in June last, twenty-four boys passed; of whom nine juniors and three seniors obtained Honors [sic – must be a misprint, unless a maverick American got loose on the typewriter for the last paragraph].

Top of the league then – and three times running. Not bad going for a school born barely nine years before. No wonder the Directors called their Report 'favourable'. It shows commendable understatement. Among the others schools beaten were lions like Manchester Grammar School.

Note the odd reversal of names: not 'Oxford and Cambridge', as everyone says today, but 'Cambridge and Oxford'. Where, when, and why did that reversal take place? Or was it a mere quirk of Devonian phraseology? You know – Devon has a view of England not like that of other Englishmen: everyone else goes 'up' to London; Devonians go 'down Lunnon'.

It is easy to sneer from the vantage point of the twenty-first century, and say, 'But look how small the school was. Only thirty-six passes.' True, but the school was only nine years old, and total numbers must have been barely a hundred, if that.

The critics still would not be finished. 'But what sort of exams did they have to take? Pretty primitive, eh?' Well, if you want a definitive answer, you can still buy a reprint of the original papers from the very first exam in 1858. The Exams Syndicate will sell them to you. Take a look, and see if they are really that primitive. See if anybody would fancy taking them today.

'All right. But just how many schools went in for this exam? If the whole system was that young [it had started, like West Buckland, in 1858], the level of competition couldn't have been that high.'

Well, once again, look at the exam papers. There they are. How many sixteen-year-olds could knock them off today? Come to that, how many adults?

And there is one fact that no critic can get away from: No matter how many schools were involved, no matter how hard or easy the exams actually were, West Buckland beat the lot of them – three times. Whichever way you look at it, top is top.

Look also at those two boys who had the best results. 'First and Second *in England*' is surely something to be proud of. And, surely too, to have the first *and* second boys *in the whole of England* is something for the school to be proud of.

A propos exams, only a year after this report, the *Register* printed a plaintive plea
which makes one recall the recent scandals in the press about lost papers and re-sits and misprints in Maths exams.

'An Oxford and a Cambridge Certificate have been mislaid. [They got the order 'right' this time. Perhaps they weren't so rigid as we are today – flexibility again. Spelling too – look at the varied ways of rendering Shakespeare's name.] If they were put by mistake into any boy's box at the end of the half-year, Mr. Watson will be glad if the boy will let him know.'

I bet he would.

It sets off a train of thought. Suppose that boy in whose box they were found (if indeed they ever were) was a modest performer with the usual boy's share of original sin, and a smidgin of quick wit. . . what a windfall. What a temptation.

Some careful erasure of the operative name, a smudge of camouflage, a spot of meticulous, tongue-sticking-out fancy writing, and one's reputation could take a 'leap forward' which would have cheered Chairman Mao's heart. And what a foundation for a career. The possibilities were endless. . .

Straight bat

WE ARE BACK TO the theme of flexibility again. Well, if not flexibility, certainly the constant presence of uncertainty. Cricket writers continually tell us that in the 'old days', pitches were not the shirt-fronts we are used to now. So there was, as I said, uncertainty, in large dollops. All the more credit then to those batsmen who kept their eye on the ball and dealt with the vagaries of bumps and holes and tussocks of grass.

Balls could hit one on them, and rear like a cobra or fly straight along the ground like a bullet. And the danger was not confined to rural club and school wickets. The mighty W.G.Grace once stopped four of these 'shooters' in a row, and Lord's gave him a standing ovation.

However, my point is that good batsmen could still deal with these wickets, and get high scores. This applied not only to giants like W.G., but to schoolboys as well. In 1896, one school opening batsman notched up two centuries in a fortnight. Can any cricket master find evidence of that feat having been repeated – on these premises?

Seven years later, Talbot Henry Watts scored 145, which, to the best of my knowledge, remains the highest score ever made by a West Buckland batsman. Watts also held the school record for throwing the cricket ball, an event which remained on the athletics day programme until well after the Second World War. Watts managed 105 yards, 3 inches. Again, can any cricket master produce evidence that any WB boy has exceeded it? I suggest it would challenge the majority of adult club players too.

That was not the end of Watts' talents; he went on to play football for Notts County. Sadly, he was one of the millions of victims of the First World War.

Before leaving Grace and bad wickets, mention must be made not of another schoolboy, but of a headmaster. John Challen was clearly a gifted performer. Played for Somerset. In 1898, his batting average in local club cricket was twice that of the Master himself, and Grace, at fifty, still had ten more years of first-class cricket left in him.

Home Run

THE ANNUAL CROSS-COUNTRY RUN, the *Exmoor* (six miles out and nine miles back), remains the most evocative event of the year at West Buckland. It may not always evoke gently pleasant memories, but everybody who has ever had anything to do with it remembers it, and has something to say about it. It is like asking a very old soldier about the War.

I was rarely short of material about the *Exmoor* to put up on the notice board.

The writer R.F. Delderfield, who attended WB between 1926 and 1928, was similarly smitten (for better or worse), and, being a writer, he had little trouble in reminiscing about it.

Before reading this extract, one needs to be reminded that one of the landmarks on the course was the village of Heasley Mill. Further along one came to the hamlet of Charles, and the declivity called Charles Bottom (more familiarly known as 'Charley's Arse').

You did two things when you got back: you had a bath (somewhat mud-filled if you were one of the last finishers), and you devoured a plate of pea soup.

I need not explain to readers of your scholarship the references to Tom Brown, Tom the Sweep, Carver Doone, and Crusoe.

'At Heasley Mill there was some unlooked-for encouragement. A row of pinafored children [this was the rural 1920's, remember] lined the route and set up a piping cheer. You were very surprised to see them. You had forgotten that the fringes of the moor were inhabited. But then they were behind you, and, about the same time, you lost sight of everyone else, so that you were either away out in front (which was very difficult to believe) or a long way behind, perhaps at the very tail of a procession now strung out over a span of miles.

'A long time had passed since I had seen the last marker and even from the top of the downsloping field I could see no other runners. Away on the left there was a cluster of off-white buildings and I thought it might be Charles Bottom, a hamlet within scrounging distance of the school, so I went on down, trying to head in that direction and using the only signpost I had, a red, heatless sun, hanging somewhere over Barnstaple Bay.

'Emerging from yet another coppice I saw that it was indeed Charles Bottom and tackled the last fold in the landscape and there, right ahead, was a feature I could not fail to recognise, the long thin plantation that buttressed the school on the east. Tom Brown, Tom the Sweep, and even Carver Doone were behind me now. I was Crusoe coming ashore from the wreck and finding firm sand under my feet.

'I was quite right about my position at the very tail. The checkers were there in the middle of the rugby pitch, but everyone else was in the dining hall or the bath-house. I reeled into the hall and they put the plate of soup in front of me. To compare it to ambrosia would be to insult it. The dictionary defines ambrosia as "a finely flavoured beverage". That pea soup was resurrection, served in a shallow plate.'

Sign of the times

IN THE *REGISTER* OF 1983 (they came out only annually now; right up to the 1960's they had come out three times a year), there was an announcement:

'Last year saw the opening of "The Gables", the girls' boarding house. At first there were only four residents, who were later joined by four other girls who, while alterations were being completed, resided at a local guest house.

'The rooms are well furnished and serve as studies as well as sleeping quarters. The house has central heating, its own kitchen, sitting-room and laundry facilities, consisting of an essential washing machine and tumble-drier. During their spare time the girls can listen to music, watch colour television, cook and sew. They join the rest of the school for meals and other extra-curricular activities.'

It is very often the smallest, unobtrusive items that can provoke the most comment.

For a start, it is difficult in these multi-sex, uni-sex, bi-sex, transex, and I-don't-know-what-else-sex times to appreciate the seismic impact of the arrival of these disturbing creatures on the campus. Ever since the opening of the school in 1858, females had been almost as rare as four-leaf clovers – a matron, maybe a nurse, perhaps a head cook, and a scattering of chambermaids. And that was about that. Even the school secretary in the early days was a man. No female member of staff appeared till the 20th century.

Nearly all the pupils were boarders. Day pupils were regarded as a sort of second-class citizen, for all that they may have walked three or four miles to school every day. (Imagine doing the *Exmoor* after that. And then walking home again.) It was hard – porridge every morning; no central heating; oil lamps; outside toilets, and so on.

This was not purely a nineteenth-century phenomenon; it went on in the twentieth: still the outside toilets; permanent hunger; no central heating in the dormitories till 1987.

It is a common characteristic of the survivors of a spartan regime to regard their upbringing as worthy, positive, better than other effete systems, and pretty generally superior. 'Never did me any harm' just about sums it up. It is the sort of camaraderie you would expect in Colditz.

So the rearguard action to keep out the distaff side was vigorous. It fuelled the opposition to the reforms of the new headmaster who came to power in 1968, and, in conjunction with other issues, was to lead to his early resignation.

Before the dust had settled, some governors had resigned; a phalanx of traditionalist old boys had threatened never to cross the school threshold ever again; some long-serving, often bachelor, teachers had either been persuaded to take early retirement or had offered resignation on their own initiative; and the headmaster had been persuaded to withdraw his resignation. (He was to remain for ten years.) It is quite a saga, and the definitive account of it is still waiting to be written.

So the girls were in. This was the 1970's. It was going to be only a matter of time before the first female boarders arrived.

George Ridding, the maverick headmaster, had his point. In fact he made two. One, as I said, was the entry of girls. The other was the great rise in the number of day pupils. That produced a tsunami of traditionalist dismay as well. Boarding was 'part of the West Buckland tradition'. 'Boarding is the spirit of West Buckland, makes West Buckland what it is.' That sort of thing.

Ridding was relentless. His brief was to save the school. If tradition had to give way to necessity and expediency, so be it. Numbers were down. He had to get bums on seats and fee cheques in the bank. If it had to be achieved by taking in more day boys and by the heretical means of accepting girls, so be it once again.

He said in effect, 'You either take in more day boys, and these funny creatures called girls, or you die.'

It cost him a lot of sedition; it cost him a resignation and a re-instatement; but he won in the end, and the corner was turned. There would be no going back.

Incidentally, the same principle applied to corporal punishment. The most reactionary partisans of tradition had to agree that you could not inflict corporal punishment on girls. If you couldn't cane girls, you couldn't cane boys. QED.

So the point was made, and the remaining, more liberal, governors took the necessary decisions and wrote the necessary letters, and made the necessary alterations in the prospectus.

However, the principle may have changed, but unconscious attitudes lingered for a long time. Take the remarks about the wonders of girls' accommodation in the extract above. One press article pointed out with a dash of wonder that the girls would be provided with 'common rooms, showers, a kitchen, laundry facilities, *all for their exclusive use.*' [My my.]

The entry in the *Register* went further. Look at the top again: 'The girls can listen to music' [my my again], and 'watch colour television' [wow]. And, as a special treat, they would be allowed to 'cook and sew'. [I wonder how many girls pestered their parents to let them come when they heard that.]

Such a good likeness

ON THE WALL IN the Memorial Hall hang two portraits. Well three actually, but I am concerned here with just two of them. They are of a strikingly handsome couple – the Revd. Joseph Lloyd Brereton, the school's founder, and his wife, Frances.

Brereton has the classic good looks of the ideal scholarly young lion, with just a hint of vanity in the carefully-choreographed locks of hair about the ears. Serious, earnest, a searching look about the eyes, as if they missed nothing, and a silver pencil poised to make yet another learned note on the pad in his left hand. Frances looks serious too, but there is a richness and fluidity about the lips to give the impression that a full smile would light up a whole room. A radiant blush in the cheeks. A perfect English rose.

We have no idea of their market value. To try and find out, the school's head of Art once sent prints of them to Agnew's of Bond Street, which was having an exhibition of the artist's paintings. He received a reply, which was what I put on the Common Room Notice Board. It stated that it was not possible to give a valuation based simply on photographs. One would have to see the originals, as 'so much depends on the condition, and this is never clearly discernible, even from the best photographs'.

Well, fair enough. To my knowledge, nobody has since (or before) attempted to find out, so we have no idea how valuable they are. We do know, however, from a book about the artist by Raymond Lister [*George Richmond*, 1981], that Lord Fortescue paid the artist £200 for the two.

We know that Richmond exhibited regularly at the Royal Academy, and we know that these two were shown there in 1868.

Richmond was one of the most successful portrait painters of the mid-to-late nineteenth century. It makes sense; anyone who can get a hundred pounds a throw for his work in Victorian England is clearly no amateur dauber. Many of his earlier portraits were in water-colour too, which must have been fiendishly difficult. His reputation stood so high that Prime Minister Gladstone offered him the presidency of the Royal Academy – twice. And unsuccessfully – both times.

This sense of daring and independence must have been evident quite early. When he was only twenty-two, faced with the opposition of his fiancée's father to their marriage, he eloped with her to Scotland and got married at Gretna Green. He was so widely recognised that he received honorary degrees from both Oxford and Cambridge, was a fellow of the Society of Antiquaries, an honorary fellow of both University College, London and the Royal Institute of British Architects, and a member of the Company of Painter-Stainers of the City of London (whoever they were, or are).

One way and another, quite a big name. It says a lot for Fortescue's affluence, and influence, that he was able to secure two commissions like this from such a celebrity.

It also speaks a lot for the esteem in which Fortescue held Brereton. We know that they had a stormy relationship, arguing regularly, about money mostly (Brereton was a great spender – of other people's). But the bond was strong and deep: Brereton once described Fortescue's friendship as 'the salt of my soul'.

Presumably Fortescue presented these pictures to the school, in recognition of Brereton's work. Frances got up there probably because she was just lovely. I can't remember where I saw it, but there sticks in my memory a comment that the picture of Frances was reckoned to be one of the most beautiful portraits Richmond ever painted. Also worthy of comment on her beauty is the fact that, when this portrait was executed, she had already had, by my calculations, eight children. Poor soul – she was to have eight more. Hardly surprisingly, her husband outlived her. He had come down to Devon because of poor health.

Hard luck story

I THOUGHT THAT THIS story might have resonance at a time when the World Cup was being played, and England, as usual, were not doing very well. It is taken from the *Register* off November, 1896.

The Football Season, 1895-1896
RESULT OF MATCHES
Matches played 13. Won 12, lost 1.
Goals scored 101 – 12. .

The Season will always be looked upon as one of the most successful ever enjoyed by the School. The Teams representing the Masters and Boys were strong at all points and under favourable conditions it would have taken a good lot to have beaten either.

The crowning point of the School's success was the victory over the Somerset County School by 5 – 2, a win for the Devon County School being scored for the first time in the history of the Matches. [Somerset County School had had a foundation similar to that of the Devon County School – as it then was – owing its existence to Brereton and his dream of secondary education for 'the middle classes'. Just a little younger, and only fifty-odd miles away. Understandably therefore, there was a pretty sharp edge to the matches between them – a bit like Glasgow Rangers and Glasgow Celtic.]

Although the boys had not played together in an out Match before [presumably an 'out match' was an 'away match'], a great many of them had helped to pile up the big score of 22 – 0 which the Masters and Boys had compiled against South Molton and the 8 – 0 *v*. Mr. Townsend's Team. [Poor Mr. Townsend.] Therefore the journey to Wellington was taken with the firm determination to keep an unbeaten record of 45 – 3 (as it then stood), and to do or die – They didn't die, they **do-ed!**

When one and all played so pluckily [they were very fond of the word 'plucky' then; it was felt to embrace so many qualities that a schoolboy of the time was expected to show on his way to worthy Victorian manhood], it would be invidious to particularise, but a word must be said for our stalwart pair of backs and also to Captain Kempton who led the team to victory, setting an excellent example by his speed and clever passing.

The excitement at the School on receiving the news, and, later, on the return of the Team, baffles description; we wish however to take this opportunity of confuting the statement, on his authority, that the holiday which was given a few days after was in anyway connected with the victory.

After this the Boys beat South Molton four times, scoring 23 – 4, although they had a little trouble on the last occasion. The Masters' XI after defeating South Molton, Dulverton twice, and Mr. Townsend's XI twice [Mr. Townsend must have been gnashing his teeth by now], had to put up with a reverse at the hands of the Somerset County School Masters who, after postponing the Match on account of the weather chose about the worst day possible to imagine. [The bounders.]

We do not grudge our friends their victory [not much they don't] for one single instant, but we do think that had the game been played in anything like favourable weather we should have won.

For the first half we played with the terrific gale that was blowing and simply pressed our opponents from start until the whistle blew half time, being prevented from scoring more than once owing to the skilful manner in which our opponents packed their goal. [Most unsportsmanlike.]

In the second half to add to our discomfort heavy sleet began to pour down into our faces and with the wind increasing in force we were at a double disadvantage. They scored three times, two of the goals being kicked by our backs, who instead of seeing the ball proceed up the field towards our opponents' goal as they might naturally expect, had the mortification of watching it ascend in the air and come sailing back over their heads and through the goal which was some 30 yards behind them.

And then, too, most of us thought that the second half was much longer than the first. [My God – how low can you stoop?]

Both sides deeply regretted the unfortunate weather that prevailed, ourselves especially, as, with such few Matches available, we had earnestly looked forward to a good and even struggle.

The Match was played throughout in the best possible spirit [after all that?], a marked difference to our experience with the Dulverton Football Club a month before, who for crass ignorance of the general rules and the spirit in which Football should be played were hard to beat. Better no Football at all than that, say we, and the fixture this year is conspicuous by its absence.

[So – bad behaviour was not only not cricket; it was not football either.]

Few Words

Not a man, but a notice, of few words.

ON THE LAST PAGE of the *Register*, every term, was printed the schedule for the start of the coming term.

Compared with the avalanche of computer-generated bumf that political necessity, and health and safety regulations, make compulsory today, this documents is a masterpiece of succinctness.

NOTICES

All Boarders are expected to be in residence on Thursday, July 24th. [There were very few day boys, and presumably they walked in every morning. There were no buses, no motor cars, no bicycles, and the Exeter-Barnstaple line did not come till just after the school was founded. The Taunton to Barnstaple line was not opened till the 1870's.]

Any who may find it more convenient can be received the preceding day: but it is requested that no one will be absent on Thursday night, unless in case of real necessity, and with leave obtained previously from the Head Master. [This may be been because some pupils had a long way to come, and the railway system was not comprehensive in 1876. There were some boys who lived so far away from the school that they did not get home for every holiday, and special arrangements had to be made to keep them at school. It makes you wonder why parents sent their sons here. Even how they came to hear of the school in the first place.]

Mr. Llewellin, one of the masters, will be in Exeter on the Thursday until the departure of the train from St. David's Station at 4.8 p.m., for Barnstaple. His address will be the Railway Hotel, near St. David's Station.

Mr. Thomas [another master] will leave Bristol on that day by the 10.30 train. [So you had to look slippy to make it from, say, the Midlands, or else stay the night before in Bristol. Teenage boys, on their own, in a hotel in Bristol? Or did Dad also make the trip to see them off?]

[Note that term *started* on July 24th. This was because, in the early days, the school ran on a four-term year – Christmas, Lent, Summer, and Michaelmas.]

Prize Day

WHEN THE OPPORTUNITY PRESENTED itself, and I had recently come across a document which reflected something that was going on at the time, I would put it up on the notice board.

On this occasion, we were coming up, in 2002, to Speech Day; it was scheduled for 21st September. By good fortune, the very earliest Speech Day programme that survived in the Archive was one which told one and all that the proceedings for 1876 were to take place on Wednesday, 20th September. So – only one day out. We do try in the Archive.

Incidentally, when did the name change? When did 'Prize Day' give way to 'Speech Day'? (I was terrified when I was told, at eleven, that I had been awarded a prize; I thought that all prizewinners had to make a speech.) Anyway, this is what the programme looked like:

Devon County School,
WEST BUCKLAND.
PRIZE DAY AND OPENING OF NEW BUILDINGS,
1876

[Note the meticulous punctuation. We would regard it today as over-fussy.]

The PRIZE DAY is fixed for Wednesday, September 20th..
EARL FORTESCUE will take the Chair at Two o'clock.

Among those who will take part in the proceedings will be EARL DUCIE, Lord Lieutenant of Gloucestershire, Sir T.D.ACLAND, M.P., the Rev. Prebendary PERCEVAL, Head Master of Clifton College, Rev. Prebendary BRERETON, and others.

[Fortescue had extensive property in Gloucestershire, and so may well have been instrumental in inveigling the Lord Lieutenant to come. Fortescue knew everybody. Prebendary Perceval was presumably invited to present the prizes. Acland was a local landowner and benefactor; he helped to set up the very first *Exmoor* cross-country race – if you call that benefaction.]

The new Buildings will be opened at the same time.

[This is a bit of a mystery. The date on the school clock is 1873. – well actually, it is MDCCCLXXIII – and the Karslake Hall was opened in 1878. So what arrived in between? I don't know.)

Luncheon tickets (price 3s. 6d – 17½p) can be had of Mr. THOMAS, at the School. [No event ever took place at West Buckland without its 'luncheon'.]

An Omnibus or other conveyance will start from the Fortescue Arms Hotel, Barnstaple, for the School at Half-past Twelve.

[Presumably this 'other conveyance – or the 'Omnibus' itself – involved horses. To give everyone time to board, descend, be shown to their seats, and peer at the programme, only 90 minutes. The horses would have to go at a fair old clip. One wonders what the springs were like.]

The Down Express will stop at Castle Hill Station, at 5 p.m.

[All sorts of thoughts occur here. Why announce the expected arrival of a train at five o'clock when the proceedings were due to begin at two? Did it mean that the arrivals would have to find accommodation at the village of Filleigh? Hardly a metropolis. Or were the Fortescues at Castle Hill going to offer B. and B. at their stately home? Or did these visitors have to hire an 'Omnibus or other conveyance' to take them to Barnstaple for the night, and then hire another to take them back again in the morning? If so, they must have had wanted to come pretty badly. Oh – and, if they did plan to stay the night at Barnstaple, why didn't they stay on the 'Down Express' all the way to Barnstaple?

[We know that, in addition to these arrivals, and the obvious parents and general wellwishers who came from Barnstaple, Speech Days then were attended by a hefty contingent of journalists. The DCS, in these early times, was still living on its celebrity reputation as a pioneer school – the very first secondary school for the 'middle class'.

[Finally, the nearest railway station to the school was at Filleigh, because the Fortescues did not want the Taunton to Barnstaple line to run through their property. Well, OK – that happened quite a lot. But then it seems that the station was still called 'Castle Hill', when the whole *raison d'être* of the station was to get it *away* from Castle Hill. It seems the Fortescues had it both ways – privacy and celebrity. Anonymity and clout.

[And look at the last sentence. The London train – the 'Down Express' – this giant of shatter and bang, with its hints of *Mallard* and the *Flying Scotsman* – was going to stop specially at a wayside halt on the edge of Exmoor. Was there no end to the Fortescue influence?]

The secret of West Buckland health

NOBODY WOULD EVER CHALLENGE the assertion that the general health of West Buckland pupils is 'rude'.

By way of example, I offer the following extract from the *Register:*

Swimming Notes

Owing to the very low rainfall since January, the swimming bath contained no more than a few inches of water and all hopes of its filling were unfulfilled.

The opportunity was taken to repair the bath and the surrounds, and when the rains came in August, the bath quickly filled with crystal clear water.

Swimming commenced on September 24th, and is still in full swing at the end of November.

I like that – 'the rains came'. In August! It makes it sound like the monsoon, or something out of a Somerset Maugham short story about rubber planters.

Notice that swimming didn't *start* till late September. And it was still going on at the *end* of November. That was when the editor composed this item. For all we know, it went on till the end of the Christmas term.

This is West Buckland, remember – North Devon, Exmoor, and 'the rains in August'. And the pool was in the open air.

I came across this piece in the *Register* for October, 1960, but an item like this could easily have appeared in any number of the magazine going right back to its first edition in 1863. At first there was a 'pond', replaced in 1906 by the pool. Not covered till the 1970's.

A cynic may argue that cavorting in the pond/pool went on in all weathers because there was damn-all else to do. Some truth in that, maybe. The most partisan of West Buckland supporters would have to admit that WB, for a long time, was not exactly a holiday camp chock full of diversionary delights. But it is unlikely that boys at the time felt hard done by, because they didn't know about other treats that were missing from our 'modern' scheme of things. They didn't feel 'deprived', any more than kids playing cops and robbers on bomb sites in London after the War complained about the lack of playgrounds or recreation parks.

That was what there was. You got on with it.

No wonder one medical report after another made mention of the robust condition of the inmates. One went so far as to remark that 'the general Physical Education is producing a virile set of boys'. So there.

At an ever-increasing rate

WE ALL KNOW THAT things are not what they used to be (they never were), but it is a shock now and then to discover *to what extent* things are not what they used to be. Take prices. Everybody knows about inflation, but look at this cutting from a local paper:

Bishop launches school appeal

TARGET OF £50,000

West Buckland School's endowment fund appeal was launched by the Bishop of Crediton on Monday. He addressed governors, staff, boys, parents, and old boys who were attending the school's traditional Whitsun gathering.

He stressed the importance of proportionate giving. Instead of this being merely an appeal for funds, he said, it was a challenge to parents and others interested in the school to support the independent education in which they believed so far as they could reasonably afford.

Regional committees have been set up so that, as far as possible, every old boy and friend of the school shall be approached individually with a personal explanation of the aims of the fund, which has a target of £50,000.

Before the official launching took place, covenants and gifts amounting to over £16,000 had been obtained.

The campaign will end in the late Autumn. Early projects include new sixth form accommodation and a new library and art room.

Fifty thousand pounds. How many teachers' salaries, never mind libraries and art rooms, would you get out of fifty grand today? And this was not the eighteenth century, nor yet the nineteenth. It was 1965 – barely more than fifty years ago.

In the last decade, we have seen a sports hall for £2.1 million, an art and drama block for £4.6 million, and a whole new complex of library, boarding block, and study centre which together cost £5.6 million.

If you happen to have the back of an envelope handy, you might work out what percentage inflation rate that would represent.

Mr. President, Sir

JUST AFTER THE TURN of the 19th – 20th century, inspectors descended upon the Devon County School. Their report was, on the whole favourable as regards the teaching and sport. (All that bracing air.)

But it had some criticism to offer about the school's provision for science, for positive recreation, and for cultural development. The Headmaster, Mr. W.A. Knight, must have been somewhat stung by these comments. Within a few years, the school had some new laboratories and a new (open-air) swimming pool to replace the 'pond'. A rifle club was formed. In addition, a Reading and Debating Society was set up, which did what you would expect – it laid on talks and provided debates. We have the Minutes of this society right back to its formation in 1903. (One volume was lost in the fire of 1930.)_

They make engaging 'dip-in' reading, and offer many a quote to put on a notice board. An observer today would perhaps smile somewhat patronisingly at the subject matter, and at the actual wording of the talks and speeches, which of course reflected the limitations of the life the boys led at that time, and reflected too the assumptions and attitudes of Edwardian England. But they were genuine for all that. The attendance numbers were indeed modest, but when you take them as a percentage of the whole school, it is most creditable.

Again, a cynic may be tempted to remark that, stuck out there on the edge of Exmoor on a cold winter's evening, they had not much else to do. But the boys were proud of their school and of their country – witness their support of the school sports teams, their willingness to turn up year on year at old boys' gatherings (many of them had attended the school for only two years or so – even eighteen months), their finding time, while shivering and trembling in a world war trench, to write to the Headmaster and tell him how they were getting on – shelling, gassing, and all..

And look at the motions that they debated in their first decade. Yes, hunting, votes for women, and the Yellow Peril – you would expect that. But they also tackled subjects which could easily provoke animated debate today:

On 23rd September, 1908, 'L.G.H. Major moved a resolution in favour of a republican form of government as opposed to a monarchy'.

On 5th October in the same year, 'Mr. E.M. Bagshawe [a master] moved "that the nationalisation of railways would be of benefit to this country".' And the motion was carried.

In the previous year, debates had been held on reform of the House of Lords, and on a Channel tunnel. You can't get much more modern than that.

And don't forget that, in 1914, all over the country, boys like these joined up in droves because their country needed them.

The collective noun for eccentrics

LIKE MANY COUNTRY BOARDING schools who had a common room seething with long-serving bachelors, West Buckland had its share of eccentrics. Perhaps this explains the high percentage of nicknames in those days compared with today. You don't make up nicknames about people who are ordinary and just do their job.

A fine example of this phenomenon was Ian McLintock, who served the school from 1939 to 1970. He boasted not one nickname, but two. 'Mac', obviously. But I also discovered a second – 'Tick-tock'.

Now where do these names come from? Sometimes they reflect a chance happening early in the teacher's career, and the name stuck long after anybody could remember the original incident. In my school we had a French teacher called 'Wiggy'. But he didn't wear a wig; he was completely bald. But he *had* worn one when he had first arrived. Perhaps he got fed up with being teased about it. Anyway, he gave it up. But the nickname stuck, and remained around to puzzle generations of schoolboys.

Between the wars, there was a French teacher at West Buckland (French again) called 'Inky'. Now why? It was ages before the penny dropped. His surname was 'Bellot'. Nothing remarkable in that. But, when you stopped to wonder how it should be pronounced. . . . with the stress on the first syllable? – '*Bell*ot" or the stress on the second – 'Bell*ot*', you got it. Bell*ot* – Blot – Inky. QED. (And I know I have already told you this.)

Anyway, Ticktock was a school character, much laughed about (not laughed *at*). Like many eccentrics he was a good scholar. He got up to all sorts of things besides teaching. He ran the cadet force. He took parties abroad. He wrote, and received, hundreds of picture postcards, which are still in the Archive. You don't write and receive all that unless you are well liked. He had adventures doing fire-watching during the War. Somewhere or other you feel that there is a story about cadets arresting a parachuting German pilot in the middle of the Moor waiting to be unearthed.

At the end of the year I received a letter from a retired colleague, who enclosed many scrips and scraps about Ticktock which he had obtained from Ticktock's niece. The man, it appears, was an inveterate jotter. He would get a passing idea, but, instead of letting it fly away into the ether, he would grasp it, examine it, mould it, and produce something smile-worthy out of it.

One example in this set was his playing around with the old English custom of printing 's' in the middle of a word as 'f', and some satire on contemporary phenomena. As in: The weather: 'Generally downcaft, but then there will funny periods.'

'Staff Appointments: Bright lads wanted to manage computers. And bright computers wanted to manage lads. 'You are advifed to fee your careers mafter. He will tell you whether you are a lad or a computer.'

[See also Chapter Sixteen – 'Man of few words'.]

Editorial licence

EDITORS, BY VIRTUE OF the thankless job they have to do, are rarely popular with the authors of the pieces they put into the magazine or the anthology or whatever. They have to shorten, cut, delete, transpose, modify, defuse, de-toxify, and generally knock the stuffing out of most of the material that reaches them.

They rarely have the chance to slip into the text a personal note, much less a joke. (Somebody is bound to take offence.)

But in the *Register* of March, 1920, I came across this dry comment from the Editor (I suspect the Headmaster), which gets in a sharp crack without leaving a bloody nose:

'The Sanatorium, the erection or rather putting together of which was commenced in September last, is gradually approaching completion. There are some incorrigible optimists who expect to see it finished by Easter.'

4. 2003

The Flip Side

WHEN I USED TO collect the old-type wax '78' gramophone records, I was often given a treat when I turned the disc over and heard what was on the other side; it was often better than the side I had bought.

The same thing applies to collecting old documents. Take this.

In a search for material on the early history of the school, I would visit the library and root about in newspapers of the period. One day I found an advert in the *West Briton and Cornwall Advertiser*. (That's a lovely name, isn't it – the '*West Briton*'. So redolent of ancient history and solid traditional virtues and King Arthur and John Bull. The sort of noun Churchill would have loved.)

In the edition of 11th January, 1872, I found this paean of publicity:
'THE DEVON COUNTY SCHOOL, WEST BUCKLAND

Will RE-OPEN on WEDNESDAY, January 24th, 1872.

SINCE the commencement of the Oxford and Cambridge Examinations, 406 certificates have been obtained by pupils of this school, a greater number than by those of any other school in England, and of those 104 have been in honours.

Among many other distinctions in special subjects, the following positions have been obtained in the Senior English section of the Cambridge Examinations during the last five years:- in 1866, one boy bracketed (with another), first in England; in 1869, one bracketed first in England, and another bracketed second; in 1870, the first in England. In the Junior English section, in 1869, a boy belonging to the school was bracketed (with another) as first in England among 1,299 candidates.

At the last Cambridge Examination 26 pupils of this school passed, nine in honours, among them being the only junior in first class honours in Devonshire or Cornwall.'

And so on and so on.

Crying one's wares. And why not? It is something to 'cry' about.

But, further up the same page, there was this impressive offering: Please, as they say, turn over.

Collegiate School for Young Ladies
OAKLEIGH HOUSE ST. AUSTELL
Conducted by Miss HART

THE various studies are under Miss Hart's personal superintendence; it is her earnest effort to promote the improvement and welfare of the pupils entrusted to her care, to whom she offers the advantages of a superior and accomplished education, endeavouring by watchful training to inculcate the highest principles and develope [sic] individual character and talent.

The general course of instruction comprises the Scriptures, English literature, grammar, analysis and composition, ancient and modern history, physical, political and sacred geography, chronology, etymology, natural philosophy, reading, writing, arithmetic, use of the globes, plain and ornamental needlework, &c.

French is constantly spoken.

The house is well adapted for a school, standing in its own grounds, with croquet ground, &c; the schoolroom and dormitories are airy and cheerful; great attention is paid to the health and comfort of the pupils.

Select classes for French and German on Mondays and Thursdays, at Twelve and Seven o'clock. Drawing – Tuesdays and Fridays, at Four.

A preparatory school for little boys.

A vacancy for a young lady as governess pupil.

Terms strictly moderate.

Prospectus, with references to parents of present and former pupils, on application.

School Duties will be RESUMED (D.V.) on THURSDAY, January 18th, 1872.

Miss Hart was clearly a very busy lady, though we have no idea of how many staff she employed. But if the whole school was accommodated in one house, it couldn't have been many. And it was customary for staff to live in. That 'young lady' who was appointed as 'governess pupil' would certainly have earned her keep.

'French is constantly spoken.' What – all around the school? Did girls learn to say 'Pass the sugar, please, Ursula' at breakfast? Or only on Mondays and Thursdays, at 'Twelve and Seven o'clock'?

And one odd subject – 'Sacred geography'. Useful for summer holidays in the Holy Land, presumably.

Catering for everybody

EVERY SO OFTEN, I would come across something which was not necessarily relevant to West Buckland, but could be relevant to education generally. If it wasn't, it might still be worth pinning up on the board, because a smile is relevant to everybody.

And again, it might induce people to glance at the 'Archive' spot on the N.B. now and then. With any luck, the *next* notice would be about West Buckland, and they would all learn something.

Even if they come up to you and say what a load of corny rubbish it is, it means three things:

They have looked at the Archive spot.

They have remembered what they saw long enough to come and tell you.

You have made contact.

Here it is:

In preparation for the Earth Summit hosted by South Africa, the UN conducted a world-wide survey. The only question was:

'Would you please give your honest opinion about solutions to the food shortage in the rest of the world.'

The Survey was a huge failure. . . .

In Africa, they didn't know what 'food' meant.
In Eastern Europe, they didn't know what 'honest' meant.
In Western Europe, they didn't know what 'shortage' meant.
In China, they didn't know what 'opinion' meant.
In the Middle East, they didn't know what 'solutions' meant.
In South America, they didn't know what 'please' meant.
And in the USA, they didn't know what 'the rest of the world' meant.

The civil service misses nothing

WHAT FOLLOWS IS AN extract from Government legislation about schools:

Ventilation and Heating

38. – (1) Every room in every school building and in all boarding accommodation shall be provided with means of ventilation capable of securing that the amount of fresh air available to each person for whom the room is designed shall be not less than the amount specified in this Regulation as appropriate to the cubic space available per person or six air changes per hour, whichever is the less –

Cubic space per person cubic feet	Appropriate amount of fresh air per person in cubic feet per hour
180	1,100
200	1,000
300	720
400	600
500	420

(2) In every Kitchen and in every other room in which there may be steam or fumes, adequate measures shall be taken to prevent condensation and to expel noxious fumes.

What instrument measured the amount of fresh air coming in per hour?

How do you change the air six times an hour? And do you have to change all of it, or can you get away with just half?

The topic could give Maths teachers ideas for a Year 7 homework. . .

Still on Record

The collective noun for rural rectors

EARLY SPEECH DAY REPORTS in the *Register* (and, quite probably in the local press too; they always gave value for money) were meticulous in their recording of the names of those who attended. By way of example, look at this report on the 'Prizegiving' of 1877:

'. . . Soon after two o'clock luncheon was laid out in the spacious dining hall. [West Buckland and its luncheons again – and this was before the Karslake was built.] It was a most tempting and abundant spread, such as the catering of Mrs. Miller never fails to provide at these annual festivals. [Mr. and Mrs. Miller owned the nearby farmhouse in which the very first pupils of the schools were housed and taught – all three of them. Their family has sent generations of their relatives to the school.]

'The chair was taken by one of the directors of the School, the Rev. Prebendary Karslake, Chairman of Quarter Sessions, and Rector of Meshaw [he was the one who built the present dining hall shortly afterwards; look at the plaque outside it].

'Among the large company ['large' – poor Mrs. Miller] present were – The Right Rev. Lord A. Hervey (Bishop of Bath and Wells), Right Rev. Dr. Benson (Bishop of Truro), Sir Thomas D. Acland, Bart., M.P., Samuel Morley, Esq., M.P. for Bristol, W.K. Wait, Esq., M.P.for Gloucester, Hon. T.C. Agar Robartes (Lanhydrock), Rev. John Russell (Swymbridge) [yes, *the* Jack Russell], Rev. C. Haggard, and Mrs. Haggard (Filleigh), Rev. W.J. and Mrs. Edmonds (Highbray), Rev. R. Martin (Challacombe), Rev. J.H. Thompson, Head Master, Rev. J.V. Roberts (Chittlehamholt), Rev. R.A. Whalley (Mariansleigh), Rev. F. King (Southmolton), Rev. E.G. Sandford (Landkey), Rev. J.H. Copleston (West Buckland) [a formidable performer on the cricket field against the school], Rev. W. Martin (West Buckland) [*two* priests from West Buckland], Rev. C.W. Holley and Miss Holley (Okehampton), Miss Hamlyn (Bridestowe), Rev. R. and Mrs Prentis, Rev. J. Luxton and Miss Luxton (Bondleigh).'

[Note the details of this punctuation. Believe me, it is a worry merely to copy it, never mind compose it. But it is so loyal to the rules and so 'spot on' that one can almost derive aesthetic pleasure from contemplation of such a passage.

[And that was just the VIP's. Look at them: two bishops, three M.P.'s, a judge, a celebrity dog-breeder, a knight of the realm – indeed a baronet, an 'honorable', and fourteen vicars. And notice how far they had come

– Okehampton, Bristol, Truro, Gloucester. How did they all get there? And why were they so willing to make the trip to attend the prize-giving of a remote boarding school on the edge of Exmoor? If Exmoor even today has enough wilderness to threaten life and limb to careless wanderers, what must it have been like 140 years ago? It would appear that, because of its origins, its modern philosophy, and its early unique appeal to the 'middle classes', the Devon County School, nearly twenty years after its foundation, was still a celebrity.]

[Nor was it merely the 'quality' that came.]
'...J. Luxon, Esq., Reginald Martin, Esq., Lieutenant J.H. Martin, Miss Louise Champernowne, Miss Margaret Champernowne, Miss Harriet Mallock, Miss C. Martin, Miss L. Martin [there were six Martins in this audience], Mrs. Wooldridge, Dr. Hatherly (Southmolton), W. Avery, Esq., Ex-Mayor of Barnstaple, Mr. W. Smyh (Barnstaple), Mr. Chope and Miss Abbott, Mr., Mrs. and Miss Edbrooke, Mr. and Mrs. Maunder, Mr. and Mrs. Pearse, Mr. Lovelace, Mr. Hammett, Mr. Trounson (Penzance), Mr. Baker, Mr. Bitson, Mr. and Miss Haynes,, Miss Galsworthy, Mr. and Miss Potbury, Mr. Stone (Sidmouth), Mr.R. and Mrs Bowhay (Calstock), Mr. Vellacott, Mr. and Mrs. Turner (Ross), Mr. R. Mogridge (2) [father and son?] (Molland), Mr. Dovell (Combmartin [note the spelling]), Mr. Pike (West Buckland), Mr. Dodd, Mr. and Mrs. Thomas, Mr. G.T. Llewellin, Mr. J.G. Shain, Mr. C.H. Harris, Mr. W.E. Calvert, Mr. Stone (St. John's College, Cambridge), besides several 'old boys' and a good many other friends..'

[Did the journalist or the secretary run out of paper, pencil, patience, or time when he came to the 'good many other friends'? If he did, he can be excused; it is a very worthy effort. And how did he, whoever he was, collect all these names? Waylay them as they got out of the carts and 'other conveyances'? Stop them at the door like a commissionaire? Squeeze along the rows as everyone waited for the proceedings to begin? Or did he cheat by putting out a huge sheet of paper and hoping that everybody would be obedient enough to sign? If he did this last, his sin would catch up with him, when he came to decipher the handwriting. And think of the details of typing and prodigies of proof-reading that they had to go through. Whichever way you look at it, it was a sterling effort by *somebody*.

[The names of the teachers – Thomas, Llewellin, Shain, Harris,

Calvert – came very democratically at the end. Stone was one of the school's very brightest boys, and mopped up no end of prizes. He was one of many who won a place at St. John's College, Cambridge. Over the years, the school built up quite a connection.]

A final contemporary touch

1877 WAS THE YEAR that Prime Minster Disraeli bestowed a fresh title on his monarch – 'Empress of India'. It was clearly much talked about. Among the many toasts and replies, somebody proposed the health of, naturally, Her Majesty the Queen. But that was not the end of it. After three 'hearty' cheers had been given for H.M., one of the pupils called out, 'And one for the Empress.' Needless to say, there was 'another hearty cheer'.

It is easy to smile tolerantly, amusedly, even patronisingly at these proceedings, as a parent would at children's games. It all seems so far away from what we do, or don't do, today. It all seems so innocent, and jolly, and nice. Time has deleted from our view of the past all the impatience and fatigue, all the sweat and fidget, all the strict Victorian formality, all the keeping up of appearances – there was so much 'correct behaviour' that had to be followed. Surely it couldn't have all been genuine. Was it really like that? I don't know.

But we must give these people credit for being human. They are only five generations away from us. Because they were human, we must also credit them with genuine feelings, loyalties, aspirations, worries, prejudices – just like us today. We wouldn't like it if future generations labelled us as witless innocents.

And look at us today. True, there are many who are sceptical, and critical, even hostile, about royalty, but there are many more who are dotty about it, and who turn up in the Mall in their hundreds of thousands to cheer weddings and jubilees – and travel far and wait a long time in order to be able to do it. Billions all over the world watch them.

We take our schools for granted. We moan about them, complain about them, try to change them, become convinced that they are going to the dogs, or whatever, but we do not try to abolish them. They are part of our very being.

Now consider 1877. A national system of secondary schools was only nineteen years old – nineteen years. My guess is that those parents and pupils who used it were tickled to death about it. Another guess is that they would have been as grateful for it as we were about the NHS, only nineteen years after its introduction.

So they embarked on long journeys to a remote part of the country, and put up with much discomfort to visit and champion an experiment which was just beginning to make its point. So they cheered. And they meant it.

Today, the school goes on show once a year, and parents come from far and wide, and we clap the prizewinners – countless times. Prefects look well gowned and well scrubbed, and we take pride in what the school has made of them. We listen patiently to the speeches and reports, and we gather in the Karslake afterwards (for 'luncheon') to sip coffee or scoop curry and rice standing up, with a quivering glass of wine clipped to the plate.

Parents and pupils – and staff – may have plenty to say about the heavy traditions, and the heavy-handed protocol, and the need for great powers of endurance, and they may question the very *raison d'etre* of it; but the spirit is there just as it was all those years ago. We shake our heads and we criticise and perhaps we laugh at ourselves, but we still do it every year, and go to some trouble to do it. And underneath it, just like those parents and rectors and 'honorables' all those years ago, in our way, perhaps we still mean it.

Bring back Latin

YOU OFTEN HEAR THE comment 'Bring back National Service' these days. But you will very rarely hear the sentiment 'Bring back Latin'. (Although there are some schools who have in fact done just that. Even Greek as well, we are told. How many I haven't the faintest idea. But not a lot, I would venture to guess.)

Yet Latin once had a far tighter stranglehold than soldiering on the problem of preparing the young for life. National Service lasted only about fifteen years. Latin was around in England for an incredible nineteen centuries. Of course, in many ways it still is – in our language, our habits of writing, our church protocol, our systems of law, our botanical studies, and a host more. It is in our bloodstream just as surely as our red and white corpuscles – though of course we are not aware of it. It was Latin (and the Gospel) which was the weapon used by the Church to keep civilisation alive when it looked for centuries as if the light of learning kindled by the Romans and Greeks was going to be snuffed out in the holocaust of violence, crudity, ignorance, and fear which overwhelmed the Roman Empire.

So Latin has impeccable credentials – of longevity if nothing else – and there are countless reasons why it should continue to be studied. It isn't, and the most ardent classicist has to admit that Latin (and Greek) now linger at the bottom of the league of subjects which cling – just – to the edges of the syllabus in a small minority of schools. Is it simply out of fashion? Is it now considered irrelevant? Is it thought to be too hard? Too soulless? Has it simply run out of steam, as the thousand-year-old system of monasteries ran out of steam in the 1530's?

Whether this is to be welcomed or deplored is a matter for debate far beyond the scope of this chapter. I simply state it as a fact.

What has all this to do with West Buckland?

Well, it is another fact that Latin has had a chequered career in West Buckland. When Brereton and Fortescue, the founders, set up their school, they had in mind something completely new. Secondary schools up to 1858 were, in their opinion, pretty barren places where dog-collared clergymen with Oxford and Cambridge degrees in Classics presided over a syllabus of Latin and Greek, more Latin and Greek, a lot of Bible and beating, and very little else. (Only for the sons of gentlemen, you understand, who were 'privileged'. But, looking at a syllabus like this today, one would wonder whether it was a privilege or a sentence.)

They wanted something new – lay headmasters, modern subjects, no Classics, and a much more liberal approach to the whole question of education. True, there was to be religious instruction, but it was not to be strangled by conformity to one denomination or another. Considering that Brereton was himself an Anglican clergyman, he deserves credit for being light years ahead of his time.

Then the school became the victim of its own success. (I am telescoping the events of several decades here in order to make a point; after all, I am not writing a history of the place.) Their exam successes and growing numbers induced them to lift their head in the company of the more fashionable public schools. Put another way, they felt they were now fit to join the nobs.

Little things, over the years. Senior pupils in positions of authority stopped being called 'Monitors' (which today smacks of the boy or girl in charge of the pencil-sharpener), and became 'Prefects'. Dormitories were re-christened 'houses'. The school's greatest headmaster was in fact in holy orders. So was another in the 1960's. Even the very first headmaster, who was appointed because he *didn't* wear a dog collar, took it into his head later on to study, and be accepted, for the priesthood.

And Latin appeared on the timetable. It looked a bit like the pigs in *Animal Farm*. The school became a member of the Headmasters' Conference, and, after a short lapse, still is – and proud of it.

I do not have documentary evidence for Latin's career here in detail. No syllabuses survive from the nineteenth century, no school registers, no administrative correspondence, no minutes of staff meetings, no records of 'Directors'' boards before about 1900. The only way to get close to the detailed truth would be to wade through every single page of the school magazine, which, on two mornings a week, I have not had time to do.

But Latin most certainly came back. I came across an exam paper for 'Form IVA' from March, 1926.

Get a load of these questions. Bear in mind they are for fourteen-year-olds.

1. Decline in full together *Magna urbs; curvum cornu.* [Of course, if you have not 'declined' Latin nouns and adjectives before, it presents problems. But they had.]
2. Give in columns the accusative singular, nominative plural, and

ablative plural and gender of: *Cor, hiema, ordo, crus, domus, os,* (a bone) [very helpful, that], *filia, senex, lex, portus.* [Do you know what accusatives, nominatives, and ablatives are?]
3. Compare: *difficilis, audax, facile, acriter, diu.* [And 'compare' doesn't mean what it means in everyday speech.]
4. Give the Latin for: 20 girls, 3,000 Romans, 4 each and 4 times. [Well, at least you can understand the question this time.]
5. Write out the Future Simple Active of *moneo*; the Future Perfect Passive of *rego,* the Imperfect Subjunctive Active of *audio,* the Present Infinitive of *fio, possum,* and *fero.* [I bet you don't understand this one]
6. Give the principal parts of: *Vincio, seco, sterno, volvo, tango, sepelio, nascor.* [Well, go on then.]

West Buckland was not a highly selective school, but it was assumed that this was within the scope of ordinary fourteen-year-olds. And don't forget that perhaps it was; we do not have the records of what marks they scored.

However, it was recognised that Latin was a difficult subject, and provision was made for those boys who found it beyond them. They were relieved of Latin, and given English lessons instead.

English! I have seen a 1920's printed proforma report where 'Latin' has been crossed out and 'English' written instead. 'English' was not printed on the report in the first place.

So it looks as if boys who found Latin too difficult were relieved of the pressure of it. They were 'not up to it'. By the standards of the school and of the world of education, then, they were a mite backward. Better give them some English. At least they speak it, and shouldn't find it so hard. And they have to do something.

Latin rumbled on, till well after the War. Then the rot set in, from the point of view of the classicists. Oxford and Cambridge ceased to demand it as a qualification for entry. There was no shortage of reformers who crusaded to remove this barrier of dead languages which was standing in the way of Biology and Geology and Social Studies and General Studies and Personal Education, and Integrated Studies and the rest of the never-ending stream of subjects whose partisans produced unanswerable arguments to prove that their particular bonnet bee was the key to progress for the nation's young.

Nothing stays constant; the wheel turned again. It is an irony that it was a Greek philosopher who pointed out that everything is in a state of flux.

Latin came back – again. Though this time somewhat furtively, transparently disguised as 'Latin Studies'. Latin was to be made 'accessible'. So instead of learning every single conjugation and tense and case ending, pupils were told all about what went on in an Ancient Roman's house and what he had for breakfast. Cicero and Catullus did not get much of a look-in.

It didn't last; there was more flux. The shade of Heraclitus would have been pleased to see his theory vindicated yet again. Latin Studies faded away. This may have been due to the retirement of a classicist headmaster. Any new headmaster has to make changes, so.... But this is only a guess.

However, I think it is a fact that, at the time of writing, hardly any members (if any at all) of the academic staff have had training in Latin or Greek. Even from a general knowledge point of view, it would be interesting to find out how many of the staff could handle the Imperfect Subjunctive of an *English* verb, never mind a Latin one. And how many of us would care whether he can or not?

So anybody who wants to see 'Latin' printed again on a report proforma will have to work pretty hard.

I say, I say, I say. . .

THIS IS ANOTHER STEP in the 'getting-them-to-look-at-the-notice-board' campaign If nothing else, it helps to clobber the cliché that nothing frivolous or light-hearted ever comes out of an archive.

You would be surprised, wouldn't you, to be told that Tommy Cooper spent some time as a pupil at WB. Even more surprised to be told that the Archive found these jottings in inside the back cover of one of his English exercise books:

'A jump-lead walks into a bar and asks for a drink.
The barman says, "I'll serve you this time, but don't start anything." '

'A sandwich walks into a bar and asks for a drink.
The barman says, "Sorry – we don't serve food in here." '

'Two hydrogen atoms walk into a bar.
One says, "I think I've lost an electron."
The other says, "Good heavens – are you sure?"
He said, "I'm positive." '

'A man walks into a bar with a roll of tarmac under his arm.
He says, "A pint, please – and one for the road." '

'Two aerials meet on a roof, fall in love, and get married.
The ceremony wasn't much, but the reception was terrific.'

'Answer-phone message: "If you want to buy marijuana, press the hash key." '

Still on Record

Everyone chipping in

IF EVER YOU WANT proof that West Buckland is a family affair, the list of original shareholders offers it. There were a hundred, it seems. I have found details of the second fifty. Each share was worth five pounds. A hundred on the list: first capital-raising then – five thousand pounds.

That doesn't sound much, but allow for inflation. A day-boy's fees then amounted to £5 – for the year. The Headmaster – the *Headmaster* – was paid a hundred pounds a year. You get the general idea.

However, anyone who has tried to extract money out of people – for whatever reason and no matter how worthy the motive – knows how difficult and thankless it is. The actual sums may be wildly different from those of today, but the amount of work that went into raising them would have been, I submit, the same.

We don't know how widely the school project was advertised, but it seems pretty telling that, apart from the nobility (more of them in a minute), everyone on this list came from Devon – Torrington, Totnes, Tiverton, Barnstaple (of course), South Molton (or, as they wrote, 'Southmolton'), West Buckland (but that was the Headmaster; one would hope that he would show confidence in his own school), Parracombe, High Bray and Meshaw (near South Molton), and Copplestone. Oh – and one renegade from Cornwall on the other side of the world.

Who were they? Two clergymen – who were not as a rule well off; look at the number of West Buckland lunches they turned up for (an improvement, no doubt on the level of catering in their lofty rectories). Three solicitors, one of whom gives his name to a practice that survives to this day in Barnstaple. The Headmaster, as I said. Two bankers. Well, you can't get much more respectable than that. The steward of Earl Fortescue decided that he would have a flutter – if only to the tune of one share.

Four gentlemen described themselves as just that – 'gentlemen'. I wonder what would be the reaction if a shareholder described himself as that today. (It could provoke a nice little diversionary debate: just what was a 'gentleman'?)

Then two names that would have caused consternation by their absence – the Revd. J.L. Brereton and Earl Fortescue. Dammit, they were the founders; it was their idea. They had to give proof of their faith in it. Brereton, incidentally, went one stage further; he was prepared to commit two of his sons (and, for all I know, more – he had four) to the experiment of 'middle-class education' – which puts to shame those reforming socialist politicians who legislate about abolishing privilege in the righteous name of equality and then quietly send their sons to expensive public schools.

Finally, the Earl of Devon (well, it was Devon) and, unbelievably, the Duke of Bedford. Conclusive evidence of Brereton's honey tongue and Fortescue's clout. For his next school in Norfolk, Brereton conjured money even out of the Prince of Wales.

Collecting celebrities

THERE IS NOTHING NEW under the sun. For its Speech Day of 1868 (just under a decade after it was born), this tiny little school in the back of beyond, the Devon County School, went celebrity-hunting, and didn't do too badly.

The Revd. Prebendary Brereton – well, of course; he was a founder, and turned up regularly, everywhere. He didn't have to be persuaded. He was an inveterate networker.

Lord Taunton – hardly a household name now, but in 1868 he was; he had just compiled a landmark Government report on education. He was that most attractive of celebrities – topical.

The Revd. W.H. Karslake – whose name was one to conjure with for every pupil who has ever had a meal in the school; he was the builder of the Dining Hall. Though how a country clergyman managed that we are not told.

The chaplain of a Cambridge college. Posh, famous, and holy – a perfect combination.

The Revd. Jack Russell, the renowned dog-breeder from Swimbridge. A 'personality' by any standards. What did he talk about in social gatherings, one wonders.

The novelist Thomas Hughes, the author of *Tom Brown's Schooldays*. Quite a coup; it would be like getting J.K.Rowling today.

Two more sent their apologies, because they had been prevented by 'unavoidable circumstances' from attending. Well, that's what they said. The Master of Trinity College, Cambridge, and Sir Stafford Northcote, M.P., Secretary of State for India. But worth showing off about, with their names in the magazine – the two heavyweights who *nearly* came.

The epic habit

THE *REGISTER* OF JUNE, 1914, reported a rarity in the cultural life of West Buckland:

'During the term, by a special arrangement, the kinematograph film, *Quo Vadis*, was shown for the benefit of the School in the Dining Hall. It proved of very great interest to everyone, and much light was thrown upon the customs and habits of the Romans; for days after boys might be seen greeting each other from a distance with outstretched hand after the Roman fashion.'

The more you think about this, the more comments and speculations spring to mind.

The 'kinematograph' film. 'Kinematograph' – isn't that lovely? Inured as we are now to the endless wonders of modern technology, it is difficult for us to appreciate, even estimate, the depth of awe and excitement such an event would provoke in those early days – and in a rural boarding school where nobody ever went anywhere. One gasps at the ingenuity and resource, not to say imagination, of the member of staff who engineered it.

Where did he find it? How did he get it? How did the local postman deliver it? And how was he able to project it, when the school had no electricity (that didn't come till 1923)? Did some tireless, and hapless, individual turn a handle all that time?

It was a silent film of course. Was it *projected* in total silence? (Apart from the projector.) Did the school have available a pianist who could keep up a non-stop accompaniment to a multi-hour Roman Empire epic?

If only one could have been a fly on the wall, how many surprises would there have been in witnessing the audience's reactions?

Was this the very first film the boys had ever seen? Could have been. No wonder it made an impact.

And before we smile patronisingly at the 'Roman fashion' salute craze that followed, let us remember how phrases like 'May the force be with you' and 'Shaken, not stirred' have passed into our folklore – not just 'for days', but for good.

5. 2004

Read what it says

THIS IS AN OLD schoolmaster's joke. The fact that I found it printed on quarto-sized paper dates it. But old jokes can often still raise a smile.

THIS IS A TIMED TEST – YOU HAVE THREE MINUTES ONLY
1. Read everything carefully before doing anything.
2. Print your name in the upper right corner of this paper.
3. Circle the word "name" in the sentence no. 2.
4. Draw 5 small squares in the upper left corner of this sheet.
5. Put "X2" in each square.
6. Sign your name at the top of this paper.
7. In front of your name, write "YES, YES, YES".
8. Put a circle completely round sentence no. 3.
9. Put an "X" in the lower left corner of this paper.
10. Draw a triangle around the "X" you have just put down.
11. Draw a rectangle around the word "corner" in sentence no. 4.
12. Punch three small holes in the top of this paper with your pencil point or biro.
13. LOUDLY, speak so that everyone can hear you, and say: "I AM NEARLY FINISHED, I HAVE FOLLOWED INSTRUCTIONS".
14. Now that you have finished reading everything carefully, do only numbers 1 and 2.

I doubt if a joke like this would occur to many teachers today. Attitudes change. This one falls in line with the apocryphal report penned by a weary teacher about his whole class: 'I am totally free from prejudice. I find all my pupils equally stupid.'

From the Archive

Certificate for Burial of ashes of a body cremated at Weymouth Crematorium, pursuant to the Regulations made by the Secretary of State for the Home Department 1930

Issued by the
WEYMOUTH AND PORTLAND BOROUGH COUNCIL
Municipal Offices, Weymouth
(Telephone: Weymouth 785101)

Cremation No. 3444 B

THIS IS TO CERTIFY that the Certificate of registry of death of _Eleanor Harries_ aged 99 years who died on 7th December 1985 at Greenbushes Nursing Home, Dorchester registered at Entry No. 184 on the 9th day of December 1985, by the Registrar of Births and Deaths, Registration District _Weymouth_ Sub-District _Dorchester_ has been produced to the Medical Referee and filed by me in accordance with the Regulations made under S.7 of the Cremation Act, 1902 (2 Ed. VII, c.8.).†

Dated 11th December 1985

R. E. F. NORMAN
Registrar (C.S.)

† A Certified Extract from the Register of Cremations can be obtained at the Municipal Offices at a charge of 20p.

A batch of burial certificates came our way recently. Here's a link with the past. Eleanor Harries ('Ellie') was the widow of E.C. Harries (HM 1907-34), who had been born in 1865, only 10 years after the School's foundation.

Visit from the Bard

Thoughts during the *Exmoor:*

'For this, be sure, tonight thou shalt have cramps,
Side stiches that shall pen thy breath up.'

GCSE English

'Here will be an old abusing of God's patience and the King's English.'

Tuckshop at the end of term

'Let us, like merchants, show our foulest wares
And think, perchance, they'll sell.'

'O' Level results by post

'Read o'er this:
And after, this: and then to breakfast with
What appetite you have.'

REPORT ON
West Buckland Farm and County School,
READ BY THE MASTER, MR. THOMPSON,
ON THE
OPENING OF THE NEW DORMITORY, MAY 24, 1859,
AND
PRINTED BY THE DESIRE OF THE COMPANY
ASSEMBLED THERE

'MY LORD FORTESCUE,
Before commencing my report of the operations of the Farm and

County School, permit me to express on behalf both of masters and pupils, our high sense of the honor [sic] your Lordship has conferred upon us, in consenting to engage in the proceedings of this day. To your Lordship's liberality we are indebted for the room which we are now met to inaugurate, and that liberality receives an additional value from the manner in which your Lordship and my Lady Fortescue have condescended to take part in its opening. I trust, my Lord, that either within these our "wooden walls", or in a more durable and substantial building we may again and again have the honor and pleasure of welcoming your Lordship, and of rendering an account of our proceedings and of our progress. . . . '

And so on and so on. All very orotund stuff. One wonders how it would have sounded in the voice and presence of a young man of only twenty-one years of age. Because that's how old Thompson was when he was appointed, and the school was only six months old on 'MAY 24, 1859'. It cannot be coincidence that the date chosen was Queen Victoria's birthday. It all added to the general wave of lush loyalty and complimentary goo that drenched the occasion.

But it was the way people did things. And, to a certain extent, still do them now. In cold print long after the event, it looks pretty cringe-making, but people then understood matters of form just as they do now. We still tolerate 'Yours sincerely' at the end of letters. How many of us mean it?

Note the original name of the school. The 'farm' component soon fell away, because it didn't work. The founders adopted the 'County' name because they did not want their school (and the others they were going to found – and did) to be linked to the church in any way. No bishoprics need apply. Astoundingly liberal for the time, especially considering that Brereton, one of the founders, was an Anglican priest.

The school was going to be organised in 'two parts: the Upper and Preparatory'. The dividing age was thirteen. The 'Prep' had a chequered career in West Buckland history. Here it is, at the very outset. But before long it seems to have faded away, and was simply tacked on to the main school. For years the entry age was kept at eleven, though there are individual instances of boys below that age entering.

This habit too seems to have died in the early and mid-twentieth century, and a fairly rigid cut-off at eleven became standard. It was not until the 1970's that a proper 'Prep.' emerged again. That was followed by the 'Pre-Prep' and, ultimately, by the Nursery Unit.

Thompson put cards on the table. After all, he was setting out the wares of a brand-new school, founded, I repeat, only six months before. Senior boys were to be prepared for 'Agricultural and Commercial pursuits, for the Civil Service Examinations, for the Oxford and Cambridge [Local] Examinations [these last, known as the "Locals", were set up in the same year that West Buckland was born]. . . to fit them to occupy honourable and independent positions in life; while the Preparatory division, as its name implies, is intended to afford younger boys such good elementary instruction as may enable them to enter the Upper division with credit to themselves and satisfaction to their friends'.

Note that Thompson, ever the visionary, could not help stealthily inserting, even while he was thanking Fortescue for the wooden building, the tentative hope that a stone one might one day appear – and who did they hope would contribute to that?

Oh, yes – and fees, for the 'Upper Division', were to be £25 – a year. That included boarding. Well, it was aimed at the 'middle class'.

Finally, look at the titles – the effort and thought invested in the fonts and layouts. And the punctuation – all those commas at the ends of the lines, for example. Considering that, in the beginning, punctuation hardly existed (look at a medieval manuscript; they didn't even dot the 'i's' at one time), printers and custom had come a long way. Since 1859, they have gone a long way again – back? We don't write 'M.P.' now; we write 'MP'. We don't write 'U.S.A.'; we write 'USA'. Not 'D.S.O.', but 'DSO'. The colon is practically dead. The semi-colon is an endangered species. The apostrophe is so badly abused ('potato's'; 'its' and 'it's') that it is under threat of dying from, effectively, lack of care.

Because I once had to study 'Divinity', I am in a position to close with the comment '*Ichabod, Ichabod*'. But it wouldn't cut much ice with a modern population whose education informs us about Sikhs and Buddhists but does not tell us much about the Old Testament.

A little learning

RICHARD PEARSE CHOPE, FROM Hartland, had a distinguished career at the school as a pupil (prizes, Fortescue Medal, scholarship to Cambridge, and so on), and, after he left, became, and remained, a relentless benefactor.

He maintained a steady stream of gifts; he wrote scholarly, and very long, articles for the school magazine (which the embarrassed editors tried hard to edit without giving offence); he turned up at every public function and old boys' event (and sat in the middle of the front row for the photograph); and held every office that the Old Boys' Association had to offer.

Early in the twentieth century he set up a General Knowledge Prize, and himself composed the questions. He kept this up till his death in the 1930's.. It survived even after that, till 1965. By modern standards the early ones (set by Chope) were of fiendish abstruseness and difficulty, and one would love to have been able to see the actual marks the boys gained.

However, Chope had a sense of humour too, and (in the *Register* of course) he published some of the more outrageous wrong answers. As with pupils through the ages, they defy logic, reason, and imagination, but they are much more fun than the right ones:

- Tipperary won the Derby last year.
- The great friend of Dr. Johnson was David Livingstone.
- Kruger was an Austrian coinage.
- '*Dies Irae*' means 'the gods of wrath'. It means the wrath of the Gods. It is a zugma.
- In answer to the question 'Explain the reference to "sumer is a-cumen in" ', we had the following:
    1. It is either Latin or Scotch
    2. It is in the Somerset dialect.
    3. It is the first line of a poem by a man with a cold.
    4. It was a German song sung by Bismarck, when he was dying. It is said that it helped him to pass away much quicker.

Rising to the challenge

AT THE TURN OF the nineteenth and twentieth centuries, a team of inspectors descended upon the school. In their report, they found the provision for teaching was satisfactory, and the provision for outdoor pursuits very satisfactory (all that moor and all that cross-country running, and football, and cricket – even, for a while, rugby). But they observed that there was very little time or facility devoted to cultural or other activities.

The new Headmaster, Mr. William Arthur Knight, must have been stung, and it is no coincidence that, in the following few years, A Reading and Debating Society was founded; scientific laboratories were built; a Rifle Club was inaugurated. And a Swimming Pool appeared.

This announcement was published in the *Register* for October, 1903:

The Swimming Bath

'The Old Bathing Pond will soon, we hope, be a thing of the past. Expert advice has been obtained, plans and specifications have been drawn up, and it is found that, with a sum of about one hundred and fifty pounds, a really first-class bath may be built; and towards this a sum of over thirty pounds has already been promised by Parents, Governors, Masters, Old Boys and Friends. In addition to this the School has promised twenty pounds, and a like sum has been allocated from the Games Fund, so that already we can reckon on nearly half the required sum.

Signs are not wanting that a great deal of expense will be saved by our own efforts in the digging line. . . . '

This is typical West Buckland make do and mend, short-cutting, and DIY. Even more prudently, to shore up the side of the pool while it was in construction, they used timbers which had survived when the school cricket pavilion had been burnt down. Waste not. . .

Among the other subscribers to the fund was Mr. Knight, the Headmaster (well, it was probably his idea) and Viscount Ebrington, the son of Earl Fortescue. You have to hand it to the Fortescues; they understood very clearly that the school depended for sustenance not only on the Fortescue name and clout, but on the cheque book, and they duly chipped in.

We all know that inflation has been ever-present, and we expect to be told about low costs and prices in the 'old days' (just listen to grandparents). But even so, it still comes as a shock to be told that an entire 'really first-class bath' was obtainable for £150 – even if you dig the hole yourself.

And finally, the 'Old Bathing Pond' – which had been serving the school's needs ever since the 1870's, and which was so much a part of school life that it was dignified by capital letters in the text of the announcement. One would dearly love to have been able to see it.

Casting the net wide

BY 1904, THE READING and Debating Society was in full swing, and met regularly throughout the year. The *Register* of October, 1904 printed a 'summary of the meetings of the summer term'. (Apologies for the unavoidable pun.).

'May 9th – J. Pearce read an essay on "R.D. Blackmore and Lorna Doone". The Society has not hitherto had many literary papers, and the departure was a welcome one. The rather astonishing fact revealed itself that some of the members had not read "Lorna Doone". [How shocking! I doubt if, today, one boy or girl in a hundred has read *Lorna Doone*. But the Devon County School was miles from anywhere, and there was not even the radio, never mind television. People read. At any rate literary, grown-up, well-educated people. This applies the more so to North Devon, because Blackmore was one of the giants of Devon-inspired fiction of the time. Hence the shock. It would be as if a teenager today had not heard of Harry Potter. It seems that, then as now, schoolboys were a pretty unrepentant Philistine lot.]. . .

'May 16th – S.E. Passmore proposed a motion in favour of constructing a Channel Tunnel. . . . The bogie of invasion loomed large in most of the speakers, and finally the cause of insularity triumphed.'

[Insularity or no insularity, it is perhaps surprising to discover that a Channel Tunnel was being discussed, by schoolboys, over a hundred years ago.]

'May 23rd – G.E.L. Carter read a very interesting paper on "Buddha and Buddhism", dealing with both the history and philosophy of Buddhism.

'May 30th – Mr. Harries [later Headmaster; at this time he was the School Chaplain] proposed a motion in favour of cremation. . . . apart from the opening speeches, [the debate] was not quite up to the traditions of this House.' [Interesting that secretaries did not confine themselves to mere reportage; they felt free to pass comment as well. And 'traditions'? – the Reading and Debating Society was only a year old.]

'June 6th – J.C. Pearce [Pearce again – busy boy] read a paper on the Zulus, which was extremely interesting, as a considerable part of it was based on personal knowledge of the country and the people. . .' [Now how had J.C. Pearce got himself to Zululand – from North Devon? Was it more likely that Pearce had got himself *to* North Devon *from* Zululand, because his father and family had left South Africa after England's messy victory in the Boer War? The Boers were not going to be friendly after having suffered such treatment.].

'June 13th – Mr. Fry [a teacher, in charge of the R. and D. Soc. He read the Secretary's Minutes too, and you can still see his corrections in the margin.] proposed a motion in favour of "Conscription". . . . The cause of patriotism was lost by the casting vote of the Chairman.' [Odd; this is the high tide decade of King and Empire. Yet they all rushed to volunteer in 1914. Rather like the young men in the Oxford Union who famously said that they would not fight for King and Country. But of course they did.]

A boy of few words

WEST BUCKLAND SCHOOL.
REPORT FOR THE TERM ENDING JULY 28TH, 1924.

House: Grenville

NAME	Age	Form	No. of Boys	Average Age	General Work	Mathematics	Science	Final Form Order
Sanders, R.T.	17.0	IV.A	27	16.1	12	6	4	7

Order on Exam. Results	Latin	French	English	History	Geography	Divinity	Drawing	Handwork
	13	13			12			

LATIN: Consistently satisfactory. *Classics Master*

FRENCH: Satisfactory work & progress. *Mod. Language Master*

ENGLISH: Good. *English Master*

MATHEMATICS: Good work. *Math. Master*

SCIENCE: Good work & progress. *Science Master*

MUSIC: Steady progress has been made. *M.W. Music Master*

SHORTHAND or BOOK-KEEPING: —

Very good. Why not let him take the School Certificate in 1925.

ERNEST C. HARRIES, M.A., Head Master.

Tuesday, Sept. 16th, 1924. Boarders Return. They are required to report themselves to the Head Master immediately on their arrival, and to hand in their Health Certificates.
Wednesday, Sept. 17th, 1924. Day Boys Return. Prayers and Roll Call 10.30 a.m.
Friday, Sept. 19th, 1924. Camp Contingent return.

P.T.O.

Take a look at this report. . . .

The English teacher was the legendary Sam Howells, noted for his fierce discipline, sharp tongue, and high standards. To get a laconic 'Good' out of him was probably quite an achievement.

'MW' in Music was Mr. Watson ('Watto'), who, with 42 years to his credit, is the longest-serving member of the academic staff (at least three others, on the support staff, have beaten that). Watto played the piano for all the rehearsals and performances for the nineteen-year run of Gilbert and Sullivan operas that the school put on. Harries, the Head, was crazy about G. and S., and usually took the leading role.

Watto had a second nickname, which makes him quite rare. Apparently the other one was 'Barch'. Work that one out. . . . Music. . . keyboard. . . classical. . .

Master Sanders was seventeen years old, and nearly a year older than the class average. And they were talking about putting him in for School Certificate (GCSE today) in 1925 – the *following year*. If they were debating whether to put a seventeen-year-old in for a sixteen-plus exam a year later, and his final form order was 7th, out of 27, what does that say about the average academic achievement of the others? Perhaps sights were simply lower then. Lower expectations usually produce lower performance.

Now look at the wordage. The grand total of subject remarks comes to sixteen. The total vocabulary used in the remarks is six.

I asked one of the school secretaries to print me out a brace of typical reports from today – quite at random. The total wordage came to 1,600 – each. Does that mean that the teaching today is a hundred times better? If not, what does it mean? If anything. Does it automatically follow that a parent can get a clearer picture of their child from 1,600 words than they could from 16? One of those random reports I spoke about used the boy's Christian name forty times.

Finally, if you come to the conclusion that the teaching staff in 1924 weren't up to much, look again at their handwriting. Never mind the brevity or the unoriginality for a moment; the calligraphy is very respectable – probably a good deal better than teachers' handwriting today. But then teachers today don't have to *write* reports; they simply knock on a few keys. They don't even have to sign their name – or their initials..

Buttoned up

THE ARCHIVE NATURALLY HAS a lot of group photographs – staff, pupils, staff *and* pupils, governors, cricket, rugby, football teams, teams from every sport and outlandish activity under the sun. It is tempting to think that when you've seen one, you' ve seen them all, and it is indeed true that their interest and appeal is usually confined to those who appear in them (unless you are an old boy, stabbing a forefinger at a dimly-remembered face from forty years before).

But now and again, when you look at one, things strike you – not individuals, but general impressions. Trains of thought can be started. Particularly if you are looking at one from an evocative year.

I came across the photo of the whole school – well, half of it. It was one of those mighty panoramas, and somebody apparently had wanted only the left-hand half. But you still think things.

This one was from July, 1939. In these days when so many men go about with no ties at all – with lounge suits – one can be forgiven for wondering whether what we are witnessing is nothing less than the demise of the tie. In this picture every member of staff, naturally, is smart – lounge suits for the most part. But not a single boy either has his hair uncombed or his top button undone. Ties are tight up to where they are designed to be, caressing the Adam's apple.

No doubt boys then found plenty of other ways to express their attitude to authority and correctness, as boys always have. But the general impression created is quite striking.

Secondly, to repeat, 1939. The War was only two months away. How many of these boys had any inkling of what was about to happen – something which turned out to be the greatest single event of the entire twentieth century?

We have all seen groups like this; the fact that I have not illustrated this one in no way detracts from what it makes us think. We all know about the regimentation, the 'done-up' smartness, the moon spectacles, the long socks and knickerbockers in the front row, the pale uncreased faces, the serious frowns and self-conscious dignity among the prefects. We know what is ahead of them; they didn't.

How many volunteered as soon as they could? How many left school early so that they could join up? How many hoped that their experience in the school cadet force (the '*Officers*' Training Corps') would help them to gain a commission? How many went abroad? And where? How many saw action? How many were decorated? How many came home wounded, crippled, disabled?

How many of the boys in that picture did not come home at all?

Lucky lad

FROM TIME TO TIME, the Archive receives material from old boys, or, more often, from the *families* of old boys, as they go through Grandad's things after the funeral.

This piece is about a boy called Richard Guy Anstice Prideaux, who attended the school between 1930 and 1933, in Grenville House. It was sent by his daughter.

It looks as if it was composed by his family out of listening to his reminiscences about the War. The first person is not used at all. This is what it said:

1933 – Richard left West Buckland School.

1934 – Started an Engineering Apprenticeship at Fawcett Preston in Liverpool.

Met Joan Mary Eggleston, who worked for the same firm as a secretary.

1939 – Joined the Royal Engineers – 104 Army Troops Company, based at Chorlton-cum-Hardy, Manchester. He volunteered before call-up.

1940 – Went to France – Nantes – where he acted as interpreter as he spoke fluent French. As Royal Engineers, they were the last to leave when the army was retreating from the Germans. Their troop was to be evacuated from St. Nazaire on the Cunard liner 'The Lancastria'. After being delayed they missed the boat, and ended up with a coal ship.

The 'Lancastria' received a direct hit and was sunk by German planes at the mouth of the Loire just off St. Nazaire, with the loss of 3,000 lives, on June 17th, 1940. This was to be the worst maritime disaster in British history, but wasn't reported to the British public for fear of lowering morale.

June 29th, 1940 – married Joan Mary Eggleston, by special licence – 'relieved to be alive'.

It is neverendingly amazing what the pressure of war will do. It looks from this as if Richard was courting Joan Eggleston from 1934. He certainly considered her important enough to record the time he first met her.

War came. He had this escape on 17th June. Although he later left the Army because, as an engineer, he was in a reserved occupation, he must have been made totally aware of the chanciness of war. There couldn't have been a more tragic lesson than 'The Lancastria'. Something had to be done.

He was courting, or at least knew, Joan for six years. After he came back from St. Nazaire, it took him just twelve days to get married – 'by special licence'.

Chope's joke book

IN FEBRUARY, 1915, THE *Register* published Mr. Chope's gems of learning mined from the answer papers to his General Knowledge exam.

By the Petition of Right the King was not allowed to order taxis without the consent of Parliament.
Queen Mary had all the Protestants put under the steak.
Henry VIII was very pious, and he had a hymn-book chained up in every church.
Tennyson was the greatest writer of Roman prose, he wrote the 'Iliad' and 'Paradise Lost'.
Australia exports wine to England, made from a bird called the emu.
Cologne is famous for the odour made there.
To germinate means to become a naturalized German.
'Magna Carta means the queen has lost her garter. The French for it is *honi soit qui mal y pense*.
A refugee is a man who keeps order in a football match. [I'll go along with that.]

Chope knocked off all this (preparation, setting, marking, selecting) in between working for the Patent Office, and commuting regularly to London from Hartland. Hartland! And there were no trains to Hartland. He ran a local dramatic society, edited a local news sheet, and gave regular recitations in the Devon dialect. In this same year (1915) he published *The London Devonian Year Book*, to which the editor of the *Register* gave the sort of ecstatic review that authors dream of.

A school in every county

THE SCHOOL'S FOUNDER, THE Revd. J.L. Brereton, thought big. He envisaged not only a new type of secondary school, for 'the middle classes', which he succeeded in setting up, with Earl Fortescue, in Devon; he wanted to establish a school like it in every county in England.

To his credit, he worked at it, and schools appeared in Devon, Norfolk, Gloucester, Hampshire, Somerset, Bedford, Suffolk, Surrey, and Durham. Sadly, they did not all survive. Those that remained changed their name. West Buckland itself was, for years, the Devon County School, before being transmuted to West Buckland School in 1912. Surrey County School became Cranleigh. Somerset CS emerged as Wellington (not *the* Wellington in Berkshire). Suffolk CS reappeared as Framlingham, and the North-East County School renamed itself Barnard Castle School.

The first two were in Devon and Norfolk. Why the great distance between them?

The answer is to do with Brereton's pastoral work. Or at least it seems to be the overwhelmingly likely answer. He was the rector of the village of West Buckland. His father was the rector in a small Norfolk village called Little Massingham, only a few miles from where the Norfolk CS was born just outside North Elmham. When his father died, Brereton moved from West Buckland to take over from his father at Little Massingham.

So that appears to be the connection. He strengthened the connection by taking his Deputy Head at the DCS and installing him as the first HM in Norfolk. (He later was responsible for securing his second son's appointment as HM at the North-East CS.)

Look at the picture. There are similarities between the Norfolk building and the one at West Buckland. It would be interesting to try and find out if they were built by the same architect. (There are similarities too with the North-East CS.) It is quite possible; Brereton was a man of enormous energy and drive, and his co-founder, Lord Fortescue, knew absolutely everybody.

Sadly, the Norfolk County School failed. The HM, William Watson, died young, and the successor, Brereton's son (forced by his father to move from successful tenure at the North-East CS), was unable to keep it going.

Not only did the school disappear; the building did too – literally. I have visited the site, and all that I could see was a solitary doorstep.

It seems a shame that this magnificent-looking building, founded with so much well-meaning energy and such crusading zeal (education for the 'middle classes' – what more worthy cause could you have, except perhaps education for the 'working classes'), should have vanished so completely.

It did not disappear overnight; the building was used by Dr. Barnardo's for a while, and then became a naval cadet training academy. But the contrast still makes an impact: that great big school, and now only a doorstep, and few pitiful little gravestones in the over-shaded school burying ground.

Gazing into the future

ON SATURDAY, SEPTEMBER 17TH, 1939 (that is, only a fortnight after the outbreak of the Second World War), there was a debate in the Phoenix Society.

'The Phoenix', as it became known, was the successor to the school's original Reading and Debating Society. The transition took place in 1926, and to this day the Archivist has not been able to find out why the change took place. From the existing records, both societies performed pretty much the same functions; it seems only a matter of names. The only differences that I can discover are that the R. and D. Soc.'s members read learned 'papers' in between debates, and the Phoenix gave occasional play-readings.

Be that as it may, on the day recorded above, there was a debate on the motion 'In the opinion of this House Gas will play an insignificant part in Modern Warfare'.

As it happened, they were right, insofar as it was not used during the Second World War. Which is perhaps odd, since it was little more than twenty years since it had made its dread appearance on the Western Front during the *First* World War. In 1939, there were thousands of surviving victims of it; society must have been conscious of them, just as it was well aware of the loss of arms and legs, because so many men were seen on the streets with crutches. What was it that produced the argument that it could not happen again?

One of the answers produced was based on technology. A speaker claimed that it was no longer possible to inflict this form of attack, because modern defences against it were more efficient. Recent new anti-aircraft techniques were now able to force aeroplanes above the altitude from which gas could be effectively dropped.

Well, it may sound initially plausible, but even a scientific ignoramus might be forgiven for thinking that this argument was about as accurate as the 'expert' opinion which claimed that the new railways would never take on because they were too dangerous; human lungs would not be able to stand the pressure of being whisked through the air at speeds in excess of thirty-five miles an hour.

All this of course dwindles into mere antiquarian curiosity when one contemplates the modern techniques of chemical and nuclear weapons. What would the Phoenix Society have made of that?

6. 2005

Unidentified

ON 20TH JANUARY, 2005, I put this notice on the board in the Common Room.

'I have come across a lot of photographs of past drama productions – either undated or untitled, or both.

'I should be grateful if colleagues suffering from longevity could glance inside a buff envelope in my pigeon-hole, and offer their speculations – in pencil preferably, on the relevant white envelopes inside – and sign their speculations.'

I should confidently bet that one of the bugbears of a school archivist's working life (well, if not bugbear, nuisance) is the number of photographs that he finds which offer little or no means of identifying themselves.

Why is this? We are brought up to date letters. If we work in offices, we are made to put in dates *and* references. When we write emails today, and forget to type in a title, we get a firm reminder from the machine. Teachers, friends, and others connected with the school, know that they are taking the picture of the particular group or club or event for posterity. What use is posterity if we don't know what part of posterity is being preserved?

Even if dates and titles are put in, it does not always occur to the picture-monger to provide names. In the Archive are A4 boxes packed with shots of rugby teams, cricket teams, tennis teams, swimming teams, basketball teams, Ten Tors finishers, rock-climbers, prize-winners, drama medal gold-medallists, and cheeky also-rans.

Yes, I could ask long-serving members of staff, and I do occasionally. But staff memories are not limitless, and the task of applying this technique to the whole collection would be near-impossible, especially on a work allocation of two mornings a week. To say nothing of driving to exasperation willing colleagues who are already coping with an over-filled week.

Nevertheless, I am frequently gratified by their willingness. I am moreover often entertained by the peripheral comments that come with, or even without, the identifying information. Stories, anecdotes, and tales out of school, come freely, and provide much more enjoyment than that offered by the mere knowledge that the boy second from the left at the back is called Dallyn or Beer or Szelest or Ubogu or whatever.

I once attended an afternoon meeting of veteran staff, which was designed to elicit information about boys who appeared on various past lists of an academic nature, I think it was.

The remarks and reminiscences that came out produced a constant chorus of chuckles, sniggers, belly-laughs, and total guffaws. For a moment I wished I had had some paper on which to record it all, but, as the tide of racy recall rolled on, I realised that it would not do. Some of the contents were near-unprintable. Colleagues moreover were speaking off the record, and it would not have been fair or discreet to put down everything they said.

But what a time we had. The meeting overran prodigiously.

Foot in the door

IN FEBRUARY OF THIS year, I put up a notice about the youngest pupil the school had yet had: on the admission date, she was a fortnight short of her third birthday.

In the 1970's, the school had opened a Prep. department. There had been under-elevens at the school before, but this was the first 'proper' Prep. – separate buildings, separate staff, its own headmaster, and so on.

The *raison d'être* for this, one would guess, was to recruit children (and parents) early, and get them used to the place, and, if possible, get them to like it. Like it so much that they would be prepared to contemplate, when they reached eleven, another seven years in the senior school. In short, catch 'em early.

Before long, the penny seems to have dropped that, if we could successfully catch'em early, why not catch 'em earlier? So the 'Pre-Prep.' was born.

It does not take much imagination to work out what the logical end to this process would be. The Nursery unit made its debut, just before the turn of the century.

Records are made to be broken. Before long I had found a child who had come into the Nursery at just two years and three days.

As with the debate about the increasing difficulty of beating hundred-metre sprint records, one wonders how far this Nursery phenomenon can go. Will we see, one day, prams and crèches?

The shortcomings of education

IN JANUARY, 2005, I listened to a broadcast by a Malaysian academic, visiting his home country from Germany in the wake of the Indian Ocean disaster (it added a new word to our vocabulary – *tsunami*).

In this broadcast he offered a remark (I forget à propos of what) which I thought worth saving – worth 'archiving', if you like. Certainly worth sharing with the Common Room.

'Scholars are not trained to think of the obvious.'

We can all get compartmentalised by the nature of our work. Doctors look at the world through the end of a stethoscope. Photographers gaze at a striking view and at once think of composition. Teachers look at a boy with spectacles – they don't think of his eyesight; they wonder if he is going to be a clever-clogs.

We forget, when we examine a situation or a problem, to search for the simplest view of it. Children are often much better at this than we are, because they don't have much education or knowledge to get in the way; they rely on their own gumption and powers of observation.

An academic is prone to the same weakness as the doctors and the photographers and the teachers. Hence this Malaysian professor's comment. It struck me so forcibly that I typed it out, had it printed on card and laminated, and put it up on the softboard plaque in my office.

It also reminded me of a remark attributed to General, later President, Charles de Gaulle.

In France, one of the most prestigious educational/academic institutions of all is the Polytechnique. Its alumni, by the time they become alumni, have undergone, and survived, a terrifying regimen of study, learning, exposition, and general non-stop absorption. Chiefly engineering and general administration. By the end of it, they are universally recognised as the very tops, the *ne plus ultra*, the cream of the cream. Time and again, they win the very best jobs in their respective fields. The 'Poly' is frequently placed in the very top rank of world universities.

But Monsieur le Président (although by general consent one of the most difficult men to work with on the face of the planet) was clearly a shrewd judge of personality and character. He wanted more than just clever clogs.

He is supposed to have observed of one such 'brilliant' Polytechnique graduate, 'The trouble with that young man is that he knows everything – but he doesn't know anything else.'

How unique are we?

PUBLIC SCHOOLS – INDEED all schools – like to blow their trumpet about the prodigies that their pupils, and ex-pupils, have achieved. And that is as it should be. West Buckland is no exception, and duly promotes its triumphs in magazines, Foundation articles, old pupils' bulletins, the local press, and (for all I know, on Twitter and Face Book, and Talkchat and Gossipmode and Rumourhumour and Smartwhisper, and all the rest).

Whole countries do this, though the British are not often criticised for doing so. Their attitude is much more annoying. They do not shout about how superior they are, because they assume that everybody already knows.

West Buckland is a bit like that with the *Exmoor*. It is the oldest tradition in the school's history, and it is quite simply the oldest, longest, roughest, toughest, regular, (near) compulsory school cross-country run in the length and breadth of the realm. But WB does not bang on about it all the time. Doesn't everyone know? Nevertheless, they are quietly proud of it.

During the course of his work, an archivist naturally makes contact from time to time with his opposite number in other schools. Indeed, many of us regularly attend an annual conference of such officers – the School Archivists' Group. It started with five members; it now has over two hundred and eighty at the last count I know about. So we are a growth industry.

One such contact was with the Archivist of Sedbergh School in Cumbria. We continued to exchange notes, observations, information, and general chat until she retired.

One of these interchanges involved cross-country running. I had, of course, referred to the *Exmoor* tradition She replied to the effect that Sedbergh, because of its position in such rugged countryside, did a lot of cross-country running too.

The two traditions ran close. Ours began in 1859; theirs started in 1881. Ours had been cancelled only twice, because of the appalling winter of 1947 and because of the foot-and-mouth outbreak in 2001. They had cancelled it twice too, for the same reasons, and once more, in 1936, because of an outbreak of meningitis. In both schools, boys *and girls* did it.

That left two areas of potential rivalry. In WB, it is officially compulsory, though we all know that the receptionist's phone never stops ringing on the morning of *Exmoor* day, with tear-jerking tales of heart-broken boys and girls who are prevented from taking part owing to circumstances quite beyond their control. Sedbergh's run is not compulsory, but – and here is the rub – it is called the 'Ten Mile'. And another rub: the girls do the same length course as the boys. It is now officially measured as ten miles, 685 yards. West Buckland's senior run is about nine miles, though it has never been scientifically calculated.

However, West Buckland can take refuge behind one trifling detail: in the Senior *Exmoor*, the boys have to *walk six miles to the start*. As they say, the trial continues.

By way of tailpiece, the Sedbergh archivist sent me some extracts of an article written just after the turn of the this century by an old pupil of Sedbergh. Its details are of no direct relevance to West Buckland, but they have intrinsic entertainment value, and they serve to show that, despite what WB chooses to think, they are not quite as unique as all that.

As I said above, the race began in 1881, and was known as the Wilson Run, named after a master who organised a paper chase, later revamped as a race. (The *Exmoor* was also a paper chase, with staggered starts, and remained so until 1908, when the course was modified and the race became a 'proper' one. One some occasions, the first Headmaster, the Revd. Thompson himself, used to go out and help to lay the trail.)

It seems that other public schools fell on this idea, as a splendidly convenient way of diverting and soaking up young male energy. Naturally, these races became notorious among the pupils, and soon, as in Sedbergh and West Buckland, acquired their own names. The Leys School at Cambridge has the Klondyke; Repton has the Short Milton (one wonders what purgatory the Long Milton may have been); Eton's steeplechase dates to 1846 and Winchester's to 1872. Rugby's run beats them all with a first appearance in 1838.

At Sedbergh, the race starts in the town, goes up Green Hill, along the fellside above, and past, over, or through evocative places like Baugh and Brant fell, Catley Bridge, Thrushgill waterfall, the River Rawthey, and Muddy Slide (West Buckland has the Cleave and Charles Bottom, known inevitably as 'Charley's Arse'). It finishes, we are told, 'outside the old tuck shop'. The whole school and the town come out to greet the new champion.

The Sedbergh run was so long that runners had to be over sixteen (one WB old boy told me that he had had to do the *Exmoor* when he was ten), and the school doctor had to declare every participant fit beforehand. (When the West Buckland Headmaster in the 1930's, Commander Westall, announced that he proposed to do the same, he was, so the legend goes, met with a near-mutiny.)

As with Sedbergh, old boys, friends, and hangers-on nowadays turn up to do the run as well – slipped discs and all. One old boy at Sedbergh boasted a fine family tradition: he, his father, his three brothers, and his son all did the Wilson. At West Buckland, a boy called Tully won the *Exmoor* twice, in 1935 and 1936, and his son won it in 1968.

Tall stories stick to both races like glue. At West Buckland, one gang of reluctant runners took time out to catch, strangle, pluck, cook, and eat a local chicken. At Sedbergh in 1941, there were dark suspicions that the winner had taken over halfway from his twin brother.

For years, the runners at WB, after a mud-filled communal bath (near congealed if you were late in), adjourned to the dining hall for bread rolls and pea soup. At Sedbergh there is a concert, at which the runners walk up on to the stage in the order in which they had finished, and the last boy receives the biggest cheer of all.

Which of course is as it should be.

And so to bed

THAT SENTENCE IS PROBABLY the extent of most people's acquaintance with Samuel Pepys' diary. Samuel Pepys, the Secretary to the Navy during the reign of Charles II, spent several years compiling a diary which has become the most famous of its kind. I have no idea how popular the diary idea was before Pepys came along, or how big his contribution was to the growth of diary-keeping. Perhaps it is time that somebody wrote a history of diaries. . .

Not only people; institutions have kept diaries. Explorers, survivors, Army regiments. ships and their logs. Coming closer to home, primary schools were *required* to keep daily records of their doings.

One of the most common factors of long-lasting diaries is the interest they often generate for later generations – often miles away from the original intentions of the writers. Some didn't even want their diary read by the world. Even Pepys wrote in some kind of code. Individual soldiers at war *daren't* show them to the world (well, not at the time), because the authorities strictly forbade them.

Be that as it may, it seems to be a common fact that people reading them years later get a lot more out of them than the writers thought they were putting into them. They were simply adding to them brick by brick; they did not live to see the impression created by whole wall.

West Buckland did not, to my knowledge, ever keep a diary, or a log, or a journal. Governors' minutes of course, and the school magazine. But they are not the same. However, one energetic headmaster took it upon himself to compile a handwritten history of the school, which is the nearest we have come to a school diary.

Obviously, it is selective, and is not by any stretch comparable to a daily diary, but clumps of entries, constituting a sort of foreshortening of the past, can prove to be interesting, and revealing, just *like* a diary.

Commander Westall, the Headmaster in the 1930's (1934-1939, to be precise), took it upon himself, in the midst of the multifarious duties of headship, to compile this impressive document, in a huge leather-bound tome, which we still have in the Archive.

Here, in a sort of mini-panoramic snapshot, is his account of the year 1917. I have inserted bits and pieces of prepositions and punctuation that were left out in his telegrammatic, and no doubt hurried entries.

'Report Audit to March, 1918. Improvements to servants' quarters, £236 – 3s – 3d. [Three shillings and threepence amounted to a little over 16p.]

'Minutes of Management Committee, May. Harries [then HM] had to devise a higher scale of salaries owing to new Board of Education regulations respecting increased grants. New grant £750 as against £479. [Quite a leap. You wouldn't get governments being as generous as that today. Cuts more likely.] Harries in June recommends no increase but a bonus to 5 of the staff to cover boarding expenses during the holidays – £20 voted, £4 each. [I hope they didn't spend it too quickly.]

'Harries objects to school servants being quartered in his house – new accommodation to be dealt with in holidays. [Just imagine the reaction today of headmasters at the prospect of gardeners and dinner ladies in the second-floor bedrooms.] July, Oliver [the school architect – built the Memorial Hall] to make the necessary alterations. [So poor Harries had the dinner ladies *and* the builders in as well.]

'September, grant from DCC increased from £200 to £300. October, 122 boarders. [There were very few day boys, and they were regarded as second-class citizens.] School accommodation fully occupied.

'November, Harries said he had been offered the living of Challacombe, which he had declined. [One of the great 'if's' of WB history. What would have happened if his headship had come to a halt seventeen years earlier?]

'Minutes of Governors' meeting. July . Last year's debit balance of £565 – 10s – 7d increased to £705 – 17s – 8d. [25% up. Quite a jolt. Was it the War?]

'Unless Harries' house be used no more accommodation. [So Harries may have had to put up with those dinner ladies and gardeners after all.]

'Chicken pox and German measles at Easter.' [Outdoor toilets for the boys were the order of the day. And there was no electricity.]

Quite a portfolio of problems – overcrowding, disease, debt, discontent, to say nothing of the small problem of the Great War (the 'war to end wars' – in which 58 old boys, staff, and servants were to die out of an annual roll, remember, of barely 120).

First Lady

FROM THE *REGISTER* OF November, 1921. [The *Register* liked long paragraphs.]

'We regret to have to record the departure of Miss M. A. Tamlyn, B.A., from the teaching staff. Miss Tamlyn joined the staff in September, 1914, replacing Mr. E. Smith [killed in the War, the first – and, blessedly, the only member of the academic staff who was lost], and until her departure occupied the position of Senior English Mistress. [Must have caused a flutter or two in the Common Room, if only cleaning up language and smoking habits.] She was the first lady to hold a recognized [sic – 'z'] teaching position in the school, and her arrival caused much "shaking of heads" among the more conservative members of our community. [So it caused other ripples too – hardly surprising, in the monastic remoteness of Exmoor.] However, the war appointment – for such it was – proved a conspicuous success. Thanks to Miss Tamlyn's ready tact and energy, all difficulties disappeared and the school became accustomed to seeing a lady at the master's desk.

'The Cambridge Local Lists are a proof of the enthusiasm which she not only felt for Literature, but managed to instil into the Sixth Form. Her enthusiasm, however, was not confined to the classroom. She took an active part in all out-of-school activities, especially in the Debating Society and the Orchestra. [Quite possibly too in Harries' annual Gilbert and Sullivan extravaganzas; it must have been a rare treat to have a female part sung by a lady instead of a quavering male treble.] Her greatest success, however, was as "House Master" of the Brereton House. [The conservatives still clung to the word "Master" instead of giving in gracefully and allowing "Mistress". Nowadays they get round it by calling the job "Head of House".] She followed the fortunes of her house with zest, attending all matches, no matter how bad the weather, and stimulating the players by her presence.

'We shall miss seeing her on the touch line this Term; but we shall miss her even more next Term on the Exmoor Run.'

Those with a wild imagination may be forgiven for picturing her in shorts and plimsoles tackling Charles Bottom and the Cleave. . . . but no – surely not. Pity though; it would have been quite something.

Her arrival in the common room of a public school is an indication of the enormous impact the First War had on the labour market. The shortage of able-bodied men resulted in women appearing – and performing with efficiency and success – in the Services, the Police, factories, farming, practically every sphere of employment one could name. In the north, they even had women's professional football teams – and they drew very respectable crowds.

The Church of England is a very English church

WEST BUCKLAND FARM AND County School was founded in 1858 by a conservative aristocrat and an Anglican clergyman. It would appear from the records – putting it at its simplest – that Earl Fortescue provided the money, the influence, the connections, and the clout; the Revd. Brereton laid on the organisation, the drive, the ethos, the 'message', if you like.

Remarkably for mid-Victorian England, he did not specify that every teacher and every pupil should be a communicant member of the Church of England. In a country seething with partisan promotion of a score of Christian denominations, his tolerance was, as I have said elsewhere, light years ahead of his time.

In a way, his attitude epitomised the understated, quiet, unspectacular, simply permanent way in which the Anglican church conducted its affairs in the middle of the nineteenth century (and indeed for most of the rest of it). Such behaviour of an entire institution brought upon itself a good deal of scepticism, impatience, criticism, and downright contempt: the Anglican Church was too bland, too 'understanding', too, frankly, patient, and therefore ineffective. Because it did not disapprove of anything very much, it clearly did not stand for anything very much; it did not represent a valid point of view – certainly not one worth having. No persecution, no fire.

Well, it was a point of view, but Brereton did not bend to it. He wanted ease and comfort of the mind in his school. Years later, he was, I think, vindicated by this verdict from an old pupil of the end of the twentieth century: 'The special thing about West Buckland is that everyone is made to feel the same way, at ease with the person they are and valued because of it.'

His first headmaster, Joseph Thompson, who later took holy orders himself – in the Anglican Church – fell in with this completely. He summed it up by saying that he was concerned to inculcate 'Christian feeling' rather narrow Christian denominational correctness. The understated Christianity of the Samaritan rather than the legal, doctrinal certainty of the Pharisee.

In July, 2005, I came across this article in a 'quality' newspaper, which I thought set out this philosophy rather well. I thought it relevant therefore to the spirit of the school, and so put it on the Common Room notice board. Not all my notice board paper furniture was designed to offer merely gossip, scandal, prodigies, jokes, and general useless information, even education; now and again it was worth simply trying to make people think. Bit pious, perhaps, but it seemed a good idea at the time.

It was entitled 'I'm not devout, that's why I'm an Anglican'. It was written by Quentin Letts, to whom I am happy to give full credit. If I had been able to trace him to ask his permission, I would have done so. If he later finds out and wants me to withdraw it, I shall of course comply. This is what he said:

Last Sunday 150,000 people went to Glastonbury, la-la'd about love and peace, heard a sermon (from Bishop Geldof) and were given hours of airtime by the BBC. Also last Sunday, up and down this bruised old land of ours, at least eight times that many souls quietly entered Anglican churches and dropped to their knees, as they do every week of every year.

The dress code was slightly more formal than at Glastonbury – the evangelicals have not yet taken over completely. But these 1.2 million people, who also sang about love and peace, were given almost no media coverage.

In the mixing suites and editorial conferences of modern Britain the Church of England has few friends. Loose-shirted formulators of fashion do not think much of the Church. That is, they neither approve nor do they afford it much thought. It has been this way for perhaps 25 years.

Last month Cherie Blair helped write a book called *Why I Am Still a Catholic*. From the way the last Pope's death was reported it was as though Henry VIII had never happened. Good luck to the Catholics, though. Cardinal Cormac Murphy-O'Connor is a man of dignity. His dwindling flock was stirred. And how comic it was, amid the tears at John Paul II's passing, to see our secular politicians and newscasters draw their faces into masks of piety as they struggled to understand the deep-rooted laments in Rome.

Anyone who so much as steps foot in a church tends to be described nowadays as a "devout" or "committed" Christian. The terms are accompanied by assumptions of toothpaste sincerity. This, to use a non-ecclesiastical term, is balls. There are many reasons for going to church, and although a strong faith and holiness are greatly to be envied, they are by no means prerequisites for attendance at matins.

It is time someone published a collection of essays entitled *Why I Am Still an Anglican,* because it is time we realised how lucky we are in our official Church. It is time our vicars were thanked for their good works, their stoicism and their general lack of hysterics. It is time we stopped assailing the Church of England and, as they say at Glastonbury, bigged it up.

I go along every week primarily because I love singing hymns. There's little to beat a good blast of *Praise My Soul* or the Cathedral Psalter setting of the *Te Deum* before lunch. I suppose I also go because I love the Book of Common Prayer, which the churches in our part of Herefordshire still use, and because I want Cranmer's cadences to drip into my children's minds. This is partly a cultural thing, partly aesthetic. Religion is there, too, in the background, but I would not dare claim to understand or believe fully in every part of the liturgy.

Churchgoing is a communal affair. I don't mean that sign of peace nonsense, which makes me feel awkward, but the sense of slow-burn fellowship that can develop with one's fellow-parishioners. A pressure group was recently sniffy about how some parishes are now little more than "clubs" for their congregations. What's wrong with that? "Clubs" (a Bad Thing in 21st century-speak) are no more than another way of saying "strong communities" (Good Thing).

I go to church for the smell of the flagstones. the Rizla rustle of the Bible, the flicker of candles, the shiver of pride when the priest blesses our youngsters, the taste of the fortified wine and the sense of completeness when returning to one's pew after Communion. All these things say "Sunday" to my body and my being. In a world so full of false prophets, they help guy the week to something solid. And then comes the moment when the children can dash into the graveyard and skip around tombstones. It is something I did as a child and I am glad my children do it, too. It lends harmony to the chime of passing years.

None of this is wildly philosophical or worthy. Where's the concern for Jesus, for the Church's mission, the affirmation of doctrine? Aren't churchgoers meant to listen to every word from the lectern? Sorry, but I sometimes day-dream.

Critics often accuse the Church, particularly the Archbishop of Canterbury, of failing to show moral leadership. They say that today's Anglican clergy are weak. Archbishop Rowan is mocked not only for his beard but also for failing to froth like some fundamentalist mullah.

I prefer it this way. Maybe this is a very English and Protestant thing, but I want my relationship with God, if it exists, to be a private thing. I don't so much want to be told what to believe as to be shown how. Rowan Williams seems rather gently brilliant at that.

His stance on sexuality, tolerant but discreet, suits the age. In our area last year we welcomed a new curate, a jovial, big-haired woman who spoke up well in the pulpit and seemed a thoroughly good egg. Then a national newspaper reported, excitedly, that our new curate had started life as a man. I half expected the parish to be outraged but quite the reverse happened. Nonchalance is but another way of saying tolerance, and tolerance is a proper Christian characteristic. That's what happened.

Our curate, with her rich tenor singing voice, is exceedingly popular and is soon to be ordained. (A traditionalist friend of mine opposed to female vicars, meanwhile, is still trying to work out whether or not it is doctrinally OK for him to take communion from her.)

Fire and brimstone is still there in the Book of Common Prayer, should your taste run to that sort of thing. "Cursed are the unmerciful, fornicators and adulterers, covetous persons, idolaters, slanderers, drunkards and extortioners," growls a commination just before the Psalms.

To this the response, if not "Amen", is either "blimey", or a mumbled, "now you put it like that, Lord, is there any chance you could perhaps please have mercy on our fragile, flawed beings?" None of us, not even our priests or archbishops, is perfect. But I reckon the dear old Church of England is a fine and forgiving institution, and way less feeble than strangers and critics presume.

Named and Numbered

IN 1801, IN THE middle of its great war with France, the English Government found time to organise the very first census. Estimates of population before that had been random in the extreme; nobody had much reliable information to go on.

When it turned out that the population of England and Wales came to over nine million, the Government were staggered. Almost frightened. All those people. Nobody had been used to numbers like that before. Everyone had soon to *get* used to them; by the end of the nineteenth century, the population had risen to thirty million; it had trebled in a century. By the year 2000, it had doubled again.

So the censuses, which came to be taken every ten years, were to provide a great deal of worry, food for thought, and resolve for planning, in addition to mere information. The effect on the history of West Buckland was much more modest, but interesting for all that.

The very first one to affect West Buckland was in 1861, when the school was barely three years old. The record sheets look a pretty homespun affair, with the entries filled in by hand. This left a good deal of room for human error, naturally. But the general outline seems clear enough.

For a historian or an archivist, these lists were invaluable. No attendance registers for those early years have survived – if indeed they had ever existed. Registers or no registers, nobody seems to have thought it worthwhile to record the pupils' names. Or, if they did, the names have gone.

It was not until 1907 that the school magazine, called (ironically) the *Register*, began the regular practice of compiling and publishing a full list of pupils. This was almost certainly the work of the new Headmaster, the Revd. Harries, who, as the new broom sweeping clean, also introduced a lot of fresh features into the life of the school in his twenty-seven years of office.

So how did an archivist or a historian find out about who was here? His only recourse was the *Register*. As the official organ of the new, and, later, up-and-coming – nay, pioneering – school, it was concerned not only to record actual events, but to publicise the young school's successes, and sing the praises of its more successful or virtuous pupils. A bit of trumpet-blowing, if you like – and why not?

So, first and foremost, exam successes received pride of place. Justifiably too. In the mid-1860's, when the school was less than a decade old, it came top of the exam success league for the whole country – three times running – beating schools like Manchester Grammar.

Equally naturally, the successes of school sports teams were recorded – in the case of cricket at inordinate length. The school authorities went out of their way to record virtue as well. Those boys who were never late got a mention. So did those who were late only once, or twice. Similarly, those who had no complaints recorded against them appeared in the *Register's* merit list, as did those who had only one black mark, or two. Inevitably, speech day prizewinners received their just deserts, along, very often, with the actual titles of the books they were awarded (leather-bound, with the school crest embossed in gold on the cover). Singing in the choir was considered worthy of mention, as were the achievements of recent old boys.

So there were a lot of names on the page. But these were all the good boys. What about the rest? Is there such a thing as a school which housed only good boys? Exactly. So, if you were an unpunctual, naughty, tone-deaf, not-very-bright non-bender, you didn't exist.

That is where the census returns came in; they recorded everybody. So long as you lived in the Devon County School and were alive, you got a mention.

The census of 1861 provides a good example. It is the school's first, which makes it unique. It has errors, which are always more interesting than the bits they get right. (For example, names are misspelt. How do we know? Well, is it likely that a boy's surname is 'BALLLMET' or 'CRIDGE'? When we know that Balment and Ridge were, and are, common Devon names.) It is often informative not so much because of things it says, but because of things it does not say.

Because the school was so young, the numbers involved are low. There were only 28 pupils recorded, which doesn't look much, till one remembers that the school had begun with three. When Earl Fortescue had nobly offered to pay for the new wooden dormitory two years before, there were only 17. So the intervening years reflected that the school had taken advantage of his generosity, There may have been a small handful of day pupils too, whose existence would have been recorded in their own homes. Using only these figures, the census showed over a 900% increase in pupil numbers since 1858. Only three years. Not bad going.

In the late 1850's and early 1860's, public transport was pretty rudimentary, and this is reflected in the fact that only 6 came from outside

Devon, and all bar one of those were from neighbouring counties. The one from Northamptonshire is a bit of a mystery. The furthest traveller, oddly, was the Headmaster himself, Joseph Thompson. He was a Yorkshireman. But, as one of the graduates from the new teaching training colleges (which were the object of a good deal of suspicion by prospective employers), he was probably willing to travel almost anywhere to get a job.

He being a Yorkshire lad, his first meeting with 'they little tackers from Deb'm' must have been a bit of a culture shock – for both sides. Did they even understand each other?

The only member of teaching staff to get a mention was Arnold Thorne, and he was listed as a 'Pupil Assistant'. Did Thompson do it all, every day? With an age spread of four years, from thirteen to seventeen? And a solitary 'pupil assistant' of only eighteen? Again, as with possible day pupils, perhaps there were one or two teachers who lived out.

Only two servants appear in the list, clearly only serving girls; one was sixteen and the other twenty. Once again, other domestic staff almost certainly came from either East or West Buckland, each of which was only half a mile away, in opposite directions. The parish boundary ran right through the middle of the school.

Mysteriously, the school had found the opportunity, and the resources, to recruit a man who was described as a 'Drill Sergeant'. A drill sergeant! What on earth did *he* do? He was fifty-five years old. And he had come from Westminster. Were there no drill sergeants between London and Devon? Or did nobody else apply? Incidentally, Physical Education used to be described as 'Drill', so that partially explains it. But 'sergeant'?

Among the pupils, familiar names were easy to identify, whether scrawled or misspelt. Balment and Ridge have already been mentioned. Also in evidence were Thorne (two of them), Bennett, Bridgeman, Dendle, Hearson, Huxtable, Loosmore, Mortimore, Snell, Bowen, and Waldron. They crop up time and again throughout the history of the school.

It all adds to the impression that Devon gives to students of it – that nothing much changes. Devon goes its own way. In the course of some other research, I discovered that the population of East Buckland has stayed so constant that, at the end of the twentieth century, it was slightly *lower* than what was recorded in Domesday Book. After 900 years. Pretty well everywhere else, it has risen by 3000%.

Presiding over this – this pioneering school in the middle of nowhere – pupil assistant, servants, drill sergeant, 28 'scholars' and all – was a young man of twenty-four.

The New Broom

HERE IS ANOTHER EXAMPLE of the titbit you can find on the back of the documents you are actually using. When I stapled the two sheets about the census, I had used a random piece of paper I picked up by chance to use as backing to help hold the pieces together.

Glancing at it before I threw it away, I found this evocative reminiscence of a headmaster by one of the boys who had survived his care. It must be mentioned that this headmaster had served many years beforehand in the Royal Navy. The Navy must have made a deep impression on him; among other things, it induced him to keep the 'Commander' rank before his name even in civilian life.

Apart from shortening the paragraphs for readers' convenience, I have left it pretty well as that old boy wrote it.

'Commander _____ brought the school into the twentieth century. We were released from our Eton collars into suits tailored by Harrods, who were appointed the official outfitters. [Harrods!] There was immediate revision of the "School Rules" which had always been posted on a notice board near the door of the Headmaster's house. The one and only rule was to be "Any breach of commonsense is a breach of school rules".

'Within a year there were various other notices laying down items of "commonsense" which one or other of us had obviously disregarded. Another (to us) sweeping reform was the abolition of tuck boxes, which were replaced by lockers, about one foot square, one to a pupil, available only at certain set times.

'The Corps of Drums soon had new drums, new pianos appeared (also from Harrods, we were told), the Pearse Chope workshops opened [closed only in the last decade or so], kitchens sported a new "Esse" cooker, the two tennis courts in front of the School were laid and we suddenly had to wear caps and scarves whilst watching the 1st XV play rugger. Not all of us took kindly to this latter rule as we could not bring ourselves to regard it as "commonsense", never having been accustomed to these items of clothing.

'Night-lights, in the form of marine-type bulkhead lamps with dim bulbs were installed in the dormitories, the intention being that the prefect in charge could nip any untoward behaviour in the bud. This, however, failed to prevent one of the more adventurous pupils from trying out the newly-installed fire escape. A further naval tradition, that of swimming in the nude, was also instigated.

His years as a naval officer had clearly given him a natural air of authority which enabled him to carry off all these changes. He also envisaged a school chapel. And he was only here for five years.

[The school handyman, reminiscing many years later, said,] "he looked a headmaster"; his typical stance was that of a naval officer with hands in the jacket pockets of his double-breasted jacket and eyes fixed on some far horizon.' [Steely, no doubt.]

Always good for a laugh

TEACHERS, WHEN THEY MARK exam papers, never fail to home in on the more outrageous of their pupils' mistakes. If they publish them, those mistakes also never fail to evoke anything from a smile to a belly laugh. Well, it is human enough, isn't it? On all sides.

The Prep., properly founded in 1970, duly produced its first crop of howlers in the Christmas General Knowledge Competition of Christmas, 1971. In no particular order of nail-head-missing, here are some of them.

In what year was Jesus born?	A.	1066
What is the name of a female sheep?	A.	A mummy sheep
Who sailed in the *Mayflower* in 1620?	A.	Winston Churchill
What is the name of a baby swan?	A.	A singlet
Who is President of the U.S.A?	A.	David Nixon [a favourite TV personality of the time]
What was St. Paul's original name?	A.	St. Paul's Cathedral
Which football team plays at Goodison Park?	A.	Filleigh
Name the capital of South Africa	A.	Cake Town

Still on Record

Winning wars on the playing fields

FROM THE *REGISTER* OF Michaelmas, 1876.

ATHLETIC SPORTS.

The annual Athletic Sports were commenced on July 28th, when the Cottage Garden Show was held in the School Ground, and, as they were not quite finished on that day, they were completed on September 7th.

[The suspense waiting for the final results must have been unbearable – nearly 6 weeks. And isn't it a lovely juxtaposition? Coinciding with the Cottage Garden Show. So intimate, so 'family', like the Archers.]

The following is the result.

THROWING THE HAMMER

Above 15 1. J.A. Potbury…….. 60 ft. [Not even the length of a cricket pitch. And the boy who won the Under 12 event managed almost exactly one-third of a cricket pitch. One wonders how much it weighed. And did everyone use the same weight?]

THROWING THE CRICKET BALL

/Above 15. G.Hallifax………….94 yds. 7 ins. [Very respectable by club standards today.]

PUTTING THE WEIGHT

Above 15 J. P. Wilkinson……..42 feet. [14 yards. A little more than half a cricket pitch.]

STANDING LONG JUMP

Above 15 J.P. Wilkinson ………8 ft 6¾in. [You can't get much more traditional than this; this is what the Ancient Greeks used to do in the 'real' Olympic Games.]

[And why did Putting the Weight survive in school athletics, but not the other three?]

7. 2006

Brereton's Crystal Ball

THE REVD. J.L. BRERETON was, as explained above, the rector of the village of West Buckland. Besides founding a school up the road, and publicising it in every medium he could get access to, and travelling widely for it, and fathering sixteen children, he turned his attention, and his many energies, to running his parish. No mere absentee priest, this. He pioneered new ideas in farming; he ran a farm himself; he succeeded in getting a local railway built to serve his new school; and he published a year book about his village. Only two numbers survive, from 1857 and 1860. (Perhaps they were the only two he did.) One suspects that he wrote most of it himself. Indeed, he took the opportunity to publish a selection of his sermons. Oh – and he wrote the words for the school song, which was sung till the 1960's.

In the Year Book of 1857, he produced this piece of innovation:

Decimal Weights and Measures

'No farmer needs to be told how inconvenient the present system of weights and measures is. Two different markets have two different measures. The first thing to be wished is to have an [sic] uniform system all through the country. But it is also important that the system should be the simplest, that is, one by which all calculations may be made most quickly and easily. And the decimal system is the simplest, because we already use it in our system of enumeration – the first thing that children learn at school – the system of units, tens, hundreds, &c. Thus in 1800 each figure has ten times the value of the figure next to the right. Now supposing that we called ten pecks a bushel, and 10 bushels a bag, 1800 pecks would make exactly 180 bushels, or 18 bags. No time need be wasted in calculation. With the decimal system we should have the numbers we want always ready. And the same thing applies to money. If with our pounds, shillings, and pence, 10 pence made the shilling, and 10 shillings made the pound, we should be saved a world of trouble.'

A school for the middle class, more emphasis on science and maths, freeing education from the stranglehold of the church, schooling for girls, a layman headmaster – there was no end to this man's inventiveness. And he did not stop with education.

Looking back, it seems almost inevitable that he would have turned his attention to decimal coinage sooner or later. All right, so he was not the only reformer to take up this particular cudgel. Nor was he the first. But it fitted the pattern of his thinking so neatly – simple, fair, reeking of common sense, shining with tolerance, in many cases unarguable, and yet doomed to frustration and, in many cases, failure – at least in his lifetime. And not all his fault. It was a wonder that West Buckland, founded in 1858, survived. It took much longer for decimal coinage to see the light of day.

Bright periods and showers

IN THE EARLY TWENTIETH century, the *Register* got into the habit of printing weather reports in each of its numbers.

For example, in the CXXVII number, of May, 1905, it informed eager readers that the 'last week of January was fine, and on three successive days the barometer readings were higher than any previously recorded at West Buckland. February was an average month, with no special features. March was very rainy, especially from the 4th to the 17th, rain falling on every day between those dates. April up to the middle of the month gave us 11 rainy days, but the amount of rain was small. There has been very little sunshine.'

The day which brought the highest rainfall came in early April, which tipped nearly half an inch on to the school. Not much, perhaps, for Caribbean hurricanes, but pretty significant for North Devon. So, typical *Exmoor* weather.

In fact, taking things all round, nothing much seems to have changed since 1905. Cleary global warming didn't figure very largely in West Buckland thought or conversation.

I am left with half a page empty, so I thought it might help to fill it if I inserted another piece of 'nothing-to-do-with-West-Buckland' information. For the hell of it.

A recipe for stress

Just in case you have had a rough day, here is an 8-step stress management technique recommended in the latest psychological texts:

1. Picture yourself near a stream.
2. Birds are softly chirping in the cool mountain air.
3. No one but yourself knows your secret place.
4. You are in total seclusion from the hectic place called 'the world'.
5. The soothing sound of a gentle waterfall fills the air with a cascade of serenity.
6. The water is crystal clear.
7. You can easily make out the face of the person you are holding under the water.
8. See? You're smiling already.

NB Do not try this at home.

I remember, I remember

OUR MEMORIES ARE NEVER as good as we like to think they are. This can sometimes lead us into trouble, or at least into inconvenience or frustration. Not, however, with reminiscences. They may be partial; they may be incomplete. But they are usually fond, and therefore harmless. They can often be entertaining too, even if the reader or listener can guess at once that they are indeed partial and incomplete, even wrong. They can also be souped up beyond all sensible credence. But that does not matter. A literary old boy, R.F. Delderfield, said that the very fact that these memories are cherished, burnished, and trotted out at every opportunity is evidence of how high in the affection and esteem they remain.

This little bunch came from an ex-pupil who had left the school in the 1950's.

'... [I remember] the magnificent hand-made dining tables, crafted in the School Workshops. [Still in use, and recently given a facelift. Crafted by the woodwork teacher, Mr. Davey, who now has a plaque in his honour up on the wall in the Dining Hall.]

' [I remember] the Hong Kong flu and I being among the first to recover. Picking up stationery supplies from "behind the green door". Complaints from Mr. D.G. Smith because we'd made a great ice slide in the snow outside his art room. The biology teacher Mr. Pickering and his habit of flinging things at the inattentive boy in the biology lab and our hope that he would hit the display cabinets one day. . . The reaction of Major Corless when he came in to take Maths and discovered we had a life-size pin-up of Brigitte Bardot pinned to the front wall of the room. Mention must be made of Mr. R.G. Pearce whose insistence on us reading five books a week meant a great grounding in literature, and the marvellously idiosyncratic and successful methods used by Gus McClintock to teach French.'

[I forget now what triggered all this, but I think he had come across one of my books about the school, or the Foundation had reached him in Australia, because this is how he ended his lengthy letter:]

'In March, 1959, I was dragged kicking and screaming to Australia, and until now [this] has just been a treasured, fragmented dream of a long gone world. A halcyon memory of an eternal summer.'

Which exactly echoes the point I made at the beginning of this piece. 'A halcyon memory of an eternal summer.' What a lovely phrase.

Is this why so many summers of our childhood are so long, hot, and sunny?

Another likely lad

I'VE AN IDEA I have used this little squib before. I certainly shared it with the Common Room, because this whole book stems from 'memory notices' I have been putting on the notice board for nineteen years. Besides, all the best jokes stand repetition.

This came from a headmaster's report on a boy from, I think, the 1960's or 1970's.

'_____ has been for most of his life in a variety of "scrapes", not of a very serious kind taken separately, but collectively adding up to an unsatisfactory record. Earlier this year he was given a final warning. . .

'In spite of his past I find _____ fundamentally a likeable boy. . . I hope he will be given an opportunity to emigrate. . . . '

Ding-dong

THINGS HAVE A HABIT of just turning up in the Archive. One week they are not there, and the next week they are. I had occasion to seek enlightenment about the following:

'A bell has come into the possession of the Archive, and resides temporarily in my pigeon-hole [quite a deep one]. Can any member of staff with a long memory [we have quite a lot of them] confirm its provenance?'

I never cease to be surprised at the variety of things that find their way to a school archive: a bell, a bass drum (complete with leopardskin for the drummer), glass photographic slides a century old, a cast-iron hole-punch, a pair of racing binoculars, rifle club records, a ninety-year-old school blazer. . .

Fellow Academy

THE NORFOLK COUNTY SCHOOL, AT ELMHAM, 1874

THE REVD. J.L. BRERETON envisaged a nation-wide system of boarding secondary schools for the 'middle class', and he christened them 'County Schools' because he didn't want the whole project hijacked by the Church.

One of his earliest foundations was the Norfolk County School. Its first headmaster was the Revd. William Watson, who had been the caretaker head of West Buckland while the Headmaster, Thompson, was away reading for holy orders and gaining a degree. So getting him into the top seat at 'Elmham' [look at the caption] was almost certainly Brereton's work.

When Watson retired owing to ill health, Brereton once again stepped in and persuaded his second son Francis to abandon a healthy headship in yet another county school and come down to rescue the Norfolk school. He failed, and Elmham closed. (By an incredible piece of luck, Francis got his old headship back, because his successor died suddenly.)

The Elmham school re-opened as a Barnardo's Naval School. One of its headmasters was a Mr. Mills, and he had a son who was born there – Lewis Ernest Watts Mills (later the actor John Mills).

The naval school closed after the War, and underwent decades of neglect (the chapel was used as a piggery and is now a private house).

Nothing remains of the school above ground except a tiny group of small gravestones and a doorstep. (And I know I have said some of this before too.)

Those were the days

WEST BUCKLAND SCHOOL.

Mr A. L. Cummins for D. L. Cummins

	£ s. d.
To Fees 1st Term 1949	35 0 0
Travelling Expenses	19 4
Games Shop	
Advances:—	
Matric Exam	2 6
Games Fee	1 5 0
	37 16 10
Fees Insurance Premium	3 6 8
By Scholarship	£34 0 2
Outfitter attached	1 6 3
	£35 6 5

RECEIVED 25th March 1949
p.p. WEST BUCKLAND SCHOOL

Payments to be made to The Secretary, West Buckland School. Cheques crossed National Provincial Bank Ltd., South Molton. Money Orders to be made payable at South Molton.

MOST SCHOOL ARCHIVES OF any appreciable age are usually awash with pieces like this, and are good for an airing on the notice board when inspiration is lacking.

These were the fees being paid for a senior boy in 1949. The '2.6' means two shillings and sixpence – twelve and a half pence today. Only it used to be called 'half a crown'. The old crown – worth five shillings, a quarter of a pound, had long gone out of circulation, but often figured in the coin collections of small boys. It was a mighty hefty piece; you knew you had a coin in your hand.

One of the casualties of decimalisation was the demise of coinage slang. All our coins are now the same – pence and pounds. Before 1971, we had bobs and tanners too. We don't even use the slang for money – 'bread'. Cockney rhyming slang – 'bread and honey' – money. Only 'quid' has survived – and not much of that.

Anyway, to explain further: that half-crown referred to 'Matriculation Exemption', which meant that the boy had passed his School Certificate (then 'O' Level, now GCSE) with five credits, which had to include English Language and Maths.

Look at the cost of a full school uniform – enough to make today's parents drool.

Note the stamp bearing the head of the late King George VI. He died in 1952. And the cost '2d.' That meant that you could send 120 letters with stamps like this for a pound.

To keep this in perspective, a deputy head in a grammar school would not have made it to £1,000 a year till the mid-fifties. A young teacher in the late fifties was being paid less than £700 a year

One of the great might-have-been's

MY GUESS IS THAT there exists between public school headmasters a sort of freemasonry the activities of which do not reach the annual reports on speech days. (To misquote Voltaire, if it doesn't, you would think that man would find it necessary to invent one.) It's not exactly an old-boy network, though a lot of them of course do know each other, if only because of their regular attendance at the Headmasters' Conference (the prestigious 'HMC' – representation at which entitles a school to call itself a 'public school'). It is not necessarily a mutual-help organisation, though naturally they do each other favours. It is not exactly a grapevine, but I reckon that a fair amount of gossip and useful information filters and trickles between them. It would be surprising if it did not. Dammit – they're all on the telephone.

Whatever you care to call it, it makes obvious sense that they talk regularly to each other, and, like professionals the world over, discuss things in outspoken manner which might cause a tremor or two if revealed to the light of day.

One unsurprising way in which this manifests itself is in the matter of troublesome pupils. A boy – or a girl – is giving the staff on a particular school a lot of grief. The most drastic remedy, of course, is to expel him, or her.

But then mother or father will try to get him in somewhere else. Favours are asked. On occasions favours are exchanged: 'I took Smith last term ; can you take Jones come January?'

Another strategy is, simply, moving him (I can't keep on saying 'or her'). It could of course be for the above reason, and but there are scores of others. Headmasters' files are well supplied with correspondence between themselves and other heads discussing the expedients adopted by worried, or desperate, parents who can end up doing the rounds, in order to get their offspring 'in' somewhere.

There are other circumstances, many of which do not necessarily involve naughtiness. Is he simply unhappy? Is he a fish out of water? Would he respond to a change of surroundings? Is he to be given the chance to escape bullying? Would a change of school enable him to shake off, for instance, his vulnerability to anorexia? (Boys get it as well as girls. Such a boy appeared for this reason in my tutor group in a nearby comprehensive school, and did very well.)

Anyway, one day I came across this warning from one head to another. This was an instance of a mother with, apparently, sole responsibility for a wayward son. He was such a bad case that the headmaster in question not only wrote direct to the mother; at the same time he sent a copy of the correspondence to the next school of mother's choice – West Buckland. Below are extracts from what he wrote:

'Madam,

'Before very long _____ may be in the hands of the police. I feel that I should write and tell you bluntly my opinion of this boy's behaviour during the short time that he was here.
'I regret to say that I found him to be an inveterate liar and thief. During his last three days here I believe that he stole three cars and went driving around in them. . .
'He continually used disgusting language in Persian and Turkish to my other students. I found that his manners in general, and his table manners in particular, were simply revolting. He was a thoroughly unpleasant boy, undisciplined in every way, and a nuisance from beginning to end.
'A detailed statement of account will be sent to the Bursar of West Buckland in due course.'

Presumably there was a student or member of staff sufficiently fluent in Persian and Turkish to be able to judge the offensiveness of his language. The headmaster wanted to give warning that _____ was an expensive pupil to contain – or that staff at West Buckland should raise the security standards on their cars.

At any rate, either the Headmaster or the Bursar took the hint – or Mum did – and the boy never reached the school.

We all know that boys will be boys, but they seldom come quite as bad as this.

Home from home

In 1860, the *Barnstaple and North Devon Times* reported on the sixth annual meeting of the West Buckland, East Buckland, Filleigh and Charles Agricultural Society. (Filleigh and Charles are villages close to East and West Buckland.)

[I have broken it up into paragraphs to make it a little more digestible. Newspaper articles could be then, and can still be now, a mite daunting.]

'The principle feature of interest in the day's proceedings was the ceremony of laying the foundation stone of the new buildings for the Devon Farm and County School by the Lord Lieutenant of the county [the second Earl Fortescue].

'The position which, within these two years, the West Buckland School has assumed among the public and private educational establishments of North Devon is unparalleled. [So it was a sort of celebrity from the word go.] It owes its origin to the Rev. J.L. Brereton, the rector of West Buckland and prebendary of Exeter Cathedral. The school was established in order that two experiments might be tried, viz:-

1st. Whether a public school would be supported by the middle classes;

2nd. How far it would be possible to connect a system of instruction in practical agriculture, with the other branches of education, the value of each boy's labour being applied to reduce the cost of his board and tuition.

'It was commenced in November, 1858, and up to Christmas of that year it numbered only three boys – Henry Dendle, James Ley Walden, and Henry Tyte, of Bishop's Tawton. The parlour of the farm house of Mr. Miller was the first school room of the Devon Farm and County School. The second quarter the scholars increased to ten boarders and one day boy, and a house, with a few acres of land, was then nobly offered to the prebendary by Lord Fortescue; but as some time must have elapsed and considerable expense been incurred, to adapt the premises to the purposes of a school, it was decided that a small farm in Mr. Brereton's occupation, should be the cradle of the scheme. At Tideport – a quiet sequestered nook in one of the those picturesque vales which lie embosomed in the beautifully-wooded amphitheatre of hills around Buckland – accordingly some wooden erections were constructed in the simplest style of Arcadian architecture. ['Embosomed' – isn't that lovely? And in an 'amphitheatre'.

How many new rural buildings are embosomed in amphitheatres today? And who thought up 'Arcadian architecture' – albeit the simplest style – in the wilds of North Devon?]. . . There, in January, 1859, the second quarter's scholars assembled.

'At Easter a Preparatory division was formed in the school in order to afford those boys too young to enter the upper division, a sound elementary education. In the third quarter the school was further increased to seventeen. It now became necessary to provide additional accommodation, and on the 24th May a new dormitory was opened by the Countess Fortescue. At Midsummer, the number of attendants was doubled; at Michaelmas and Christmas there were further augmentations, and with the subsequent additions during the present year the school now consists of about fifty scholars, day boys and boarders, in the upper and preparatory classes.

'This gradually increasing popularity having at length outgrown the rather circumscribed limits of the "wooden walls" of Tideport, Lord Ebrington [Fortescue's son, later the third Earl] kindly placed his farm premises at Middle Hill at the disposal of the school, and at that place the project will now be carried on under the title of the Devon County School Association (limited) till the building of which the first stone was laid on Thursday is completed.

'The proceedings of the day were commenced by divine service at East Buckland Church, under Lord Fortescue's endowment of £1,000. The officiating clergymen were the Rev. W. Martin, curate of East Buckland and Chaplain to the School [I have an idea that Brereton had married his daughter Frances], and the Revds. J.L. Brereton and Richard Blackmore of Charles [related to the author of *Lorna Doone* – Devon's homegrown literary classic.]'

Notice how generous the Fortescue family was (and has continued to be) – grants of land, provision of farm buildings, underwriting the wooden dormitory, and endowing East Buckland Church. For all Brereton's inspiration, energy, and drive, it is very doubtful if the school would have lasted very long without them.

And look how quickly the school grew. This was North Devon, one of the most sparsely populated counties, traditionally remote and off the beaten track. It was a remarkable achievement.

However, Brereton had to give up one of his dreams very early. His original conception was that the boys would contribute the fruits of their labour towards the school's economy. But it clearly didn't work. The 'Farm' dimension very soon disappeared from the school's name.

The County School Association ('limited') carried on running the school till it was wound up in 1912, and finally re-emerged in the incarnation one sees today.

The foundation stone laid by the second Earl still sits prominently beside the entrance, with an inscription which reflects Fortescue's masonic connections and beliefs:

'In humble hope that the Great Architect of the Universe the Maker of Heaven and earth the Giver of all Good, will bless and prosper the work this day commenced, and that the School to be raised will prove, under the Divine blessing, an institution for the promotion of God's glory in the extension of sound and practical education, in the diffusion of useful knowledge, upon the imperishable foundation of Divine truth.'

The building was completed in remarkably quick time; it was opened only twelve months later. Sadly, the second Earl died just before he could perform the ceremony, which was, naturally, carried out by his son, the new third Earl. He and his friend Joseph Brereton worked tirelessly for the school for the rest of their lives.

8. 2007

One of us

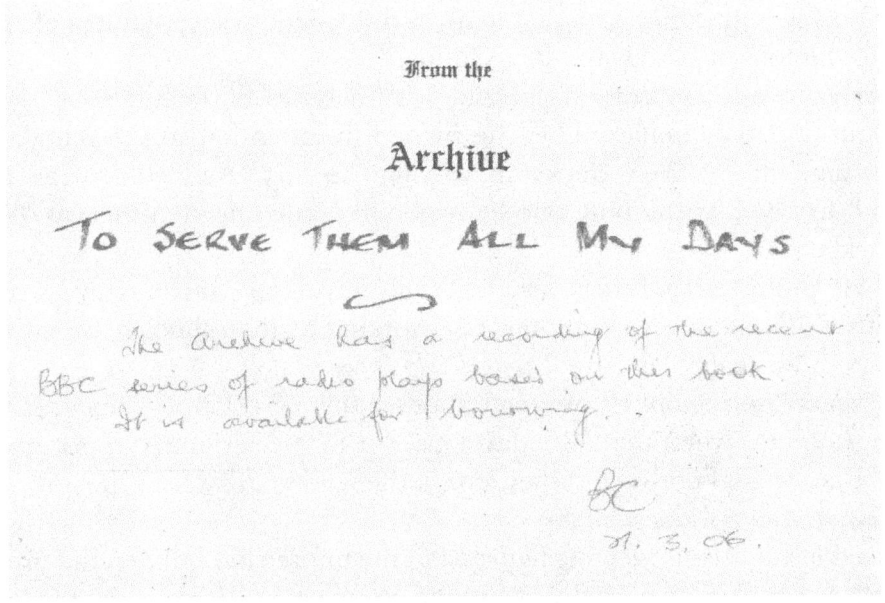

From the Archive

TO SERVE THEM ALL MY DAYS

The archive has a recording of the recent BBC series of radio plays based on this book. It is available for borrowing.

BC
31.3.06

IT IS DOUBTFUL IF anybody in the present generation has ever heard of the play *Worm's Eye View*. Which is hardly surprising; it opened in 1945.

I first saw it during its out-town trial run, during an Easter holiday with my mother at Cliftonville. I was not old enough to catch all the references and the innuendo, but I do remember laughing a great deal. So did a lot of other people. When the play opened at the Whitehall Theatre in London, it ran for five years.

It was of its time, and it would creak a bit now, but for years after the War, it was staple fare for amateur dramatic companies up and down the country. The author, clearly a courteous man, said he had lost count of the number of such performances he had attended. Huge numbers responded; they had served in the War, they had been bombed in the Blitz, they had survived the austerity after War, they had had to tolerate food rationing of one kind or another right up to 1953. Of course they responded; it was about them.

It made the name, and the fortune, of a youngish playwright called R. F. Delderfield ('Ronnie' to his many friends). In fact RFD already had a goodish literary pedigree to his credit; he had been turning out novels, plays, and varied historical work for years, but it was *Worm's Eye View* which turned him into a celebrity. He did not maintain that high profile, but till his death he continued to offer a pretty sizeable output – more plays and history books, on offbeat subjects like Napoleon's brothers and sisters (he had rather a lot of them), and the fictitious adventures of that most famous of castaways, Ben Gunn.

He hit another sort of jackpot with a series of fat novels – sagas about country families. Then he turned his attention to the school he had attended – West Buckland. He had in fact attended several, but said, firmly, that the only one he harboured any affection for was West Buckland.

He produced (another) very hefty novel (you got your money's worth with RFD), about a young teacher working at the school between the wars. It was called *To Serve Them All My Days*.

Years later again, he attained another sort of celebrity (albeit, sadly, posthumous) when the BBC dramatised it for television. And not just a routine, one-off pot-boiler; they gave it the works – a saga of epic proportions, 13 full episodes, no less.

I don't know the viewing figures, but my impression is that it did pretty well. It was well cast, and was immensely viewable. I spent my working years in the classroom, and the one thing I didn't want to watch in the evening was anything to do with education. But I watched TSTAMD, as it was referred to in documents at West Buckland. (Well, it was theirs.)

I thought it was a gentle, fond series. And it fitted West Buckland. As the School Archivist, I have naturally spent a good deal of time reading documents about the school's past, and one strong impression I have received is that the school, over the years, has displayed a remarkable facility for engendering affection. Not smiling recollection, not loyalty, not pride (though those too are there). Affection. There are many instances of old boys who come back (not to London restaurants; all the way to North Devon in the early days) to share reunions, and some of them were at the school for barely two years, some even less. And the school was a pretty rough place, not for frail flowers. All right, not everybody loved it, but I fancy that the haters are outnumbered by the likers. And the liking usually is strong.

The actor who played the part of the Headmaster, Herries (in real life

Harries), was Frank Middlemass. He was invited to the school to attend a dinner. He is supposed to have remarked that in a mysterious way he felt completely at home.

As one would expect, the school basked in the attention and the fame. For a long time afterwards, little phrases would be added to publicity hand-outs to the effect that West Buckland was the 'home' of 'the popular drama series, *To Serve Them All My Days*'.

In the event viewers didn't see much of West Buckland. The school itself, that is. The BBC sent a team down to give the place the once-over, and they decided that there were too many newer buildings which got in the way of atmospheric camera angles, so they took it somewhere else. But they used the surroundings. There cannot be many places with better views and panoramas all around than West Buckland. And they had the wit to use that.

The school of course obtained a set of the videos, and, in due course, I bought a set of the DVD's for the Archive. Then the BBC had another bite at it, and produced a new dramatisation for radio. Just as the original was very viewable, so this radio version was very listenable to.

And that's what this notice was about.

A neat tribute

AMONG THE TYPES OF people who write about their past, two seem prominent.

One is the public figure who wants to put the record straight. Their works can be interesting, spiced no doubt by some racy comment on those who had done them wrong in the deep past. But they rarely generate warmth. Heat, yes; but not warmth.

The other is the individual, not necessarily famous, musing on his, or her, personal past, and, with the perspective of years, beginning at last to give credit where credit is due. The weight of those years goes into the scales of judgment, and mysteriously tends to become distributed quite evenly between the dishes of praise and censure. Put another way, older people get better at judging themselves.

If you are looking for warmth, you are more likely to find it here.

This tribute was written by an old boy who was looking back over half a century to his time at the school in the first ten years of the twentieth century:

'The physical atmosphere was nearer to that of Sparta than is the rule today. . . . [but] I acquired enough English, French and Latin to make the reading of the classics of all three a pleasure that has lasted a lifetime, enough Mathematics to get an Open Scholarship at Corpus Christi College, Cambridge – with the joy of occupying rooms inhabited there by Christopher Marlowe – and enough common sense to let somebody else blow my trumpet.'

A sharp little sally at the end, well timed – another sign of a good education. Note that he carefully says that he read the classics '*of*' all three languages, not '*in*' all three languages. But who can cavil at an undergraduate who has lived in rooms once used by Kit Marlowe? For all that Marlowe came to a sticky end.

This verdict bears comparison with the shorter, but no less proud, compliment offered by another Cambridge graduate – this time to his university:

'Six of the twelve most important discoveries since the birth of Christ were made within half a mile of my rooms.'

G. and S. at WB
Roll up, roll up

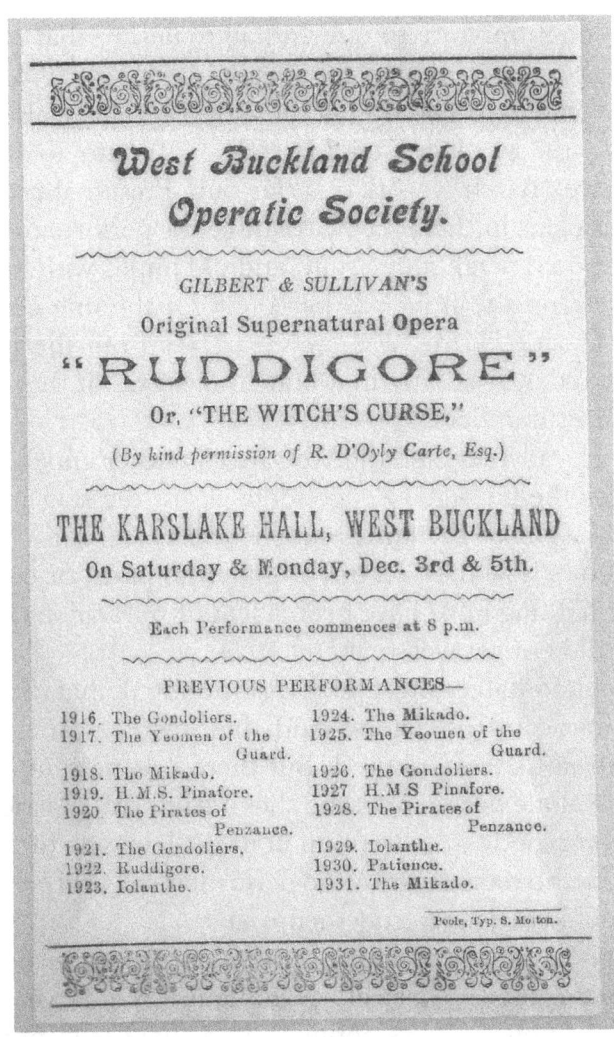

As is clear from the 'previous performances' footnote, this was an annual tradition at West Buckland. It owed its inception and its longevity, almost entirely I should think, to Headmaster Harries. He started it, bravely one would imagine, in the middle of the First World War, and it stopped in the year of his retirement in 1934. In between those dates, he organised, drove, inspired, and generally oversaw, every production.

One is tempted to wonder whether one incentive was that he could play a starring role – which he did in nearly every one. We have a splendid portrait-size photograph of him as the Mikado.

His wife was with him all the way, encouraging, nannying the young members of the cast, providing timely teas and buns, and dollops of castor oil or cough mixture to one and all to ensure that nobody was ill on the night (there were no understudies).

The school had no orchestra; all the music at rehearsals was provided at the piano by the Music master, Mr. Watson ('Watto; to one and all, or, as an alternative, 'Barch' – work that one out). Presumably they cajoled a few adult musicians in the area to assemble for performances. Similarly, those well-disposed neighbours, staff, and old pupils with any semblance of a voice took on the principal parts (except the one commandeered by Harries). Female chorus was easy – trebles from the junior classes. No doubt the older boys sang in a bunch of keys, but they drowned the discords by sheer numbers.

The school handyman and the Woodwork master knocked up the sets. The staging of the passage of a gondola across the stage was a saga in itself. In *Iolanthe*, one of the fairies caught fire.

Heaven knows how they acquired orchestral parts, or costumes come to that. Stage lighting must have been a feat of miraculous inventiveness, as the school did not get electricity till 1924.

The school had barely more than 200 pupils, if that. Schoolboys are not natural musicians or actors. And they tend toward the Philistine rather than towards the Cultured. But there was nothing much else to do. They were alone out there in the sticks. And with Harries as the irresistible force everybody was swept up in it. Well, he was the Headmaster.

Alas, we have no recordings of the performances, and certainly no film footage. It would have been truly memorable.

The chances are that the actual *standard* of the productions was irrelevant. It was the biggest project of the entire school year. There was dressing up, and noise (always popular), and changes from routine (with any luck a few lessons to be missed for dress rehearsals). For a country boarding school on the edge the Exmoor wilderness, from which boys were able to escape only twice in a term on a half-day excursion to Barnstaple, it was a sensation.

If it was bad that didn't matter; everybody was having such a good time. Crises and dramas and disasters only made it better. Devil take the audience.

Cheap at the price

WE ALL KNOW ABOUT inflation, and how prices in the 'old days' (or, if you prefer, the 'olden days') can look ludicrous, even, frankly, unbelievable.

We all have our favourite examples. For instance, my mother was fond of telling me that, round about the time of the First World War, you could buy a fish-and-ship supper for three old pence ('tuppenny piece of fish and a pen'orth of chips'). That comes out today at 1.25 p.

I can tell you, because I am a historian, that William the Conqueror ran the whole country on an annual budget of £10,000 – and made a profit.

The other side of the penny (forgive the pun) is, of course, the fact that wages were correspondingly lower. Everything was lower. When I was at primary school, my mother was raising me on less than three pounds a week. And I don't ever remember going short of anything. Careful, maybe, but not short.

The very first old age pension in 1908 was five shillings (25p.) for a single person and seven shillings and sixpence (37½p.) for a couple. If we simply marvel and don't look at the context, we might cast scorn upon it; but it looks different if we are reminded that, before 1908, old people got no pension at all. Nothing.

And that did not die with the 'olden days'. Young National Servicemen, conscripted to serve for two years, received 20p. a day as late as the 1960's. My father, when he joined up at the beginning of the Second World War, got 25p. – a week!

All we can do is shake our heads and wonder.

Now and again, however, we come across an example which sounds so outrageous that it hits us all over again. We laugh at the incongruity of it all. In the *Register* of November, 1937, under 'Old Boys' News',

'It was decided that an effort should be made to hold periodical gatherings in London to give members (especially the younger ones) the opportunity of meeting School friends more frequently than had been the case during the last few years. Before the War [the *First* World War] similar gatherings were much enjoyed and proved to be very inexpensive. . . .

'The next gathering will be held on December 2nd next, and we have arranged with the Chesham Hotel [in the Strand] to supply an excellent supper at the low cost of 1s. 6d.'

Not the old Bromley's in Barnstaple; not the local Wimpy, not Wetherspoons. This was a posh hotel in London – in the Strand. For 7½p.

Beat that

PEOPLE LOVE BEING THE holder of a record. No matter how off-beat, unlikely, or believable. I, for example, have a rare record. I claim to be the very last person in the world who has not seen *The Sound of Music*.

How's this? My maternal grandfather held the record for length of service for a bus driver. When he was a lad, buses were still pulled by horses, but he wanted to be a bus driver, and was so keen to get stuck in that he lied about his age, and had two years' service under his belt before he was legally allowed to drive. Well, they couldn't stop him when they found out, because he was legal by that time. So, when he retired, he had two years' more service to his credit that any other bus driver could possibly have – hence, a record. Moreover, a record that could not be broken.

Take the *Exmoor*. If it has been said once, it has been said a hundred times: the *Exmoor* is the oldest, longest, roughest, toughest, regular, compulsory, scheduled school cross-country run in the length and breadth of the realm. Naturally, West Buckland shouts about it. Perhaps surprisingly, nobody yet has got out his measuring tape and tried to prove us wrong. West Buckland may not be the home of royalty, the womb of genius, or the cradle of prime ministers and film stars, but people do know that it is the place where they have 'that run'. So, another record.

And recently, there has appeared a refinement to it. A few years ago, a boy ran in the *Exmoor*, who, according to his father, was the *ninth* member of his family to have done so. That will take some beating, I fancy.

Rosalie Priscott did not run in the *Exmoor*. She served for many years in the Bursar's 'outer office'. Not many boys or girls knew her, but she was one of the few vital, if unsung, members of the support staff who keep the finances of the school in a healthy state. Without the Rosalie Priscotts of this world, there wouldn't *be* a school.

Well, Rosalie is the *tenth* member of her family to have served it. That will take even more beating.

At the cutting edge

IN NOVEMBER, 1924, THE *Register* announced that the Governors had initiated, paid for, and oversaw, ' the installation of the electric light'.

Note – not 'electric light', but '***the*** electric light'. The definite article gives the game away. People did the same with television in the forties and fifties. They didn't ask, 'Have you got television in your house?' They said 'Have you got *the* television?'

Bully for West Buckland; it was only forty years after the first London theatre got it. It was not an undiluted blessing; one school servant lost his job. He had till then been responsible for trimming all the oil lamps.

Trade secret

HERE IS ANOTHER OF those 'useless and irrelevant' pieces of information which nevertheless deserve to be preserved.

'Science is what we do when we don't know what we are doing.'

[From a BBC *Horizon* programme.]

Health and hygiene

IN THE *REGISTER* OF 1982, an old boy reminisced about a school servant called Bill Cockram. (Known to one and all as 'Yannah Bill'. He did no end of jobs about the place, from basic sanitation and driving the school's venerable Austin to ground maintenance and serving in the Karslake Hall.)

'Prior to dishing out the cream buns... Yannah would clean the central lavatories. The urinal section had an appalling smell due to the chlorine in the water. The water was fed from the swimming pool... Yannah dosed the chlorine into the pool and removed the dead newts when the water was clear enough to see them.'

There is another story like this, probably an alternative version of the above:

In addition to keeping the pool as clean as possible (notwithstanding the dead newts), Bill was also responsible for maintaining the filter beds and soak-away in the school septic tank (the school is still on septic tank drainage).

He would usually tackle this towards the end of the afternoon. When he had finished, his next duty was in the dining hall. In the interests of general health, Bill generously changed from his brown overall into a white one – and served out tea and buns still wearing his wellington boots.

Concert

A *REGISTER* OF 1914 offered the following report:

'A Concert, with Dramatic Performance, was held in the Karslake Hall, on Thursday, December 10, in aid of the National Relief Fund, and as the result the sum of £10 was realized. [We don't know who or what was being relieved, but, as the war had broken out only in August, there must have been countless funds, projects, charities, and collections for equally countless worthy causes, embarked on by eager patriots, anxious not to miss anything, because, as everyone knew, the war would be over by Christmas.]

'The whole of the musical programme was rendered by members of the School. The boys were in good form, and the choruses and part-songs were excellently done. Mr. Davey, who is new to West Buckland audiences, possesses the voice that is generally styled "sympathetic" and charmed his hearers. The Head Master, in rendering "The Admiral's Broom", adapted the words to suit our recent victory off the Falkland Islands. [Not 1982, remember; this was 1914. And we weren't fighting the Argentinians.] Romberg's "Toy Symphony" was very well done, and aroused great interest. Mr. Innis's ideas of the ways in which men of different nations might recite "The Charge of the Light Brigade" caused great amusement.'

Mr. Innis, who hailed from Trinidad (what on earth was a West Indian doing in North Devon in the second decade of the twentieth century?) was a colourful character in every sense of the word. He was fond of composing skits on recent events or occasions in West Buckland life. Here he demonstrates that, in addition to his satirical skills, he also had dramatic ones.

Studying the records of a school like West Buckland provides never-ending evidence of the range of activities to which members of staff would turn their energies.

I suppose, when one contemplates the isolation of the school in Darkest Devon, before regular motor cars and buses, it is hardly surprising. Shortage of basic facilities produced a diminution of critical faculties. There wasn't anything else; you lumped it. And it was fun. One is reminded of the endless entertainment expedients employed by the inmates of a Second World War prison camp – if half the films we see come close to the truth.

A good read

THE SPEECH DAY REPORT in the 1907 *Register*, as usual, recorded all the prizes presented to successful boys. Here is a selection of them. A modern reader of it would not come away from it with the impression that the school authorities went out of their way to encourage boys to read for recreation. It all had to be 'good for you'. Look at these titles.

THE EDMONDS DIVINITY PRIZE.

J.B. Harrris. "Helps to the Study of the Bible."

THE ACLAND SCIENCE PRIZE

J.B. Harris. "Starland", by Sir R.S. Ball.

THE ACLAND MATHEMATICS PRIZE.

W.L. Armstrong. "Pioneers of Science", by Sir Oliver Lodge.

THE MICHAEL SNELL ENGLISH PRIZE.

S. Bendall. "New Land", by Sverdrup. 2 vols. [With 2 volumes of it, Master Bendall certainly got his money's worth.]

THE CHOPE GENERAL KNOWLEDGE PRIZE.

W.L. Armstrong

"Alexander's Empire", by Mahaffy.

"Chaldea", by Ragozin.

"Phoenicia", by Rawlinson. [So Master Armstrong got even more of his money's worth. Served him right.]

THE HEAD MASTER'S LANGUAGE PRIZE.

J.B. Harris. Shakespeare's Plays.

CAMBRIDGE LOCAL HONOUR PRIZES. [The Cambridge 'Locals' were one of the predecessors of GCSE. In fact the very first predecessor, being started in the same year as the school – 1858.]

J.B. Harris, Senior, Class III. "Highways and Byeways in Devon and Cornwall", by Norway.

W.L. Armstrong, Junior, Class I, distinguished in French and Mathematics. "Wanderings in South America", by Waterton.

[Almost a clean sweep for Messrs. Harris and Armstrong. It's wonder anybody else bothered to turn up. But I don't suppose anybody else was consumed by jealousy at not being able to curl up during long winter evenings in the dorm with "Chaldea" or "Highways and Byeways of Devon and Cornwall".]

Centenary happenings

IN 1958, A SMALL fleet of boats was pushed out to celebrate the school's hundredth birthday – and why not?

1. Sir Leonard Rogers, an old boy of the school, opened the 'new' Physics Laboratory. (Sir Leonard was a most distinguished medic. He was credited with discovering a cure for leprosy. He had come to the school in 1879. That's right – 1879. Seventy-nine years before.)
2. West Buckland laid on some typical weather: the cricket match against the MCC was abandoned because of rain, but Speech Day, on 18th October, enjoyed 'perfect weather'.
3. A pupil, Geoffrey Bayles, was selected to play for England over-15 schoolboys against Wales. (Odd to have '*over*-15'; it is usually '*under*-16' or '*under*-19' or whatever.)
4. The chief guest at Speech Day was the Duchess of Devonshire, Mistress of the Robes in the Queen's Household, and Chancellor of the University of Exeter. (Crumbs!)
5. There was a 'historical exhibition' at the school. One of the chief attractions was the set of gold spurs presented to Bertie Hill (1939-41), after his Olympic success at the Stockholm games in 1956. (Only equestrian, presumably; the main Games were held at Melbourne. Bertie later coached the successful equestrian team at the Mexico City Games in 1968.)
   He certainly started young; as a pupil, he used to ride a horse to school.
6. The speaker at the Centenary Dinner was Mr. H.L. Brereton, a grandson of the founder and Headmaster of Gordonstoun. (The Breretons were a most fertile family; and they got everywhere.)
7. The only non-West Buckland speaker at the Dinner was Mr. James Lindsay, the MP for North Devon. The *North Devon Journal* reported that at the end of his speech, 'he added, "If they are destined by a true and proper criteria, then their future is assured." '

(Which is an eloquent comment either on the public speaking skills of our MP's in 1958, or on the education level of our journalists.)

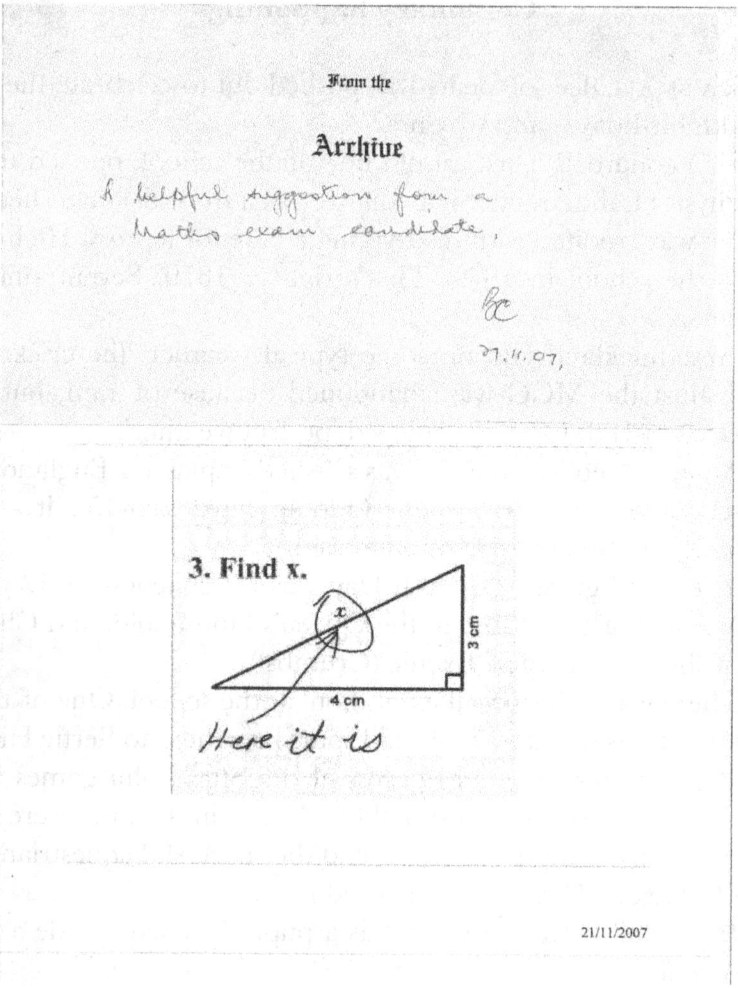
From the

Archive

A helpful suggestion from a
Maths exam candidate,

BC

21.11.07.

3. Find x.
x
3 cm
4 cm
Here it is

21/11/2007

Christmas cheer

THE *REGISTER* OF FEBRUARY, 1908, reported on the Christmas festivities and proceedings from the end of the previous term. It was the Revd. Harries' first term as Headmaster. As a very new man, he had had only one term to make his influence felt, and the chances are that he had made few changes by this time. Secondly, he had spent three or four years at the school between 1901 and 1904, as Chaplain, so understood the general ethos of the place.

Moreover, Christmas being Christmas, it is unlikely that a head who understood how the school worked was going to do anything to upset the traditions of such a modest little, inward-looking establishment – there were fewer than a hundred pupils. It was a boarding school in the back of beyond, so it was necessary to nurture the feeling of family and belonging. Incidentally, it is quite common for pupils leaving today, from a school well over 600 strong, to state that they valued and cherished the family atmosphere that still prevailed.

'On the last evening of the Christmas Term, December 16th, 1907, after the usual Special Prayers and Lesson in Big School [now two Modern Languages classrooms], the Head Master read the Form Order for the term, and the lists of promotions and prizes, recorded elsewhere in this number.

'He afterwards entertained the School to supper in the Dining Hall [Built by the Revd. Karslake in 1878, and named after him now. When did the name change?] Mrs. Harries [the Headmaster's mother, not his wife. When he married – at fifty – Harries chose a sister of his current Head Boy, Sidney Bendall – see below. His brother married another sister.], Miss Hickman, Mrs. Lutley, Miss Denny [the Matron], Miss Haywood, and Mr. W.L. Miles were present, besides the masters and boys. The School Cups and other trophies adorned the scene, all of them, by the fortune of war, being placed this year on the Courtenay tables. [Brereton must have been a bit glum with a bare board.]

'After supper, Mr. G.C. Fry [the chief, and only, Science Master] proposed the health of the Brereton Dormitory [they called them 'dormitories' then, not 'houses', and there were only two.], which was enthusiastically drunk by their rivals at the other side of the room. S. Bendall [the Headmaster's future brother-in-law] responded in a very felicitous valedictory speech, this occasion being his last appearance as Head of the School.

'Mr. A. Taylor [choirmaster, secretary, and long-serving teacher of nearly everything] then proposed the toast of the Courtenay Dormitory, which was also enthusiastically received. J. B. Harris made an able speech response.

'The Head Master [written as two words, note] then proposed "The Visitors", for whom Mr. W.L. Miles, our one "official spectator" at football and cricket matches, responded with a very effective speech, both serious and humorous.

'The whole evening was, on every side, voted a great success.'

9. 2008

ONE OF THE VERY earliest school prospectuses. Note the name: West Buckland Farm and County School. The 'Farm' dimension soon disappeared.

The Preparatory section soon faded too, not to be formally revived till the 1970's.

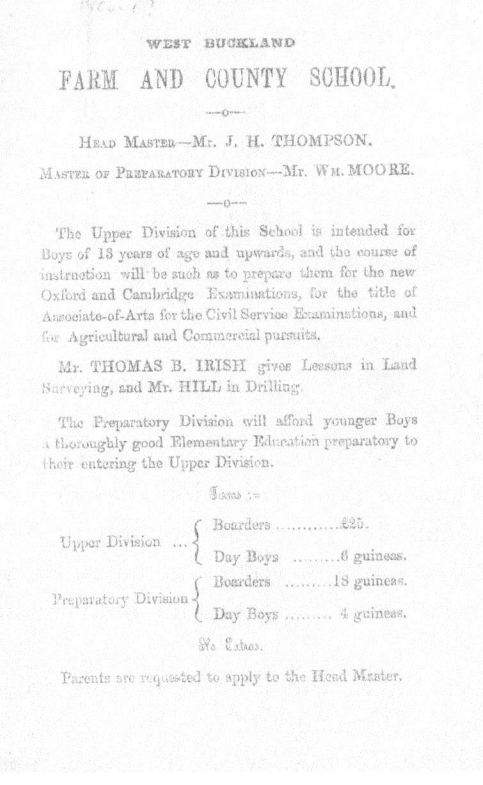

Four guineas for a primary day boy's education for a year – not a bad deal.

One wonders what 'Drilling' was. Probably a forerunner of the lessons we now call P.E. – Physical Education. (In my school it was simply 'Gym.') There exist many photographs of schoolgirl classes from many old schools doing 'Drill', complete with long stockings, long hair, and gym slips.

The 'Lessons in Land Surveying' were a symptom of Brereton's philosophy about getting away from the stranglehold of the Classics and introducing 'modern' subjects. The products of the new County Schools were not being prepared to run the Empire, but many of them were going to help run the country. The records of the time show a predictable percentage of boys who went back to run father's farm or father's business. But they also showed a solid percentage of others who went into careers in spheres like science, medicine, and marine engineering. More and more, steadily, were encouraged to aspire to university.

The 'new Oxford and Cambridge Local Examinations' – known familiarly as 'the Locals' – were the gateway to these universities. They were the earliest ancestor of GCSE. Until these came along, no boy (or girl) from the 'middle class' (Brereton's target) was able to produce academic qualifications to enable him or her to be considered for Oxbridge, for the simple reason that, till West Buckland appeared, there was, quite simply, no school to prepare him for it. Well, all right, a few, but no *system*.

This is the significance of Brereton's (and Fortescue's) dream: a nationwide coverage of new schools to fill that gap. It had never been attempted before. To my knowledge, never even considered. West Buckland was the very first, the pioneer.

We are so used to a national universal education regime – it is so much part of our lives – that it may come as a surprise to realise that it is barely six generations old, if that. The absence of such a regime, by the same token, had also been so much a part of people's lives that we may not fully appreciate what a leap of the imagination Brereton's idea was.

And that was not all. Brereton's contribution ran further. So did that of three other trail-blazers. It is no coincidence that the year of the school's foundation, 1858, also saw the very first national secondary examinations – the Locals.

Even more remarkable, the four men who drove this initiative – Brereton (of course), Fortescue (of course again), Sir Thomas Dyke Acland, and Frederick Temple, were all closely associated with West Buckland. Brereton and Fortescue we know about. Acland was a prominent North Devon landowner, school director and general benefactor (he it was who had helped to lay out the course for the very first *Exmoor*). Temple, Headmaster of Rugby, later Bishop of Exeter, Bishop of London, and finally Archbishop of Canterbury, was a great champion of the *raison d'être* of the school. He was moreover a strong friend of Brereton, and once visited, in 1873, to present the prizes. (The second Primate of all England to do so.)

In a wider perspective, what these men did by setting up the Locals was to establish the principle of competition. There were university degrees, of course, but they were for 'gentlemen'. Nobody, or very, very few, had got anywhere much on sheer talent. What these four men did, in effect, was to invent exams, to enable young people to *show* their talent. To show their fitness for promotion – on level terms. They had never had the chance before.

It is no coincidence either that, within a year, Charles Darwin had published his bombshell, *The Origin of Species*, in which he introduced a shocked world to the principle of the 'survival of the fittest'.

Boys of the old brigade – in 2009 the school cadet force celebrated its centenary.

1909 marked the high tide of imperialism in Britain. British was best. Boys' adventure stories were all about clean-limbed, wholesome young men performing heroic prodigies in far-flung corners of 'the Empire'. The world map was soaked with splashes of pink. Britannia still ruled the waves – just (despite the fact that the dastardly Germans were daring to catch up on our warship production).

Cadet forces were breaking out like the measles all over the country – in the *public* schools, you understand – where they were not called mere 'cadet forces'; they were 'The Officers' Training Corps' – for obvious reasons.

Everyone was familiar with the music-hall song, which had appeared as early as the 1880's: 'We don't want to fight, but by jingo, if we do, we've got the men, we've got the ships, we've got the money too.' Jingoism is a dirty word now, but it wasn't then.

Headmaster Harries had started a cadet force when he was on the staff at Blundells, and when he became Head at West Buckland, he couldn't wait to start one here. On cadet days, he saw no incongruity whatever in exchanging his dog collar for a Sam Browne.

As it says, RAF and Navy sections made their appearance in due course, so the whole force became known as the 'Combined Cadet Force'. My understanding is that the Navy and Air Force contingents have faded away, but, perversely, the whole unit is still referred to as the 'CCF'.

It is easy to laugh at it all now, but read what they said at the time, and see how patriotic they were, and how sincere. They weren't arrogant; they simply meant it. It was true. They were proud of it. And they volunteered in their tens of thousands in 1914. Fifty-eight of them from West Buckland did not come home – to a school whose average roll in the years running up to the War was less than 120.

WEST BUCKLAND SCHOOL

COMMANDING OFFICERS 1909

Capt. E.C.Harries	–1924	Officers Training Corps
Capt. T.C.Bellot	–1927	
Maj. J.E.Corless.T.D.	–1940	1940
Capt. W.A.Davies	–1944	Junior Training Corps 1943
(Air) Fl. Lt. W.F.Dale	1943–	Junior Training Corps
Maj. I.S.McLintock	–1951	and Air Training Corps
(Navy) Sub. Lt. G.E.Hern	1955–	1948
Lt. Col. J.E.Corless.T.D.	–1959	Combined Cadet Force

THE SCHOOL CONTINGENT of the Officers Training Corps took part in a Royal Review of the Senior and Junior Divisions of the O.T.C. at Windsor Great Park in 1911.

In 1912, at the request of the Fourth Earl Fortescue, the Contingent formed a Guard of Honour to H.R.H. Princess Henry of Battenberg, who was paying a visit to the Earl and Countess Fortescue.

A Flight of the Air Training Corps was formed in 1943 and an R.N. Section of the Combined Cadet Force in 1955.

At present the Contingent consists of R.N., Army, R.A.F. and Basic sections with Signals.

The playing fields where our battles were won

I AM SURE MOST schools find a place on their Sports Day programme to print some athletic records. This selection is taken from a Sports programme of 1938. As you would expect, after a time lapse of eighty years, most of the records have long been broken.

But two stand up very respectably today. We don't throw the cricket ball now, but look nevertheless at the distance – 106 yards. That's longer than a football pitch. A pretty sterling effort by any standards. How many club cricketers can beat it today? How many county players, come to that?

And look at the Long Jump – 22 feet. Prodigious for a schoolboy. W.E.L. Wall. He was known in the school as 'Eustace' – presumably because it was his name. If memory serves, I think he came from the West Indies – and he was not the first boy at WB to do that. We had a teacher from Trinidad too.

Wall dominated the Long Jump for three years (1922-24); nobody could touch him. For over twenty years, no West Buckland athlete came within two feet of his record.

SCHOOL RECORDS.

EVENT	TIME OR DISTANCE	HELD BY	YEAR
100 Yards	10 one-fifth secs	D. N. Cornwell	1930
220 Yards	24 four-fifths secs	D. N. Cornwell	1931
440 Yards	54 secs	J. H. Wyatt	1919
880 Yards	2 min 9 one-fifth secs	D. N. Cornwell	1933
Mile	4 min 49 one-fifth secs	H. Tully	1935
Hurdles	17 one-fifth secs	W. E. Wall	1922
High Jump	5 ft 5¼ inches	W. E. Wall	1924
Long Jump	22 feet 1 inch	W. E. Wall	1924
Cricket Ball	106 yards 2 inches	M. S. Farara	1934
The Weight	33 feet 3½ inches	R. J. Langford	1937

Coming up to scratch

IN THE 'BAD OLD days', there were – and, for all I know, still are, though their prevalence, I hope, is not so marked – many rituals, trials, tests, penances, forfeits, and generally unwelcome procedures to which new boys were subjected by the veterans in their dormitory. Some were harmless enough; others could verge on the cruel and demeaning.

It is likely that most of them don't exist in West Buckland now, not because of any increase in the average schoolboy's or schoolgirl's share of virtue, but because West Buckland is not primarily a boarding school any more. Opportunities were legion in the days of huge barrack-room dormitories, slack supervision, and the very human desire to make later arrivals suffer in the way that you had – or at least to tolerate it. Elderly old boys have told me that, in their day, nearly everybody got bullied one way or another, and at one time or another, largely because there was damn all else to do.

Nowadays, sleeping units are generally smaller, better heated, better furnished, better equipped with recreating facilities, and better supervised. There are many more attractive ways of passing the time.

Does that mean that people have stopped looking for ways of making life a misery for those they have taken against? No, of course not. Ill disposition is always fertile ground for growing ways of producing fears and tears in others.

One of the less objectionable rituals to which new boys were subjected was recalled at an Old Boys' Dinner in 1923. The speaker was William Stradling – a most distinguished alumnus: he had won every prize, medal, scholarship and distinction in the school's gift. But he had been new once, and so recalled this little episode quite sharply, as would anyone else have done who had been through it.

The point of the exercise was to discover whether the new arrival was a 'true Devonian'.

Two brothers called Balment (a very old Devon name) conducted the proceedings. One would ask the other: 'Where's your brother?'

The other, right on cue, would reply, 'Up Turchin 'ood digging' tetties wi' a tuball.'

If the new boy could translate that, he was considered a real son of Deb'm.

The anecdote does not recall what the penalty was for failure. So it could have been anything.

Stradling was lucky; he came from Chittlehampton.

A just beast

CHARLES BLAND WAS THE second headmaster, appointed in 1888. His *curriculum vitae* embraced Cambridge and a spell at Ipswich Grammar School.

He soon became noted for his stern discipline. In his favour, though, he was remembered as having been 'a beast, but a just beast'. He had the Victorians' passion for sport, and played regularly with the school football team.

He did some valuable rebuilding of numbers, which had slipped badly in the earlier 1880's, because of the severe agricultural depression. Farmers knew where to make economies. He did well enough to win the headship of Ripon Grammar School in 1895.

Victorian rectitude, Victorian fashion, the stringencies of office, high collars, pince-nez spectacles, and Wyatt Earp moustaches, combined to make a lot of headmasters look older than they actually were. Bland was only in his thirties; he played football, and, in his seven-year sojourn at the Devon County School, sired four children, including twins. By an extraordinary coincidence, so did the Revd. Harries, one of his successors, in about 1920.

1889 — 1895 Mr. C. C. S. BLAND, M.A.

Compulsory culture

Nowadays, schools do, for the most part, try to provide a spot of genuine entertainment to all those willing parents who make the trip to see their offspring receive prizes – or perhaps simply to be seen seeing them receive prizes – if only a school orchestra, band, group, combo, or whatever laying out their musical wares on a temporary dais in the hall, gym, or marquee, as circumstances permitted.

Before the War (and, for all I know, for some time after it, if the experience of my own school speech days is anything to go by), the audience did not get off so lightly. During the headship of Commander Westall (1934-39), this is a sample of what they got.

Still on Record

Speeches

Latin In Verrem Actio II *Cicero*
W.G. Turpitt (This was the boy who had to recite it, conjugations and all.)

(Verres, the Governor of Sicily, on his retirement was impeached for maladministration. Cicero, the prosecuting counsel, enumerates some of the offences: the theft of public statues and general ill-usage of the provincials.)

[In the days of Latin as a regular item in the curriculum, audiences still had to have the reference to Verres explained to them. And hardly surprising. One suspects that, today, they would (many of them anyway) have needed similar explanatory notes for Cicero. Or, to put it more bluntly, 'Who the hell was Cicero?']

French Le Bourgeois Gentilhomme *Moliere*
A.D. Taylor and W.G. Turpitt [Master Turpitt was certainly earning his keep.]

(Monsieur Jourdain, who has made a fortune, is desirous of taking a position among "people of quality". He summons to his assistance a professor of philosophy. The latter attempts a course of logics [sic], ethics and physical science, but, finding his pupil unresponsive, is finally reduced to a lesson in vowel pronunciation. He however assists M. Jourdain in the composition of a *billet doux* to a certain Marquise.) [And *bonne chance* to M. Jourdain.]

English The Proposal (Pride and Prejudice) *J. Austen*
[I like that – 'J. Austen'. No preferential treatment for the women. Strict equality.]

English The Snake Queen (Queen of the Air) *J. Ruskin*
[No notes offered here. Did they assume that everyone would know? Optimistic.]

English Kitchener (The World Crisis) *Winston Churchill*
[Shouldn't it be 'W.Churchill'? Sauce for the goose. . . .?]

Where do I come from?

AT SOME TIME OR other in our lives, we get curious about this. By extending the idea, it is possible that all those countless poor souls who are regularly subjected to the curse of exams may have speculated about how the damned things came about in the first place. Well, they would; they were suffering from them.

They weren't always there. There are many things that are woven into your lives so ubiquitously that it may never occur to you to imagine what life might have been like without them, or before them. You may not have suffered from them, but you used them, all the time, and you got used *to* them. You never thought of them as 'not there'. Like castles, and villages, and hedgerows, and wheels. Nevertheless, they had to be invented. It was the same with exams.

When tradesmen and farmers wanted to win promotion for their sons (all you had to do for a daughter was find a husband for her; a kind, affluent husband was as good an investment as any, if you wanted to avoid the nursery or the kitchens or the streets), they had to write some oily letters or suck up generally to the local bigwig. But when the Industrial Revolution produced a demand for engineers and scientists and architects, these new men clearly had to be equipped with some kind of education, and that education had to be measured to ensure that the engine worked or that the bridge did not fall down. It was no longer enough to be a likely lad. Hence, exams. QED.

Oxford and Cambridge had long had degree exams for sons of gentlemen, but nobody else got much of a look in. It was Brereton's great flash of insight to imagine a system of schools for 'the middle class', to teach subjects which would give pupils more skills than the ability to quote Aristotle and Juvenal and the Book of Samuel, and know what colour wine went with the fish, and the dates of the various hunting seasons. By the same token as above, the way to measure the usefulness and effectiveness of this middle class education was to set exams, to find out what boys (and a few girls) had learned.

As with so many worthwhile reforms, it was a battle to get the establishment to accept this idea, but at last they succeeded, in 1858. (This is a telescoped version of what actually happened. For more information, try my chapter entitled 'Tried and Tested' in *The Natural History of a Country School* [Woodfield, 2005, pp. 118-134]. That too is a telescoped version

– it's a big subject – but it does take you a little further.)

Oxford and Cambridge Universities each set up their own local exams, which any boy or girl from any school could enter for. They became known universally, and succinctly, as 'the Locals'. And they lasted till the end of the first decade of the twentieth century – quite a good run, compared with School Certificate and 'O' Level which came later.

As explained before, the four main architects of this project – Brereton, Fortescue, Sir Thomas Dyke Acland, and Frederick Temple, (Headmaster of Rugby, later Bishop of Exeter and Archbishop of Canterbury), were all closely associated with West Buckland School.

And there is another remarkable parallel. The school was founded in 1858, and received its first (three) pupils in November of that year. We still have the actual papers printed for the very first of the Cambridge University Local Examinations, printed in November, 1858. Pupils sat them the following month.

Take a look at them. All right, so Latin is still there. But so is German. (Half the Royal Family was German; Queen Victoria's first language was German.) 'Scripture' is still present; the reformers did not want to remove religion from the curriculum (God forbid – and He probably would have done); they simply wanted a better balance. History, Geography, English Grammar, English Composition. Well, OK. But look at the rest – Chemistry, Anatomy and Physiology, Heat, Electricity, and Magnetism; Geology, Optics and Acoustics, Hydrostatics, Trigonometry, Euclid, Land Surveying, Botany, Zoology, and so on and so on. You couldn't have the colours of modernity nailed more firmly to the mast.

Now look at the amount that these candidates were submitted to in a single day. From ten in the morning to eight at night. The poor juniors did not fare any better. They were on the go from nine to half-past seven or eight. All right, so they got a break for lunch and tea, and every candidate did not sit every single exam, but nevertheless it is a pretty charged week. Eight consecutive days, with a break only for the Sabbath.

As the population has gradually slipped away from Church belief and Church observance, it is curious that the Sabbath has retained its longevity of influence. It is less time ago than you might think that football matches and horse races did not take place on Sunday. And newspapers did not appear on Good Friday. It was a saloon-bar joke for years that you could buy a saucy magazine on Sunday but not a bible.

No doubt many of the traditional public schools availed themselves of these opportunities, but West Buckland was the very first 'middle class' school to enter their boys. And very creditably they performed too. In the mid-eighteen-sixties, when the school was less than ten years old, they recorded more successes than any other school in the country. Top of the league, no less. And three years running.

A final thought: as the exam papers still survive and are accessible, it might be an interesting experiment to persuade a clutch of sixteen-year-old guinea-pigs to sit these exams. All right, so they would not be expected to be familiar with all the details of the syllabuses, but they should be competent enough to tackle English Composition, German, Pure Mathematics, Drawing, Arithmetic, Trigonometry and 'Shakespeare's "Julius Caesar" ', wouldn't you say?

Is the language in danger or is it thriving?

SOME YEARS AGO I published an article about the school in a magazine called *This England*. As the title suggests, it is full of tradition, solid values, happy memories, patriotism, and tender feeling for what 'things used to be'. That is not meant as a criticism; it is simply what it is. It gives expression to a perfectly valid point of view. If you don't agree, you don't have to read it. To paraphrase Voltaire, you may take issue with its attitude, its approach, its point of view, and its contents, but in a democratic society you have to accept that it has every right, so long as it stays within the law, to say what it thinks.

In the course of an exchange of letters connected with the publication of my article, I read several numbers of the magazine, and came across this.

It appears that, in the new Oxford University Press Junior Dictionary, the following words, among others, have been taken out:

carol cracker holly ivy mistletoe aisle abbey altar bishop chapel christen disciple minister monastery monk nun parish psalm pulpit saint sin devil vicar

coronation duke emperor monarch

buttercup cheetah colt cygnet drake fern ferret goldfish hamster heron herring kingfisher lark leopard lobster magpie moss mussel newt otter ox oyster pelican piglet plaice raven spaniel starling stoat stork thrush weasel

Words that have been newly inserted include:

vandalism negotiate interdependent creep citizenship EU cautionary tale bilingual compulsory democratic Euro

The changes, it explained, have been made in the light of 'multiculturalism'. The head of children's dictionaries at the Oxford University Press is called Vineeta Gupta.

The life and times – volume three

In 2008, I published my third book about West Buckland. It was entitled *West Buckland – the Diary of an Edwardian School* [Halsgrove]. Which, I agree, is a bit of a mouthful. Moreover, a glance again at the title will tell you that it is not going to be your compulsive page-turner. Nor will Mr. Britain, or Mrs. Britain, or any other Misses and Masters Britain – or even Ms. Britain – be queueing round the block or hammering the internet keys in order to beat the rest of the world to buying a copy.

It is what the title suggests – an intimate look at a particular school's history at a particular time. It is going up so close that you can practically see the blades of grass. But I will say in its defence that detail in itself can have an interest value, and, by writing about one school like this, I am to some extent writing about all of them. And it has lots of pictures – can't beat pictures.

However, when all is said and done, I had to accept that it was not going to turn the tide of current literary fashion or cause J.K. Rowling any headaches. I was all the more gratified therefore when I found that it had received a review, in a prominent West of England newspaper. I am of course not really the person to judge it; but it struck me, coming across it again after several years, that Mr. Colin Bradley had treated me, and the book, pretty fairly.

I suppose modesty would forbid me to print it out in full, or even in bits. (Mind you, it was a temptation.) So, probably, would the laws of copyright, unless I received Mr. Bradley's permission.

But I felt gratified to discover that somebody in the trade had thought it was good enough to be given the review treatment. I venture to suggest that pretty well any old pupil of the school might derive just a little pleasure from thumbing its pages, just as one would at coming across an album of old family photographs in the loft.

After I had been the school archivist for a very short time, I realised that a sizeable part of my hours and effort was going to be devoted to raising the profile of the Archive, and, by implication, of the school. To make people know that the Archive was here, and, moreover, that it deserved to be here.

I have taken both pride and pleasure in publishing four books about the school, so I fancy that I have added my six-pennyworth to its presence, its relevance, and its worth. By offering these books, I can not claim, as I said, literature, or sensation, or drama. But it will help, I hope, to add to the school's presence. The books are out there. What you do with them is your business.

But, as I said about that Edwardian school, 'here was something'. And I put it to you also that 'here is something'.

Politically correct

NOTHING, ABSOLUTELY NOTHING, IT seems is, or is going to be, free from the attentions of those mysterious people who work continually to befog the meaning of perfectly straightforward words and phrases.

We all know about rat-catchers becoming 'rodent operators'. It is the American War Department, we are told, who have translated 'Wounded soldiers' into 'Impaired Combat Personnel'.

What is the alchemy which works this process? Who thinks these things up? Why does '*ha*rass' turn into 'har*ass*'? Why are we no longer 'fed up *with*' something, but 'fed up *of* it'? Slang usually has a reason and a neat aptness. But prepositions? What makes 'of' better than 'with'?

I'm sure that whole books have been written about this, and everybody has his or her own favourites. I bet someone has written about it in *This England*, quoted above. If it hasn't been written about, it ought to be.

Well, it seems that this process, this disease, this linguistic blight, this etymological plague, has now spread into the sheltered, fragile, reserved little world in which I operate. I have discovered that the fashionable way to refer to the School Archivist is to call him the 'Heritage Collection and Records Manager'.

10. 2009

THEY DON'T MAKE WINTERS like that any more

Or perhaps the title of this piece should be 'Global Warming'.

In 1982, according to one informant, the Barnstaple butcher Grattan's delivered the school's meat to Filleigh sawmill, where the boys collected it and dragged it back to the school on sledges.

What about 1963, which, according to the most illustrious of Devon historians, W.G. Hoskins, was the worst winter since 1740. (It is a pity that we do not have any record in Devon – well, not one known to me – about the winter of 1683, when whole fairs were held on the ice of the Thames in London.)

Those with long memories will have engraved on their slate of recollection the winter of 1947. Every one of them will have his or her own favourite meteorological titbit to talk about with regard to this. We are told, for instance, that 'gangs' of boys trudged to Filleigh on top of the hedges and brought back the bread in rucksacks.

It is also claimed that the River Taw froze.

Yet, oddly, the really bad weather did not start till 21st January. But when it did, it did so with a vengeance. Flocks and herds of animals in the fields died en masse. Root crops could not be harvested because they were frozen into the ground. Even with rationing, it looked at one time as if the nation's food supply was under threat.

It was not simply a cold snap; as late as 25th February, the temperature at Woburn in Bedfordshire fell to -21 C. It is even suggested that the freeze-up put such a strain on the national economy that the Government decided to devalue the pound (work that one out).

And it wasn't over when the thaw arrived. That too came with a vengeance; it caused widespread floods.

Soldiers were put to work shovelling away the endless snow. Even German prisoners of war. Prisoners of war! Two years after hostilities had ended, there were still German prisoners, it seems, who had not been repatriated.

The second prospectus – March, 1861

> *Prospectus 1861*
>
> ## The Devon County School, West Buckland.
>
> PATRON—Earl FORTESCUE, K.G., the Lord Lieutenant of the County.
> TRUSTEES—Viscount EBRINGTON; the Rev. J. L. BRERETON, Rector of West Buckland, and Prebendary of Exeter Cathedral; J. E. J. RICCARD, Esq., Mayor of Southmolton; the Rev. W. H. KARSLAKE, Rector of Meshaw; and GEORGE LANGDON, Esq., of Ashford.
> SECRETARY AND CHAPLAIN—The Rev. WILLIAM MARTIN.
> HEAD MASTER—Mr. J. H. THOMPSON.
>
> ### Object of the School.
> This School was started towards the close of the year 1858, under the immediate patronage of Earl FORTESCUE, the Lord Lieutenant, in order to afford, at a moderate cost, a thoroughly good education, adapted to the wants of the Middle Classes, and particularly the Farmers.
>
> ### Its Progress.
> It was commenced in temporary Premises, with only three Pupils; but its numbers have steadily increased, till at present (March, 1861) there are 45 Boarders and about 20 Day Scholars belonging to it. This, with the probability of a further increase, has rendered it necessary that new buildings should be erected, and an Association (numbering among its Members the Duke of Bedford, Earl Fortescue, K.G., the Earl of Devon, Viscount Ebrington, Sir T. D. Acland, Bart, &c., &c.) having been formed for the purpose, the Foundation-stone of the New School was laid by Earl FORTESCUE, on the 4th of October, 1860.
>
> ### Course of Instruction.
> The School consists of Two Divisions; the Upper and the Lower.
> The Upper Division is intended for boys above 13 years of age, and the Course of Instruction is such as to fit them for Agricultural or Mercantile Pursuits, for the Civil Service Examinations, for the Oxford and Cambridge Middle Class Examinations; and, in general, to qualify them for honourable and independent positions in life; while in the Lower Division younger Boys receive a thoroughly good Elementary Education, preparatory to entering the Upper Division.

NOTE THE RISE IN numbers in barely two and a half years – up from 3 to 45 boarders and 20 day 'scholars'. Good going. It looked as if Brereton and Fortescue had found a profitable gap in the market.

The school had already lost its original title – The West Buckland Farm and County School. It looks as if one of Brereton's many dreams – a school supported by the farm labour and produce of its scholars – had already evaporated. But, with Brereton, there were always plenty more dreams where the failures came from.

Earl Fortescue – the second Earl – had founded the school and provided the land, and no doubt some helpful capital, or at least preferential interest rates on a mortgage. He died just before the main school was opened in October, 1861. But he was alive when this prospectus was issued. The 'Fortescue' who was Brereton's great friend and fellow-pioneer is here listed in the trustees as Viscount Ebrington. This was the title normally enjoyed by the Earl's eldest son. The family owned property in Ebrington in Gloucestershire.

Brereton was always careful to insert 'Prebendary of Exeter Cathedral' in any formal publication of his name. A prebend is an honorary position bestowed on clergymen associated with a cathedral, and sometimes carried a nominal stipend. But it was much more likely that what attracted Brereton was not the money but the dignity and distinction of the position. One gets the impression that he liked things like that. After all, he was only a humble rector of an obscure North Devon village, and his work and interests took him into contact with aristocrats like Fortescue – and, later, the Earl of Devon, the Duke of Bedford, and later still the Prince of Wales himself. The title 'Prebendary' helped him to keep his end up.

The Revd. W.H. Karslake, listed among the Trustees, was the man who was responsible for the dining hall, still referred now in a slightly abbreviated form as 'the Karslake'.

Joseph Thompson, as explained above, was deliberately appointed as a layman, because Brereton didn't want to follow the formula of the traditional public schools. But, now that he had a growing school and its reputation among all other schools to consider, he thought it worthwhile to take holy orders himself. Brereton had also been careful not to appoint a headmaster who was a graduate from Oxbridge. Yet, at the same time as Thompson took four years off (1867-71) to study for holy orders, he read for a Cambridge degree. So had he, and Brereton, decided that having a headmaster in holy orders and armed with a Cambridge degree was quite a good idea after all? 'The Revd. J.H. Thompson, M.A.' looked so much better than plain 'Mr. Thompson'. Willy-nilly, West Buckland was joining the club. (Latin crept into the curriculum later on.)

The school, to its credit, did set out its intentions frankly. . . . 'to afford, at a moderate cost, a thoroughly good education, adapted to the wants of the Middle Classes, and particularly the Farmers'. And they stated with equal frankness that they were aiming their boys at the new Oxford and

Cambridge 'Locals' – to fit them for Agricultural or Mercantile Pursuits, for the Civil Service Examinations. . . . and in general to qualify them for honourable and independent positions in life'.

You couldn't have it clearer than that.

Worthy of his hire

THE ARCHIVE STILL HAS the original agreement drawn up between the Governors and the first Bursar appointed after the school had changed its name and its status. The new Chairman of Governors was Dudley John Campbell Bush, and the new Bursar was Edward Eastmond Hodge. (Both were to serve in those capacities for a long time.) This officer is now regularly known as 'Bursar', but then he was referred to as 'Secretary'.

He certainly had a lot of secretarial jobs – minutes of proceedings, records, statements of accounts and reports to the Governors. They kept him busy. He was to attend between 10 and 4 every day (except Sunday of course, and 'such holidays as the Governors may grant him'). So he was not to get the normal school holidays. He had to attend all Governors' meetings and Management Committee meetings. Well, you would expect that.

He had to balance the books. Well, you would expect that too. But there was a convenient extra clause which allowed the Chairman of Governors to require the Bursar to 'perform all such duties as may reasonably be required of a Secretary and Bursar'. Which could cover anything, according to the interpretation of the Chairman.

It is rather like that the old Army Act, which listed all the offences which a wayward soldier might commit, and the penalties. But the drafters, well aware of the inventiveness of the criminal mind, especially the criminal military mind, and well aware too that new offences might come into being, craftily wrote in at the end a 'catch-all' offence – 'conduct to the prejudice of good order and military discipline' – which covered absolutely everything. You could never win.

There was no question of a power-hungry bursar taking it into his head to build empires: 'He shall at all times and in all respects be under and subject to the superintendence control and direction of the Governors.' No tail wagging the dog.

The Governors undertook to pay the 'Secretary' sixty pounds a year 'in four quarterly instalments'. That is, £1.15p. per week.

We know that the Bursar had a family. This man was responsible for the financial welfare of a new boarding school, and he was getting five pounds a month. Surely he must have had another means of income.

The only perk that the agreement offered him was food 'free of expense' 'at the ordinary mealtimes'.

A mixed blessing perhaps? A 1913 school lunch for free?

Gallop to gold

It used to be a wry joke about the Helsinki Olympic Games in 1952 that the only gold medal presented to England had been won by a horse – Foxhunter. Ridden, I think, by Harry Llewellyn.

But West Buckland was represented there, and on a horse. An old boy, Bertie Hill, was chosen to be part of the English team. As I said, he didn't win a medal (that came later).

Naturally, he was very proud of the distinction, and wrote a handsome letter to the (then) caretaker Headmaster, Mr. Wheeler, to acknowledge the latter's congratulations.

Great Rapscott,
South Molton
21.5.52.

Dear Mr. Wheeler,

Thank you very much for your letter of congratulation on the honour which has come to me. I much appreciate the kind interest and good wishes of all at West Buckland, and when the testing time comes shall do my best to be worthy of them.

It is quite a step from West Buckland to Helsinki and I little thought, on my daily rides to and from school, that I was even then in early training for progress along that road!

I find it very difficult to believe in my good fortune for so many wonderful things [that] happened to me at Badminton recently.

Helsinki will be tough going but whatever happens there you may rest assured that an old West Buckland boy will have done his best for Queen and country.

With kind regards to all.
Yours sincerely,
Bertie Hill.

Bertie Hill remains – at any rate to my knowledge – the only boy who regularly rode a horse to and from school. It would be interesting to know where and how he stabled it during the day. As explained above, Bertie didn't win a medal. He didn't win a medal either at Melbourne in 1956. But he did at Mexico City in 1968, when he trained the gold-winning team.

His letter gives a flavour of what it meant to be selected to represent one's country.

Standards going in reverse?

ANYONE TODAY WHO TRIES to get into university can tell you about wading through hefty prospectuses, filling in complicated forms, discussions with one's tutor, drafting one's 'personal statement', and so on. This is followed by pressing one's nose to the window-pane in expectation of the 'offer' (although more likely now in an email) from the university of first choice (and, if that lets you down, the university of second choice, third choice, and so on). Anyone who puts down a university of fourth or fifth choice would not, I imagine, be very likely to receive a favourable letter.

If one applies to Oxford or Cambridge, there is one more hoop to jump through – an interview. The competition nowadays is so fierce that it is not enough to be good, or, sometimes, even very good. Put another way, you can't expect to walk straight in with grade A's right across the board.

It wasn't like that in the 'old days'. In my case, there was no master in charge of Sixth Form to oversee the whole process. One did not have to compose a personal statement, and UCAS didn't exist. I simply went to see my Headmaster, who gave me list of about half a dozen colleges (three in each) and said, 'Have a go at those.' So I went home and did – no vetting by my tutor (I didn't have a tutor); no forms to fill in, no typing or printing of letters. You just sat at the kitchen table and wrote out your application in longhand, stuck a stamp on the envelope, and hoped for the best.

The Archive has a letter (from the late sixties) received by the Headmaster, and which summed up the difference between now and then:

'I am happy to say that I able to offer a place to _____ without hesitation, and we shall be writing to him within a day or two. I found him lucid and coherent and was most impressed with his command of words. This is the sort of boy we always hope to find.'

This boy's 'O' Level grades were 1, 2, 2, 3, 4, 6 (out of a scale of 9).

The offer was made nine months before he achieved three B's at 'A' Level.

Note the 'without hesitation'.

He duly entered Oxford University in October, 1970.

The value of practice

Do you aspire to be a golfer? Better still, a successful one? If you do, read on...

'The first lesson to be learned... is the value of practice. This is the beginning and end of excellence... The present position I hold in the golfing world is in a very great measure due to... being able to proceed out to some quiet corner of the links, with just a couple of clubs and a dozen balls, and... [to] set myself the task of trying to find out the peculiarities... of these particular weapons... I must candidly acknowledge enjoying... an hour all alone... on the links more than the pleasure of participating in the most interesting and pleasant match one can imagine. ... A young player is apt to gain more knowledge in such an hour of solitude than he is at all likely to acquire in playing thirty-six holes against even the finest players in the land.'

Practice, practice... and enjoy it. Is not this little homily worthy of being put up in every dressing room where young people engage in any sporting activity you can name?

There are countless comments, anecdotes, and little squibs to pursue this theme. I like the one about the gushing spectator who once said to the mother of a successful runner, 'I am sure you must be so pleased that _____ has done so well. He must be very lucky.'

To which the successful athlete's mother sweetly replied, 'Yes, I have noticed that. The harder he works the luckier he gets.'

The extract comes from a book written by an international golfer called Harold Hilton, who won the Open Championship twice and the Amateur Championship four times. He attended West Buckland in the 1870's, though I doubt whether he learned much of his golf there.

One can not be sure if this is relevant, but a man who used to watch him in action claimed that, while he was actually playing, he had a cigarette in his mouth more often than not. When he didn't, he was forever chomping on lumps of chocolate. Even if this is true, it is unlikely that he would have put such advice in his book.

The phrase about 'practice... and enjoying it' struck a chord with me, because the motto of my own school is *'Bene agere ac laetari'*. Which comes out as 'Work well and enjoy it while you are doing so'.

I have always thought that was very apt.

A home of your own – at last

AFTER THE FIRST FARMHOUSE, the school had two other farmhouse premises, before this shiny new building appeared in October, 1861.

What has disappeared since then?

Carbon copy

THE FOUNDER, THE REVD. J.L. Brereton, envisaged a nation-wide network of secondary schools 'for the middle classes', one for each county. Hence the name 'Devon County School' – which was the first. This one, in Norfolk, was the second.

THE NORFOLK COUNTY SCHOOL, AT ELMHAM, 1874

Brereton installed as Headmaster the man who had been his Deputy Head at DCS, the Revd. William Watson.

Watson, sadly, died, and Brereton put this second son, Francis, in his place. The school still failed, and the building became a Naval Training School under the auspices of Dr. Barnardo's. That closed in 1953. The school was bought by a local speculator, and razed to the ground. His plans did not materialise. Some of the outbuildings became piggeries.

Much later, the old school chapel became a private house, and on the main site there are now, I understand, blocks of flats.

But there remains, on the other side of the road, a little school cemetery.

A date worth remembering

ON THE 9TH SEPTEMBER, I just had to put something up on the notice board.

Look at it: 090909. You can't get much cooler than that. Well, actually, you can. A colleague produced a baby in 2001. Not the rarest of feats, you might say. Indeed. But look at the date – 1st January. So. . . . 010101. Some birthday.

Reminds me of a soldier we had in an African battalion. He had a shocking memory. Whenever they went to the armoury to draw out their rifles for a training session, he could never remember the number of his weapon. After a lot of research, the Armourer's staff found the ideal rifle number. It had five digits – 11111. Our local amnesiac could cope with that. As askaris were in the habit of sticking a little 'y' on the end of some words, his rifle number came out as: 'Wuni-wuni-wuni-wuni-wuni.' But he didn't forget any more.

However the titbit I found to commemorate the 9th September was a near-centenary. I discovered in a 99-year-old school magazine that the school football team had played only three games that season – but what results!

They beat Somerset County School (one of the growing number of county schools being set up to perpetuate the series begun by West Buckland) by 17 to nil. They knocked off Barnstaple Grammar by the same margin – 17-1. But that was away. At home later on they blew them away 26-nil.

They must have been inspired by the huge crowds on the terraces.

And a little tailpiece of absolutely no relevance at all: One of the school's most relentless benefactors was Mr. Richard Pearse Chope, a very successful Old Boy, Governor, Secretary of the Old Boys' Association, and anything else you can think of.

He used to swamp the recipients with a regular tide of books, slides, artefacts, inexorably long magazine articles, and other memorabilia (and, to be fair, monetary gifts too). He set the General Knowledge paper, and marked it, and financed the prize that was awarded for it. It continued long after he had died, every year till 1965.

He liked collecting some of the most outrageous answers. One question was: 'How would you distinguish a land rat from a water rat?'

A candidate suggested with remorseless logic that 'if both were in water, the land rat would drown'. (Well?)

Was there international life before Jonathan Edwards?

YES, THERE MOST CERTAINLY was.

Anybody associated with sport at West Buckland knows the name of the school's most successful and celebrated athlete, Jonathan Edwards, who won every event, cup, prize, medal, and distinction in the triple-jump business. His world record, unbelievably, still stands today, after over twenty years. The school's cathedral-like Sports Centre is named after him, and was opened by him to clamorous junketings. Not to know about Jonathan Edwards would have been like attending Harrow School and never having heard of Winston Churchill.

But how many know much about the names Packer, Gimblett, Read, and Hilton?

West Buckland's first rugby international was not Victor Ubogu; nor was it Steve Ojomoh. Harry Packer beat them to it by over sixty years. Welshman. When you shook hands with him, you were being gripped at the same time by the President of the Welsh Amateur Athletic Association, a member of the Welsh Football Union, a member of the Welsh 'Big Five' (whoever they were), manager of the British Rugby Team which toured South Africa in 1924 (an early Lions task force, no less), and a member of the Monmouthshire County RFC Committee.

Herbert Jones played for England way back in 1930.

Bertie Hill rode horses for England in the Olympic team – twice. And he trained a third one – which won a gold medal. He and his horses are mentioned elsewhere in this book.

Charlotte Read was a gold medallist fencer at the Commonwealth Games.

Harold Gimblett was arguably the greatest batsman ever to play for Somerset. He appeared for his county 329 times. His appearances for England were few because his career was interrupted by the War.

Finally, Harold Hilton won the Amateur Golf Championship four times and the Open Championship twice.

Look 'em up.

Still on Record

Service or sentence?

THE
𝔚𝔢𝔰𝔱 𝔅𝔲𝔠𝔨𝔩𝔞𝔫𝔡 𝔖𝔠𝔥𝔬𝔬𝔩 𝔑𝔢𝔤𝔦𝔰𝔱𝔢𝔯.

No. 190.   JULY, 1926
School Notes and News.

The following boys left in April: -
FORM VI A.

A.C. Cooper (B), entered June, 1915. Prefect, 1923 (3), Head Prefect, 1925 (3). Examination: Cert. A, Nov., 1923. Prize: Michael Snell, English, 1926. Colours: Cricket, 1923; Football, 1922; Captain, 1924 (3); Shooting, 1923; Captain, 1925; Junior Shooting Cup, 1920; Open Shooting, 1925; Donegall Badge, 1923; Colts' Swimmng, 1920; Open Fives, 1926. C.-S.-M. in O.T.C.

They were much more pernickety with their commas and colons and hyphens and full stops then. The figures in brackets indicated one of the three terms in the school year. They operated on a calendar basis, so 3 represented the Autumn Term.

Before the First World War, boys did not, as a rule, stay very long in the school. Headmasters often referred regretfully to this fact in their Speech Day reports.

So this makes Arthur Cooper's eleven years (1915 to 1926) something of a noteworthy achievement, especially given the spartan conditions in which everyone lived. It was testimony to his resilience if nothing else. One wonders whether, when he finally left, he sought the comparative ease and comfort of the French Foreign Legion.

But times change. Now that we have not only the Prep. but the Pre-prep., and, more recently, the Nursery section, it is possible that some children can attend West Buckland for fourteen years. Indeed some have done so. In theory, of course, if you do your arithmetic properly, a boy or girl, joining the Nursery at three, can chalk up *fifteen*, but I don't know if anybody has done that – yet. .

How to get pupils to love music

THE FOLLOWING REMARKS ARE taken from the termly reports on a pupil:

Autumn Term.	Position in class – 21st	'Desperately feeble.'
Spring Term.	Position in class – 20th	'He seems to have learnt nothing.'
Summer Term.	Position in class – 21st	'Completely inactive.'

It would have been interesting to know

1. How many pupils were there in the class?
2. What did the teacher try to teach them?
3. What equipment did he have at his disposal? (In my grammar school, in the 1940's, the whole school mustered only a jaded upright piano, one record-player, and a set of spineless copies of the *National Song Book* with thread-like strings from the back bindings dangling all over the place.)
4. What teaching accommodation did the teacher have? (Again, in my school, the music master had to conduct every lesson in the main hall, through which passed a constant stream of cleaners, caretakers opening lofty windows, boys on teachers' errands, milk monitors, actual teachers on their way to another class, sixth-form boys on ladders preparing spotlights for the coming Christmas Concert, and dinner ladies putting up trestle tables for lunch.)
5. Did he have a strategy for combating schoolboys built-in philistinism?
6. And finally, what was the name of the nerve tonic he took regularly?

Behind the façade of respectability

> No. 61.
>
> SMALL LOTTERIES AND GAMING ACT, 1956.
>
> ### Certificate of Registration
> of Society under the Act.
>
> THIS IS TO CERTIFY that the Society known as West Buckland School
>
> whose [head] office is situate at West Buckland School, Barnstaple
>
> has been registered by the South Molton Rural District Council
>
> in pursuance of Section 2 of the above Act, with effect from the first day of January, 1960
>
> Receipt of the fee of **ONE POUND** is acknowledged.(†)
>
> DATED this fifth day of January, 19 60.
>
> *Clerk of the Local Authority.*
>
> (†) NOTE. A further fee of £1 is payable to the Local Authority on the 1st day of January in each year while this registration remains in force.

I bet they didn't put this in the school prospectus.

11. 2010

East India Company

EARLY IN THE TWENTIETH century an Indian doctor in Hyderabad called Shrinagesh decided to give his three sons an English education. We don't know if he visited England to have a look beforehand, and we don't know how he conducted his search for the best place for his boys from the other side of the world. (This was in the Dark Ages before the internet.) He may have been recommended the name by a friend. He may simply have stuck a pin in the page and taken a chance. We don't know.

What we do know is that all three boys entered the school between about 1910 and the 1920's. Their surname – Shrinagesh – presented difficulties to their contemporaries (maybe even to the school authorities). However, there was another name in the family – Mallannah. That was within the linguistic scope of everyone.

That took care of the surname. Christian names were a much bigger hurdle. They were Satyavant, Jayavant, and Madhukar. You couldn't call out names like that across the quadrangle or the rugby pitch, even if you could remember them, even if you could pronounce them.

The boys solved it by a piece of transparent, brilliant expediency: they called them Johnny, Jimmy, and Jackie. Satyavant became Johnnie; Jayavant became Jimmie; Madhukar became Jackie. It worked.

The Mallannah brothers became almost a school institution, and not only because of their names. I have had conversations with very old old boys, and, whenever their name came up, the eyes would mist over slightly, the head would nod wryly, and the smile would spread: 'Ah, yes, the Mallannah brothers.'

When a boy left school, the magazine would print a short account of his career – exams passed, teams played for, prizes won, distinctions and medals, and so on. The biographies of the Mallannah brothers ran into over eight lines – each.

But there must have been more to it than that. There have been lots of boys who have been good at nearly everything. Old men did not shake their heads and smile fondly just because Johnny played for the First XI or Jimmy was a good fly half or Jackie won the Fortescue Medal. There must have been another dimension, and one is forced to the conclusion that it had to do with their character, their 'presence', and maybe just a little their uniqueness. There certainly has not been a trio to surpass their achievement.

Their record after leaving school was, if anything, even more distinguished.

Jackie became a doctor, having studied at Guy's Hospital. He joined the medical branch of the RAF, and was awarded the OBE for services in the War. He did research in America on high altitude flight, and received a US commendation. He went on to become Director of Medical Services of the Indian Air Force, and later still became the Principal of the Armed Forces Medical College at Poona. He reached the rank of Air Vice Marshal.

Jimmy won his colours for rugby and athletics at Trinity College, Cambridge, and joined the Indian Civil Service. During the War he reached high rank in the government of the Punjab, the Government Munitions Department, and in the local government of a border territory between (what later became) India and Pakistan. It was there that he witnessed the appalling violence that accompanied Partition. He later ran an aircraft factory and an oil refinery, and ended his public career as chairman of a mining consultancy.

Johnnie entered Sandhurst, and won a cup for the best man-at-arms going into the Indian Army. He the first Indian instructor at the Indian Military Academy, then did war service in Burma under General Wingate. After several world postings, he returned (having been awarded the American Legion of Merit) to India, where he served as staff officer in increasingly high-ranked military organisations. In the end, with the rank of General, he became the senior officer in the entire Indian Army. He still wasn't finished. He set up the Administrative Staff College of India, and served as State Governor in Assam, Nagaland, Hyderabad, and Mysore.

Surely this will take a lot of beating.

The school made its mark on them too. They came all the way back to see the school, and they took the trouble to come together. We have a photograph of them on the playing field, with what looks like the Headmaster's dog at their feet. One of their wives (who had reached the rank of Matron in the War) visited as late as 1987. She died in 2007, aged 95.

Satyavant sent his son to West Buckland.

They must have been a bit special, and they must have had a remarkable father. And mother.

All in the family

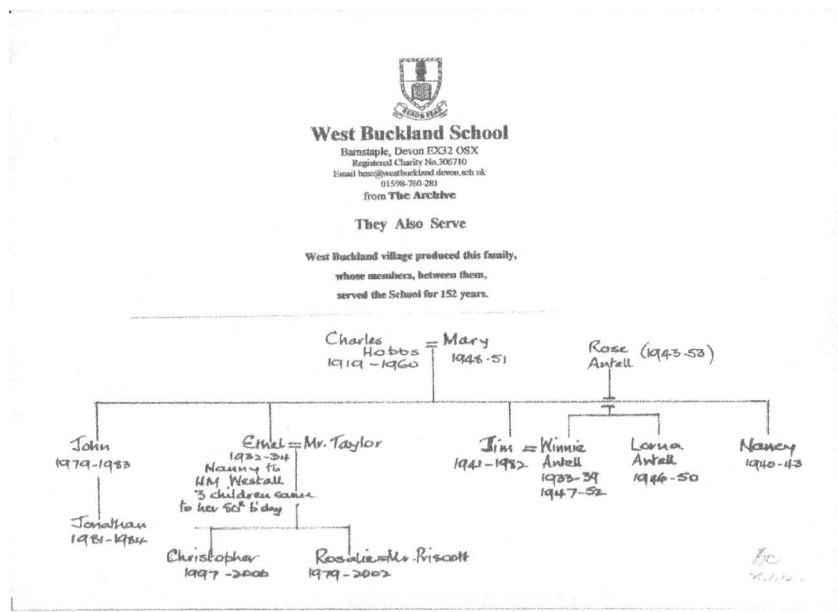

152 YEARS – THAT too will take a bit of beating.

And don't think of these people simply as humble locals who trudged in from the village in their hobnail boots and tugged the forelock.

Many of them held positions of great trust and influence. Jim, simply in himself, *was* the school maintenance staff for decades. Ethel was given the charge of the Headmaster's children, and notice that three of them came to her eightieth birthday party.

Rosalie was the chief of staff, right-hand 'man', chief factotum, and *éminence grise* of the Bursar's Office, as it says, for twenty-three years. If she had got her sums wrong – even once – the school could have been facing the receivers.

That wasn't all that Rosalie was involved with. She was an active piano-teacher, an adept accompanist, a brass band enthusiast, and a local magistrate.

It points a useful moral: never, *never* estimate a person you meet simply on the basis of what they are doing at the moment you meet them.

Still on Record

All the geese are swans

WEST BUCKLAND SCHOOL.

REPORT FOR THE TERM ENDING APRIL 9TH, 1919.

House: Treuvette (founded in 1918)

NAME: A. G. Buckingham		Form or Set	No. of Boys	Average Age	Term Order	Exam. Order
	General Work	III⁶	25	13.8	3	1
	Mathematics	F	25	13.2	1	5

Order on Exam. Results	Latin	French	English	History	Geography	Divinity	Science	Drawing	Term Order. Handwork
	2	4	4	4	1	2	1	5	8

LATIN. Excellent, he should do very well in this subject. *M.A.T. Classics Master.*

FRENCH. His work has been well done, and his progress has been very satisfactory. *E.G.W. Mod. Language Master.*

ENGLISH. Very good indeed. His work is always carefully prepared. *E.G.W. English Master.*

MATHEMATICS. Has worked splendidly + made excellent progress. *E.S. Howells. Math. Master.*

SCIENCE. A steady and sure worker - splendid progress. *A.J. Science Master.*

MUSIC. Good progress. Lacks firmness in his touch. *M.W. Music Master.*

SHORTHAND or BOOK-KEEPING.

Excellent report in every way. ERNEST C. HARRIES, M.A., Head Master.

Monday, May 5th, 1919. Boarders Return. They are required to report themselves to the Head Master immediately on their arrival, and to hand in their Health Certificates.
Tuesday, May 6th, 1919. Day Boys Return. Prayers and Roll Call 10.30 a.m.

IT LOOKS AS IF this goose really is a swan, though Harries is perhaps just a little over-enthusiastic to prove that all his scholars 'do well'.

E.S. Howells was a legendary teacher of English, so what is he doing here at Maths?

Striking how good the teachers' handwriting is, with the ironic exception of that of the Headmaster.

Le mot juste

IN THE *REGISTER* OF November, 1927, the correspondence pages threw up the following letter from (presumably) an old boy of the school who was searching for a suitable name for the Old Boys' Association:

'To coin a name for the Association with West Buckland as a starting-point is no easy task. "Old Bucks" is impossible and may be rejected at once. "West" is a difficulty, especially as *East* Buckland parish church is regarded as the School chapel. [Earl Fortescue had endowed the chaplaincy there, and even had new pews built to accommodate the growing numbers of pupils – many of whom showed their appreciation of his generosity by carving seditious graffiti on them.]

'The name Buckland means book-land, land originally. . . held by written grant (a charter or deed, Anglo-Saxon *boc* – book). . . By elimination we come to the root of the name, "boc". A possible name would be Boclandians, although " – ian" is classical and not a proper suffix for the Anglo-Saxon stem.

'We might have Boclings or Bucklandings, but again the A.-S. " – ing" has a general connotation of real or presumed blood-relationship. "Ing" has, however, dropped out of use, while " – ian" is generally used as its modern substitute, e.g. "Exonian".

'Perhaps, therefore, Bucklandians (without the "old") would be a suitable name. More exquisite is Bucklanders, on the analogy of uplanders; the word is easy to say and the accentuation is fair. It is unfortunate that there are many villages of Buckland, from Egg Buckland to Buckland Monachorum, and, perhaps, we are wrong in looking for a name from this root.

'Devon County won't take us far [WB was originally the Devon County School], but we should be wise to cherish the names of our pious founders, Fortescue and Brereton, of which Fortescue carries the tradition of dignity, benevolence, and humanity. Fortescutarian suffers from uncouthness, while Fortesconian is possibly not near enough to the original word. Fortescunians is easily possible (Manchester was "Mancunium") and is a name which may happily be suggested.'

[One could be pedantic about the punctuation, and some of the argument, but at least he is trying.]

Still on Record

Fortunes of war

THIS WAS A COMMON enough letter written by a serviceman during the First World War. Richard Chope and Cordy Wheeler were both old boys of the school.

'Dear Chope,
[Note the regular use of surnames, which, then, did not necessarily imply superior status or excessive formality. On the contrary, the most intimate of long-standing friends could, and did, use surnames. That was what you did. In the most famous partnership of theatrical history, Gilbert and Sullivan never used Christian names. Think of Holmes and Watson.]
'In case you study the casualty lists, and have seen my name there under the wounded heading, I am sending you this line to tell you that my wounds are not serious, and that, with luck, I should be back at duty by July. [This was written in 1917, not very long before Passchendaele.] I escaped broken bones, getting small bits of bomb in my left leg and left elbow. The bit in my elbow just missed making a mess of the joint, so I really was very lucky.
'There has been some quite severe scrapping out here ["severe scrapping" – this was the Western Front, and men on both sides were dying in thousands. On the Somme in tens of thousands. In the Battle of Verdun, which lasted several months, a million men died. "Severe scrapping"! Wheeler makes it sound like a dust-up in the quad.], and, as my battalion did well, and I was the senior officer surviving, I have been fortunate enough to get the D.S.O. [They used to put in the full stops then.]
'I hear Basil Harris [it was a nickname, no doubt a corruption of his middle name – Bastable.] was torpedoed on his way back from leave. [And he was in the *Army*.] He was picked up none the worse for his adventure.' ["Adventure". Harris was a great survivor. He lived to be ninety. One of his brothers lived to be ninety-nine.]. . . .
Yours sincerely,
C.WHEELER [Wheeler, in the course of a long life (another long life) was a head boy of the school, ex-teacher at WB, ex-caretaker Headmaster, governor for over fifty years, and an ex-president of the OWBA. Clearly, another great survivor.]'

The honourable member

IN 1903, THE SCHOOL set up a Reading and Debating Society. It met pretty well every fortnight during the Christmas and Easter terms. In the Archive survive the Minutes, almost complete from 1903 to the 1960's. There was one casualty; the current minute book was destroyed in the fire of 1930.

This is a selection from the debates recorded:

'This House is in favour of the fiscal reforms of Mr. Joseph Chamberlain.' [Exactly – who the hell was Joseph Chamberlain? I'll tell you – he was a household name in 1903. Think of the biggest stormy petrel in British politics today, double it, and you may get near Joseph Chamberlain.]

'In the opinion of this House the human race is degenerating.' [Well?]

'In the opinion of this House the British Empire has reached its climax.' [It had. Now how did they know it was going to be downhill after that?]

'In the opinion of this House women should be admitted to the professions and to political life on the same footing as men.' [Are they equal even now, over a century later?]

'This House is in favour of national disarmament.' [Nothing new about that; I bet there were Roman senators who stood up and said that the sensible thing to do was surrender to Hannibal. Half of Churchill's War Cabinet were in favour of surrender in 1940. Defence cuts and security still arouse bitter controversy.]

'Superstition has the support of this House.' [No use to anyone – it's unlucky.]

'This House is in favour of the importation of Chinese Labour into the Transvaal.' [You would need 'A' Level History to know about that one. But imported cheap foreign labour is just as inflammatory a subject today. It probably cost David Cameron his premiership.]

At the end of March, 1904, arrangements were made to present essays for discussion. Among the topics was 'The nationalisation of the railways.'

In 1907, the Society debated reform of the House of Lords and a Channel tunnel.

Read all the questions carefully

West Buckland School Archive

UNIVERSITY OF CAMBRIDGE.

EXAMINATION OF STUDENTS WHO ARE NOT
MEMBERS OF THE UNIVERSITY.

The very earliest ancestor of GCSE set up in the same year as WB

EXAMINATION PAPERS,

WITH LISTS OF SYNDICS AND EXAMINERS,
AND THE REGULATIONS, &c.

FOR THE EXAMINATION HELD IN DECEMBER

1858.

CAMBRIDGE:
PRINTED FOR THE SYNDICS AT THE UNIVERSITY PRESS.

CAMBRIDGE: DEIGHTON, BELL, AND CO.
LONDON: CAMBRIDGE WAREHOUSE, 32, PATERNOSTER ROW.

1858.

Write your name clearly at the top of the paper

IN 1858, THE YEAR the school was founded, there appeared the very first (true – first- ever) public examination for those over the age of sixteen. [And 'Students must be under 18 years of age on the day when the Examination begins.']

PART I. PRELIMINARY.

Every Student will be required to satisfy the Examiners in
1. Reading aloud a passage from some standard English poet.
2. Writing from dictation.
3. Analysis of English sentences and parsing.
4. Writing a short English composition.
5. The principles and practice of Arithmetic.
6. Geography:

Every Student will be required to answer questions on the subject and to draw from memory an outline map of some country in Europe showing the boundary lines, the chief ranges of mountains, the chief rivers, and the chief towns.

7. The outlines of English History; that is, the succession of Sovereigns, the chief events, and some account of the leading men in each reign.

[And this was only Part I. Wait till you see Part II.]

Part II demanded that candidates should satisfy the examiners in three out of the following six sections:

1. Section A – Old Testament right up to the death of Solomon; the Gospel of St. Luke; the morning and evening services in the Book of Common Prayer; and the Apostles' Creed.
2. Section B – English History from 1485 to 1660; the outlines of English Literature during the same period; Shakespeare's *Julius Caesar*; Physical, Political and Commercial Geography; or [they do, very kindly, say 'Or'] the outlines of Political Economy and English Law.
3. Section C – One language out of Latin, Greek, French, or German.
4. Section D – Maths – Euclid, Arithmetic, Algebra, and the 'elementary parts' of Statics, Dynamics, Mechanism, Hydrostatics, Optics, and Astronomy.
5. Section E – Facts and 'general principles' of Chemical Science; the 'elements of Analysis'; and the 'elementary principles' of Heat, Magnetism, Electricity, Physical Optics, and Acoustics. [Again, there was a little choice allowed. How kind.]
6. Section 6 [not F, oddly. Were the examiners guilty of inattention to detail? Perish the thought.] Comparative Anatomy and Animal Physiology; Botany and Physical Geography and Geology. [Again, there were one or two 'or's'. Did their generosity know no bounds?]

[This needs no editorial comment. Just look at it.]

Those were the days

ANNIVERSARIES – PARTICULARLY CENTENARIES – fascinate writers, historians, journalists, and publishers. School archivists are not immune to this complaint. Every so often I would dig into the school magazine, and come up with a titbit of earlier school life, school dramas, a snapshot in time, which might raise a smile or a gasp or a shake of the head among those who condescended to read my 'Archive' section on the Common Room Notice Board. This particular piece was put up in November, 2010.

A selection of 'School Notes' from the *Register* of autumn, 1910.

C.H. Petherick becomes Head of the School. [This was how they referred to the Head Boy in those days.]

On July 7th the Sixth Form [all 12 of them] made a journey to Barnstaple to inspect the Municipal Electric Works. [Did they get any surprises, or shocks? Ho-ho.]

On Monday July 11th, the Choir had a day off, and, accompanied by Mr. Taylor [the Choirmaster and Organist] spent a very enjoyable time in and around Lynton, which was reached by driving [as opposed to horse and cart, which had up till then been the usual – indeed the only – method].

[Perhaps the current Choir and Orchestra would like to revive the tradition – complete with horse and cart.]

Mr. R.P. Chope [an extremely clever, successful, and enthusiastic Old Boy – who has figured in these pages before] gave last term a special prize for a paper on Kingsley's Westward Ho! [He must have been swamped with entries.]

Mr. A. Taylor [Choirmaster and Organist – see above] has presented the School with several pictures, which now adorn the Third Form room. The subjects are; "The boyhood of Raleigh" (Millais); "The Pool of London", "The Victoria Falls", and 'An Athenian Audience at a Representation of of the "Agamemnon". [I bet that packed them in.]

The King is dead. Long live the King

THE OPENING YEARS OF the 20th century were not happy ones for the Devon County School. Well, they may have had their happy moments, but there were not many secure ones. The school had already survived two near-closures – just. When Mr. Knight took over in 1900, the numbers had dropped to 31, in a school built to accommodate 150 or more, and it was felt by those stalwarts who always stand by their school that Something Had to be Done. The shares in the school's limited company were not exactly soaring into blue chip stratosphere, and it was decided to go the whole hog, scrap everything, and start again. A bit like the modern cardiac technique of stopping a dicky heart, mending it, and starting it again.

What was going to keep the school going then? Fees. There had been fees of course, but there had also been share investment. This was now going. So where else was the money to come from? From local government, that's what. The authorities were slowly waking up to the fact that the nation needed a 'proper' secondary education system, and they were prepared to offer grants to schools, so long as they (the authorities) had some say in the calibre of the new pupils. In other words, the school could no longer fill it entirely with boys of their own choice (by whatever method seemed suitable to them at the time); they had also to take a proportion of 'scholarship boys' – selected bright lads whose families could not afford even the DCS modest fees. (Girls would have to wait a bit, but they did get there quite soon afterwards. For instance, my mother, who was born in 1903, was the first female pupil in her school to pass the eleven-plus, and, like Abou Ben Adem, her name was first at the top of the list on the honours board.)

That was all very well, but it meant that every shareholder would have to agree to his (or her) remaining shares being, in effect, written off. So far as I am aware, few if any objected; as explained above, they were not going to lose a fortune, and the school was, it was hoped, going to get a new lease of life. There was no point in hanging on to shares in a dying company.

But the law decreed that they all had to be asked, and we have in the Archive quite a large number of their replies. There is no point in duplicating them all, but their signatures present an item of interest, and may give amateur calligraphy experts the opportunity to do some character-analysis.

FORM OF ASSENT.

Devon County School Limited.

To the Secretary,
Devon County School Limited,
West Buckland,
Devon.

Teacher for 34 years
Secretary
Choirmaster

Referring to your Circular of the 17th August, 1905,

I, Adelbert Taylor.

hereby consent to the draft scheme formulated by the Board of Education for the resuscitation of the Devon County School, and authorize you to take such steps as may be necessary to carry it into effect with or without modification and to enable you to do so I hereby renounce all my rights as a Debenture Stock Holder against the property of the School, and agree when required to deliver up the Certificate of the Debenture Stock I hold in the Company for cancellation.

Your holding is £ 28 : - : -

Dated August 28th 1905.

When the old Devon County School Company was wound up, prior to the setting up of the new West Buckland School, stockholders were requested to indicate their agreement. We still have these agreements. It offers therefore an interesting opportunity to study their autographs.

, Henry Ind
Alas, not the Henry Ford
ereby consent to the draft scheme formulated by the

Dated 26 March 1906
Chas Chichester

I, Hugh Earl Fortescue.

Referring to your Circular of the 17th August, 1905,
I, Hugh Fortescue, Viscount Ebrington
The Earl's son

Referring to your Circular of the 18th August, 1905,
I, William Arthur Knight M.A: B.Sc.
Headmaster 1900 - 1907
Note - two degrees.

Referring to your Circular of the 17th August, 1905,
We { Francis Lloyd Brereton
      Henry Lloyd Brereton
Two of founder Brereton's four sons. Both became headmasters

Referring to your Circular of the 18th August, 1905,
I, Charles Thomas Dyke Acland,
Early Governor.
Founder & organiser of the very first Exmoor

Debenture Stock Holder against e, when required, to deliver up ck I hold in the Company for

(Signed) J. H. Thompson.
First HM - 1858 - 1588
Appointed at the age of 21.

Where did we come from?

IT IS HARD TO believe that, at a time when, in North Devon, there were no buses, trains, or motor cars (in fact even very few decent roads), that a major London magazine would have been attracted by the goings-on of a tiny, very new, and totally obscure school, in a village which no reader of the *Times* would have heard of.

But such was the case. On 9th November, 1861, *The Illustrated London News* printed a full account of the opening of the Devon County School, complete with a panoramic picture clearly drawn specially for the occasion. (Well, it was the *'Illustrated' London News*.) In the days before snap photography, my guess is that most prestigious magazines maintained a small stable of artists to provide the necessary food for the eyes. Well, the ILN did. And very good they were too. No trendy bending of the image; no arty skewed views, no idiosyncratic style – just strong, sound, beautifully observed draughtsmanship.

We have a copy of the relevant page in the Archive. I am typing out parts of the text separately. For a start, I think the picture deserves to be appreciated on its own. Secondly, it is easy to take note of what is there that is familiar, and what isn't, because it had not yet been built or planted. People enjoy deducing things about pictures, but they are not so keen to ponder paragraphs. Thirdly, captions tend to be skipped anyway, especially if they are more than a couple of lines. In this case it is a full-page effort. And finally, some passages may be conveniently omitted, so that one can concentrate on the important bits.

Take, for example, the succinct account of the genesis of the school.

'In the year 1856, the Rev. Prebendary Brereton, an energetic and popular clergyman in the north of Devonshire [I like that – not mere 'Devon', as is usual today, but 'Devon*shire*'], addressed a letter to the late Earl Fortescue, Lord Lieutenant of Devon [only 'Devon' this time – pity], suggesting a scheme of "county middle-class education". Mr. Brereton's proposal was, that in each of the larger counties a number of public schools for the middle class should be established, under the direction of a county board, of which, if possible, the Lord Lieutenant should be the patron or president; and that in connection with the schools there should be a county college, to which those youths who might be able to devote a longer time to their education should proceed, and which should have the power of granting diplomas or ecrtificates [sic] – the scheme being, of course, somewhat modified in the case of the smaller counties. [Alas, the county colleges never materialised as a national system, but Brereton did get just one founded – in Cambridge of all places – Cavendish College. Sadly, it did not survive very long. More information is available in my book *The Natural History of a Country School*, in the chapter entitled 'Founding Father'. Woodfield, 2005, pp. 73-101.]

'In order to ascertain practically the difficulties likely to be encountered, and the degree of success which such schools would probably meet with among the classes for which they would be principally designed [they loved the word "classes" in those days, and for quite a long time afterwards – even today, some would say], a school started in an unpretending manner at a farmhouse in the parish of West Buckland towards the close of the year 1858. At first only three pupils presented themselves. Patiently and hopefully, and in the face of many difficulties and discouragements, it was carried on, and every successive quarter brought an increase in its numbers.

'The farmhouse became too small to accommodate the candidates for admission, and three large wooden rooms (a dormitory for twenty boys, a dining-room, and a schoolroom) were added to it. These rooms became crowded, and another farmhouse at the distance of a mile was engaged, to which Mr Thompson, the Head Master, proceeded with the older boys, leaving a second master in charge of the younger ones.

'As, notwithstanding the disadvantages of having two separate establishments in farmhouses very ill-adapted to the purpose, both rapidly became full, and, as it was felt that the school was likely to become a much larger and more important institution than had been anticipated by the most sanguine of its friends, a number of influential noblemen and gentlemen of the county, headed by the Lord Lieutenant, formed themselves into an association of the purpose of erecting new and complete buildings in which it might be permanently carried on.'

[Just look at the length of this sentence. But, if you give it your full attention and take it in one bite, there is no trouble in understanding what it says. It has been constructed with care and precision, and so is perfectly clear – and isn't the most important feature of any piece of prose the simple matter of clarity? It offers a justification of a classical education. Most people who had been to a secondary school (admittedly not a very big percentage of the population) would have enough acquaintance with Latin to be able to cope with a sentence like this. They must have done;

journalists wouldn't have written like this if they knew in advance that most readers would be unable to comprehend it. So people were used to it, and could handle it. They may not have *spoken* like this, but they could certainly read like this. The whole literate population devoured newspapers much more avidly than they have done since the advent of radio and television and the net. And those who could not read were happy to gather round and have it read to them. So they must have understood too.

Try reading a passage from Charles Darwin or Edward Gibbon. You probably won't be able to follow the biology or the history, but you would understand what it actually *said*. The English is so elegant.]

Or, again, read this extract from the architect's description of the buildings:

'These buildings are situated on what is perhaps more properly described as an eminence or rising than a hill. The school stands in its own grounds a little to the right, on a road leading from West Buckland to East Buckland and South Molton. It has a south frontage of 180ft. in extent, and is surrounded on all sides by the peculiar woodland scenery of North Devon. The style of the building is Early Pointed, freely treated; but the most rigid severity has been adhered to in the details. Some additional effect has been obtained by the introduction of coloured bricks in the arches and dark bands of slating on the roofs. The main building forming the centre comprises – on the ground floor, a spacious entrance-hall, board-room, and library, residence for the head master, housekeeper's room, store, &c. The first floor contains master's apartments, sick and convalescent wards, dormitories, &c. The second floor is occupied entirely by dormitories, lavatory, &c. The west wing contains, on the ground floor, a dining-room capable of seating 130 boys; and over the dining-room and other offices of this wing there are dormitories for boys and assistants, lavatories, and a bathroom. The school, about 60 ft. long, occupies the entire length of the east wing and the whole height from floor to roof, which is open, the timbers stained and varnished, and the iron spans painted blue. Immediately behind the school are lavatories and other convenient offices.'

A score of observations would occur to attentive readers, so there is little point in an editor drawing attention to them. You can work it out for yourself. But it makes you think, doesn't it?]

DEVON COUNTY SCHOOL, WEST BUCKLAND, RECENTLY OPENED BY EARL FORTESCUE.

A society of many parts

IN 1903, THE SCHOOL set up a Reading and Debating Society. The Society did just that. Its members debated and read 'papers' to each other.

Gradually the 'Reading' part of it faded away. Then the Society itself faded away, because the Headmaster wound it up. We don't know why. It just went. But something else was put in its place – another debating society. We can see no reason why one debating society should be abolished simply in order to establish another one.

Be that as it may, the new society, rising in a manner of speaking from the ashes of the first, was christened, predictably, the Phoenix Society – or, often, quite simply, 'The Phoenix'. This was in 1926.

The Phoenix held regular debates, and minutes were kept. We have a near-complete run from 1926 to the 1960's, when it began to fade again. [Towards the end of the century it made a comeback.]

However, before it wasted away, the Phoenix embarked on yet another activity – drama. Play-readings were conducted, and the events recorded. In the 1950's, as you can see from the programme below, they went the whole hog and produced a full performance. Ian Hay's play *Housemaster* was staple fare for scores, maybe hundreds, of school dramatic societies up and down the country. At least the cast would kind of feel themselves on home ground, and the audience too would have some idea of what was going on, and could relate to it. The stage manager and wardrobe mistress would not be confronted by insuperable problems of sets and costume. It was ideal. They even got two boys to tackle a couple of the female parts.

THE PHOENIX SOCIETY

presents

THE WEST BUCKLAND SCHOOL
AMATEUR DRAMATIC SOCIETY

IN

Housemaster

A Comedy in Three Acts by
IAN HAY

To be performed at 7.30 p.m., on
FRIDAY, DECEMBER 11th, 1953
AND
SATURDAY, DECEMBER 12th, 1953

No charge is made for admission or this programme. Our expenses for a production like this are heavy, and we are also anxious to improve our stage lighting, curtains and other equipment. Generous support—already offered by many parents who have been unable to attend—is therefore sought, and your contributions will be gratefully received at the doors at the end of the performance.

The view from below

THE HEADMASTER OF THE Prep. was kind enough to share with me some of the gems he had culled from his experiences teaching children between three and eleven.

From the dinner ticket queue:
Secretary: Are you free?
Small boy: No – four.
Secretary: I mean, do you have free dinners?
Small boy: No – only one.

Bible knowledge:
Q. Who was it who did not approve of the return on the Prodigal Son?
A. The fatted calf.
[I'll bet. But then I expect nobody asked him.]

From a Chemistry test
Q. What are steroids?
A. The things that keep carpets on stairs.

Keen observer.
Q. What was Hitler's Christian name?
A. Heil.

12. 2011

Postcards from the edge

IAN MCLINTOCK (B. 1909, on the staff from 1939 to 1970) was one of the traditional public school bachelor schoolmasters. Well liked apparently. Teachers don't usually get nicknames like 'Ticktock' if they are unpopular; 'Ticktock' implies affection.

In the Archive are scores of postcards which friends, family, colleagues, and pupils sent him from foreign parts (more evidence of his popularity).

This one, from his mother and father, he had rather touchingly kept. The head is of King George VI, who reigned from 1937 to 1952. As 'Mac' did not come to the school till 1939, we can narrow it down just a little further.

I found all these cards in a collection of postcard-sized index-card boxes. He must have left them when he retired in 1970. So he had kept this Edinburgh card from 'Mum & 'Dad' for, at the very least, 18 years.

Look at the price of postage – a halfpenny. (Pre-decimal.)

Those were the days

AN INSTITUTION AS OLD as the *Exmoor* (first run in 1859, and cancelled only twice in over 150 years, through circumstances beyond even the Government's control) naturally builds its own legends and tall stories.

One thinks of the wettest one, the coldest one, the muddiest one, the hottest one (yes, the sun did shine now and then in March and April). One thinks of the foggy one, in which the first two boys got lost because they had not seen the markers. They knew the course well, but, in case anyone should suggest that they had cut a corner (even by accident), they refused to accept the honours due to them.

There are the multiple winners, the record-holders, the girl – *girl* – who came fourth in the boys' *Exmoor*. One would love to be able to locate the worst runner of all, who had come last in more *Exmoors* than anybody else. In an article for the school magazine, I even invented a name for him – Theodoric Lumsden-Crawley ('Creepy' to one and all).

At the end of each *Exmoor*, duly scrubbed and dressed (but not necessarily clean, because they had to break through the mud on the surface of the communal bathwater), they assembled in the Karslake Hall, for another tradition – pea soup. I bet that was exciting. But then, thinking about it. I guess that, after a six-mile walk and a nine-mile run, even a bowl of tepid Scrooge gruel would have been welcome.

In an old *Register*, dated November, 1922, I came across another sort of mini-tradition. That is, it had not survived to this day. An old boy (a very old boy), in reminiscent mood, claimed that, in the Revd. Thompson's time (1858-1888), the first twenty boys to get back to the school were treated by the Headmaster to a glass of port wine.

Not so daring as you may think. In the early days, the boys apparently were provided with beer (admittedly pretty innocuous beer). A testimony to the unreliability of the water supply.

Top of the legends of course are the phantom chicken-stranglers of Heasley Mill. A lot of boys had to be stationed out on the Moor long before the race started, in twos and threes, to mark the course. They would have to be there for hours, and food and drink would have to be planned for. Even fires and camp stoves . . . think about it.

And we just have room for the teacher in charge who had to station staff too at potential 'difficulty' areas. One spot had to be particularly well patrolled. This was in the days when runners had to wade the River Bray

– which, at bad times, could offer potholes in its bed with five or six feet of water swilling over them. This teacher clearly had a wicked sense of mischief. One of his colleagues whom he put on guard at the Bray was a young lady on the biology staff, who was barely five feet tall.

And God and the Governors said...

IN THEIR MINUTES OF 22nd July, 1923, at their AGM, the Governors reported that 'the installation of the Electric light was completed prior to the winter settling in, and had given every satisfaction'.

I should think so. It was nothing but oil lamps before. There was a school servant whose sole job was to trim them. I wonder what *he* thought of 'the Electric light'.

There is an interesting little touch of evidence here in the use of the definite article – 'the' Electric light. And note the capital letter. It was all a novelty, you see. As we became used to it, both definite article and capital letter were dropped.

Nowadays we would probably say even less: something like 'on main' or 'wired up'. Everything get elided and simplified.

While we are on the subject of facilities available, it is worth noting that West Buckland's gas supply still comes in cylinders. Central heating was not put into the dormitories until 1987, never mind 1887. Even the Headmaster's house had to do without central heating until nearly the end of the twentieth century.

And the school even now does not have any pipes for a mains sewerage system. Imagine the entry in the school magazine: 'The Governors are pleased to announce the installation of the Sewerage pipes, which, we hope, will give every satisfaction. And we shall no longer need the services of "Jim" or "Keith" or "Yanner Bill" to tend the filter bed and the septic tank.'

That'll be the day.

Cries from the heart

THIS COMES UNDER THE heading of 'things the editor thinks are worth passing on'. They are not to do with West Buckland, except insofar as the same editor passes them in order on to brighten the day of his colleagues at West Buckland.

Adverts noted during the holidays:

1. Free

Yorkshire Terrier – 8 years old
Hateful little bastard

2. For sale

Wedding dress
Worn once – by mistake

3. For sale by owner

Encyclopaedia Britannica complete
Excellent condition – £200 or best offer
No longer needed
Got married
Wife knows everything

4. Beware of the Dog

The Cat is not trustworthy either

5. No Senior Citizens Discounts
You have had twice as long to get the money

Founding Father

THE VERY EXISTENCE OF West Buckland, and of many other things (some gone, some surviving) is testimony to the fertility of Brereton's imagination. This picture testifies to his fertility in another direction.

He was himself one of a family of eleven. He married Frances when she was only seventeen, and they had sixteen children. Five died in infancy, but the others made it to adulthood. And here they all are. Well, nearly all; the one absentee is mother Frances, who predeceased her husband. After having sixteen children, it is hardly surprising that she did not make old bones.

Her husband did, dying in 1901 at the age of seventy-nine – a good age for the time. He had come down to Devon because of his poor health. Sixteen children – poor health. . .

This picture, we think, was taken in about 1894. Brereton had left the vicarage at West Buckland in 1867, the year his father died, and he moved to Little Massingham in Norfolk, where took over his late father's living.

At the back, left to right:

Eleanor, Francis, Margaret, a baby grandson (christened Munster[!] after father's regiment), Ethel the baby's mother, David, William (father of Munster), an unknown lady, and finally Joseph Thompson, the first Headmaster of West Buckland (or the Devon County School as it was at the outset). He married Anna, the eldest daughter.

On the front row, left to right:

Cicely, Jane, Henrietta, Henry, Philip, baby grandson Arthur, who was the son of Anna and Joseph Thompson on the far right. Thompson and Anna didn't get married till Thompson was about fifty, despite long courting. Brereton wouldn't let her go, because he 'wanted her for the work'.

In fact only Anna and Cicely made it to the altar. The other girls remained in the vicarage at Little Massingham, sitting God-fearedly (and no doubt father-fearedly) with their needlework. Three of the sons went into the teaching profession. Only William escaped, to the Army.

Their loyalty was truly rock-like, especially as their father's schemes and projects and failures left debts which took half a century to pay off.

Brereton ahead of his time again

BESIDES RUNNING HIS CHURCH, running his enormous family, founding schools, travelling all over the country to publicise, establish, spread his concept of a national system of 'county' secondary schools, developing farming reforms in his own village and on his own property, and charming money out of all and sundry to fund his numberless schemes, JLB found time to edit (and my guess write 90% of) a year book for West Buckland – the village. There are two that have survived – 1857 and 1861. By the standards of a 19th-century Devon village, they are sumptuous. But then Brereton knew everybody, and he was very persuasive.

One contains his diary of a long trip to Egypt (perhaps undertaken because of his lung trouble), and another prints many of his sermons.

Interspersed are other pieces which demonstrate the eccentricity, breadth, and at times staggering modernity, of his thinking. Faced with a problem, a trend, a shortage, a lack of learning, a deficiency – indeed anything which looked as if it could do with a spot of intervention, Brereton was there; he couldn't resist it.

This is typical, from his 1857 year book:

Decimal Weights and Measures.

No farmer needs to be told how inconvenient the present system of weights and measures is. Two different markets have two different measures. The first thing to be wishes is to have an [sic – 'an'] uniform system all through the country. But it is also very important that the system should be the simplest, that is, one by which all calculations may be made most quickly and easily. And the decimal system is the simplest, because we already use it in our system of enumeration – the first thing that children learn at school – the system of units, tens, hundreds, &c. Thus in 1800 each figure has ten times the value of the figure next to the right. Now supposing that we called 10 pecks a bushel, and 10 bushels a bag, 1800 pecks would make exactly 180 bushels, or 18 bags. No time need be wasted in calculation. With the decimal system we should have the numbers we want always ready. And the same thing applies to money. If with our pounds, shillings, and pence, 10 pence made the shilling, and 10 shillings made the pound, we should all be saved a world of trouble.

Where the buck stops

THE LILLYWHITE'S *CRICKETERS' COMPANION* for 1870 reviewed, among many others of course, the Devon County School cricket team of 1869. (Imagine West Buckland School getting a similar review in the *Wisden* of 2019.)

Understandably, this was proudly reproduced in the *Register*, the school magazine of the time.

Included in the remarks on the form and skill of the various players was this rare tribute to the humblest and most unsung hero of any fielding side:

W.F.E. Read was described as an 'excellent long-stop, the best ever at the school'.

Is there an Old Boy from any year since that time on behalf of whom anyone wishes to challenge that claim?

And what a splendidly unique distinction that could be put today (or any day) in a university application personal statement. That, surely, would make them sit up and take notice. Oxbridge would always be attracted by the original and the unusual and exceptional.

They would come from miles around to see such a performer, if only to satisfy themselves that it was true. It would give a tremendous boost to the attendance figures at Lord's for the Varsity match.

A class on his own

IN JULY, 1872, THOMAS Holmes Aplin left the school. His exam results deserve recording and preservation. Wonder too.

As a junior (there were two exams – Junior and Senior, roughly equivalent to our GCSE and 'A' Level), he won First Class Honours in the Local Examinations at both Oxford and Cambridge. In the Cambridge exam, he was first in all England out of 1,299 candidates.

In the Senior exams, he was first in English in all England at Cambridge in 1871, and first in English in all England at Oxford in 1872. Just by the way, he was also 7th in all England in Pure Maths and 4th in Applied Maths at Cambridge, and 6th in Maths at Oxford. He was Head Monitor, naturally (they called them monitors, then, not prefects), and won the Fortescue Medal, of course.

Two years later, he took a Civil Service exam for an appointment in the Forests of India (I thought they only had jungles in India), and came top of the lot, 'obtaining above 600 marks more than the second'. (We don't know the overall comparative totals, but, whichever way these tests were organised, a winning margin of 600 marks seems pretty prodigious.)

The entry in the *Register* (No. XLVI, Michaelmas, 1874, p. 8) adds pertinently that 'the salary of the appointment commences at £300, and increases to £1,900 a year'.

Think – in the later 19th century, nearly two thousand a year for looking after forests – in India. Some job. Some candidate.

You will see his name all over the honours boards.

[A final note. In the early days, there were four terms, not three – Easter, Summer, Michaelmas, and Christmas.]

The magic of a hundred

ARCHIVISTS, LIKE JOURNALISTS, LOVE the figure a hundred. If you're ever stuck for something to say, find out what happened a hundred years ago, and it'll be good for a page or two. In these days of the – what is it? – 'world-wide web', you can always rely on the fact that *something* relevant is caught in its meshes. The school archive, obviously, can not compete with the squillions of things out there on the net, but, with a history of over 150 years, and a complete run of school magazines to trawl through, one can usually come up with, as I said, something.

Incidentally, there is another useful way of marking the significance of a particular day that makes it worth celebrating. There can not be many dates in the Catholic Church's calendar which do not commemorate a single saint. And there you are: a ready-made story, both short and tall. What's more, one with a ponderous moral too.

Then again, people love looking at old photographs, and comparing fashions and styles, architecture, machinery, equipment, and so on. If it's in sepia too, you can hook them at once, before they've even worked out what it is a photograph *of.* By the same token, if you can persuade them to read something on the notice board, you can hook them too with hundred-year-old syllabuses, exam questions, results, reports, drama programmes, salaries, prices, old boys' dinner menus, and I don't know what. Gosh, yes, weren't they so quaint, so old-fashioned, so funny! We all instinctively bring to contemplation of past items our conviction that we are looking at them from a superior vantage point.

Take this account of the end of a typical term at West Buckland a century ago. I put it on the notice board on 13th December, 2011. I took it from the *Register* of February, 1912, which, naturally, recalled the events of the previous term.

'The Breaking-up Supper
18th December, 1911

'As usual, the Head Master and Mrs. Harries gave the Annual Breaking-Up Supper. . . in the Karslake Hall. . . The Brereton table was adorned with nine out of the sixteen trophies, the Courtenay with five, and the Fortescue with two. [Notice the, clearly, long-standing tradition of preceding the names of the houses with the definite article.] 'After a good repast, and when the health of the King had been drunk, the toasts of the different Houses were proposed by masters, and responded to by prefects.

'Mr. Key, while proposing the health of the Brereton, with his usual aplomb, complimented them on possessing the school poet. . . [poet?]

'M.R. Roberts, who responded, enumerated in detail the successes of his House, and attributed their failure to secure the Cricket Cup to bad fielding. [Michael Rookherst Roberts won the *Exmoor* twice, was top of the batting and bowling averages, president of the Debating Society, head boy, and winner of the Fortescue Medal. After leaving, he went to Sandhurst, served in both world wars, was decorated in both, and reached the rank of brigadier. He became a military historian, was a Fellow of the Royal Historical Society, served for years as chairman of the board of governors, and was twice president of the Old Boys' Association.]

'Mr. A. Taylor [teacher of practically everything for over thirty years, organist, choirmaster, and general school treasure. It was said that he had a voice reminiscent of Mr. Punch, so he was christened, almost inevitably, 'Judy']. . . said he had great pleasure and pride in proposing the toast of his old House, the Courtenay. Mrs. Taylor was a supporter of the Brereton, and now the trouble was as to which House their heir should belong. He also pointed out the benefits of a boarding school as compared with a day school. . .

'Mr. W.D. Inniss [from Trinidad – a rare enhancement of a common room in those days], in proposing "The Fortescue". . . said that the other Houses were in the habit of calling the Fortescue the "Forty Screws", and he hoped that the Fortescue would soon prove themselves to be screws in the coffins of both the Brereton and the Courtenay. . . [The Fortescue was a recent creation – a sign that Harries was hauling up the numbers after a bad time at the end of the 1890's. So the Fortescue were the new kids on the block – mostly day boys, I think – and therefore a convenient chopping block for the two boarding house – the Brereton and the Courtenay, who had been the only two houses ever since the foundation. The Grenville came even later, in 1918. By the same token, the Fortescue were keen to establish their credit and standing among the oldest inhabitants.]

'The Rev. E.C. Harries next proposed "The Visitors". . . Especially glad was he to welcome back on these occasions any Old Boys, and he therefore coupled with the toast the name of Mr. Basil Harris, who amidst his many interests at Cambridge, yet always found time to remember his School when away from it.

'Mr. Basil Harris, who responded... said that it gave him great pleasure to be there that evening, as he had not missed one supper since the custom had been inaugurated. [Harris had had a very full school career too. After Cambridge and a good war record, he became a teacher, and reached the age of ninety. One of his brothers made it to ninety-nine. Incidentally, his real middle name was 'Bastable', but the nickname 'Basil' stuck so firmly that he was clearly being addressed by it even after he had left, not in terms of tease but familiarity and affection.]

'A most enjoyable evening, both intellectually and gastronomically, was concluded by the singing of *"Auld Lang Syne"*, in which everyone joined heartily.'

It is easy to smile indulgently at this account, from our aforesaid vantage point of the twenty-first century, with our superior ways and our superior knowledge, our worldliness and sophistication. And it true that reports in school magazines tend to make everything sound wonderful. All the geese are swans, and everybody plays well, and it's all absolutely scrumptious.

Nevertheless, enjoyment does clearly come through. Everyone is together, in the Karslake, and shouting and clapping and carrying on generally. It's midwinter, it's dark, the curtains are drawn, stomachs are full, lessons and books are over, Christmas is on the way, and there is the glow and warmth of the ubiquitous oil lamps. Everyone knows everyone, and it is difficult to prevent the word 'family' creeping into the mind. The very fact that old boys came back to join in, and that Basil Harris was able to claim that he had not missed a single breaking-up supper, indicates a genuine pull of sentiment and nostalgia. People didn't flog all the way down to Darkest Devon just for the sake of form. Devon was not the Riviera, and the school was certainly not the Ritz.

13. 2012

A monstrous regiment

WEST BUCKLAND SCHOOL IS co-educational. But it hasn't always been. For approximately 75% of its life, it was for boys only. That is not a reflection on West Buckland; it is a reflection *of* the educational ideas (or lack of them) of those first three-quarters of its history. One cannot blame the Directors of the company who first ran it. You might as well blame a History teacher for not teaching Geography. Or criticise a teacher of Physics for being biased against Chemistry.

That, rightly or wrongly, was the way things were. Views on female education in the nineteenth century were thin on the ground, but nevertheless still varied. At the 'sharp' end were the pioneers who believed in sexual equality right down the line. Girls were one half of the human race, and deserved as much consideration and as many opportunities as the other half.

At the other end were the huffers and puffers who, if they thought about it at all and were pressed, would try to prove that the female mind was simply not built to take complicated ideas. It was too full of romantic ideas, vapours, flutterings, sudden mood swings, and general unpredictability, and therefore unreliable. And of course it wasn't very strong. Heroines in second-rate novels died of a mysterious complaint called 'brain fever'.

It followed then that the only things women were suited for was learning to run a home and raise a family. Even the most entrenched male chauvinist conceded that they were good at that. It was what God in His wisdom had ordained for the world, and in any case it made sense. Somebody had to run the household when the master was earning the family's keep. Men did not object to providing for the family, so why should women object to giving birth to it and looking after it? It all seemed so fair.

And what if the females in the family *did* get an education? Who was going to give them a job? How many employers would give work to female engineers, female doctors, female builders, accountants, lawyers, priests, salespersons, factory supervisors, navvies, and all the rest? The best these brainy birds could hope for was a second-rate existence as a governess, a private music teacher, a nurse, a housemaid, at best a housekeeper. Jobs like salesgirls, shorthand typists, cinema usherettes, receptionists, bus conductresses, and PA's did not exist. One did not even speak of the alternatives – the stage or the streets.

The best prospect for a young woman, far and away, was as a wife, mother, and mistress of the house. She wouldn't have to work for a living, and there was always a man to keep her. A conscientious father therefore saw to it that his daughter was taught the domestic skills that such a life demanded. That would provide the most secure and the most comfortable life he could arrange for his beloved child. By such means there was a very fair chance that she could attract a suitable husband, and then she was settled for life. Her husband meanwhile was looking for a mother for his children and someone to cook, clean, and generally care for him. So it seemed that everybody would get what they wanted.

So if you set up a new school, it was going to be a school for boys. That is what the Revd. Brereton did. Nobody would have expected him to do otherwise. However, the supreme irony is that Brereton had ideas for girls' education too. His schemes for middle-class boys' schools put him way ahead of his time. The fact that he conceived a nation-wide scheme for girls' education as well put him in the educational stratosphere.

Unfortunately, his national system for the education of girls (the GCSA) died the death, and Brereton was partially responsible for that too, because he was a shocking organiser and a terrible spendthrift (of other people's money). And he was up against a powerful force – the climate of opinion.

It took a long time for the *need* to educate girls to seep into the nation's subconscious. In West Buckland's case, it took nearly 120 years. And that was not without its hurdles, resignations, and recriminations.

However, it is generally known that girls began to appear at West Buckland, admittedly in only two's and three's, in the 1970's. By 1980, the school had its first head girl, alongside the head boy. Now, nearly forty years on, the spread is pretty well fifty-fifty.

What is not generally known – and I have got to the point at last – is that the very first girl pupils did not appear in the 1970's but the 1930's.

They were the daughters of the then Headmaster, Lt.-Comd. R.V.H. Westall (1934-39). They were of primary age, and West Buckland was a secondary school. But Westall, clearly a most persuasive man, induced the Governors to make a special dispensation for them to attend West Buckland. Since they were indeed under eleven, and the school was secondary, and there wasn't a Prep. department then, one may well wonder what sort of teaching was actually provided.

We do know, however, that they had their uniforms specially made at Harrods. (Harrods!) We know that because the elder sister, now Vyvyan Lindsay, has told us.

She also told us that, as the only girls in an establishment packed with boys, they soon found that life could be very interesting, and they threw themselves into their new school with gusto. Their one frustration was that they were not allowed to use the swimming pool. The rule for boys was that swimming gear was not needed – indeed was banned. Westall was a great outdoor enthusiast, but he drew the line at his daughters sharing such freestyle facilities.

The nearest they got was a few furtive glances over the fence round the pool from some convenient vantage point. But it no doubt enhanced their education.

First in the field

FAMOUS FOOTBALLERS. 213

H. PACKER.

Photo. by SIEDLE BROS., Newport. Copyright—HUDSON & KEARNS.

BORN at Chipping Norton, in Oxfordshire, H. PACKER, of Newport fame, learned the rudiments of the game at Devon County School. The season of 1888-89 found him not only a member of the Newport Extras, but also the Captain of the team. The following winter he got his Cap as one of the Newport First XV., with whom he has played regularly up to date, excepting in 1891-92, when he was out of Football owing to an injured leg. His International Cap came to him for the English match of 1890-91, since which time he has represented Wales twice against Scotland and Ireland, both in 1894-95. A sound hardworking forward with plenty of dash, he is particularly dangerous in the open, as he follows up hard and uses his feet well. As an Athlete he has been successful on the running track and across country. Twenty-six years of age, he weighs 13 stone and is 5ft. 11in. in height.

WEST BUCKLAND SCHOOL, AS anybody who has studied its history for only five minutes will know, was founded way out in the wilderness, so its inhabitants soon had to become resilient and self-reliant. The school was never flush with money, and the facilities were in any case *designed* to be modest so that its fees could fall within the reach of your average butcher, baker, and candlestick-maker – or, as Brereton originally intended, farmer. All this produced, predictably, a somewhat spartan regime. It is no surprise either that sport very soon established itself as a major activity in the school day. All part of the muscular Christianity which pervaded the late Victorian scene.

Perhaps it is an irony then that the school did not produce its first international sportsman till it was over thirty years old. On the other hand, it is possible to argue that, for such an obscure academy, with such modest resources, in a village that nobody had ever heard of, to secure international representation in less than forty years from scratch was quite an achievement.

A firm called Hudson and Kearns, in the late nineteenth century, produced a series of portraits of 'Famous Footballers'. It appears that they did not in fact manufacture the photos themselves; perhaps they were promoting the series as part of a commercial enterprise. In other words, were they one of the very first series of cigarette cards?

The pictures were actually taken by the firm that is credited on the bottom left of the sheet – 'Siedle Bros., Newport'. (Note the precision of the punctuation – the abbreviation and the pause both indicated.)

Anyway, there he is, in jersey and shorts down to his knees, looking away from the camera – as they always did. Heavily moustached, of course. A rather natty bow tie at his neck – rugby jersey and bow tie? Is that what they wore when they ran on to the field at Cardiff?

Because, yes, that was the country he was selected for – Wales. Harry Packer was the first ex-pupil of the Devon County School to play international sport. In the 1890's. And he played several times apparently.

A second irony it was that not only was he educated at an English school; he was born, so the caption to the picture said, in Chipping Norton in Oxfordshire. You couldn't get more English than that.

The caption went on to tell us that he was 'a sound hardworking forward with plenty of dash'. . . . and. . . 'particularly dangerous in the open, as he follows up hard and uses his feet well'.

At five feet eleven, and weighing 13 stone, he wouldn't have got far among the humanoid Sherman tanks who pound the pitches of Murrayfield and the Millennium Stadium. But times and circumstances change, and he no doubt approached the conditions of the game at that time with pragmatic common sense. Thirteen stone or seventeen stone, he deserves all credit for winning through from a tiny, unknown, rural school to an international cap. The caption also said that he 'learned the rudiments of the game at Devon County School'.

A feather in the cap of the Devon County School – forgive the pun. In fact a sort of double pun, because the badge he has on his jersey appears to be the three feathers which were the original emblem adopted by the Princes of Wales after the Battle of Crecy in 1346. Incidentally, it gives the lie to the traditional assertion that the DCS's only winter game was Association football. (Or 'foot ball', as they originally called it – and, later, 'foot-ball'.)

True, it *was* football, with or without the hyphen. The school must have been a trial to their opponents, because, secluded in their moorland retreat, with, for the most part, nobody to play against but themselves, they evolved their own rules. Rules which they expected the few visitors they received to comply with.

Somehow or other, the rugby version worked its way into the games lessons, and, later, into school matches. In the Archive there are just a few photographs of rugby teams.

Quite a few sports get mentioned in the early accounts. It was quite likely that their appearance reflected the tastes, abilities, and enthusiasms of a particularly energetic member of staff. Rugby was possibly one. In the accounts of the annual athletic sports of the 1870's, one can see 'Throwing the hammer'. Very Olympic for a tiny school in the wilderness. Early in the twentieth century, hockey got a few mentions, but it didn't last long. So that keen young teacher must have moved on.

Rugby itself also faded away, and did not reappear until the 1920's. By that time, perhaps the current Headmaster, the Revd. Harries, had decided that football – the gentlemen's game played by hooligans – did not sit well in the newer world of the fashionable public schools, who were swinging over to rugby – the hooligans' game now played by gentlemen.

Harries himself was still coaching rugby in his sixties, and insisted that the boys should tackle him. A familiar treble cry to be heard during practice sessions was 'Get the old man'.

What's in a name?

IT IS EASY ENOUGH, if you have the documents and the pictures, to find out what people in the past looked like. It is not so easy to work out what they *sounded* like. Nobody has any audio records older than about 130 years.

Specialist scholars can make informed, intelligent guesses, and obsessive antiquarians can make 'definitive' pronouncements, but, when you come right down to it, it is all somewhat uncertain, to say the least. It has to be; we have no ear-witnesses.

To be fair, I know that academics can give recitations in Chaucerian English, but I do not have the scholarship to judge their authenticity. By the same token, did the Roman writer and philosopher (and politician – he loved talking about that bit) call himself 'Sisero' or 'Kikero'? Perhaps these celebrities used different pronunciations at different times? After all, they were pretty random about the way they *spelt* their names. In modern times, Mr. Churchill must have known perfectly well how to refer to the German enemies – 'the Naatzis' – but he persistently, and perversely, insisted on saying 'Naazis'.

Take the name of the school's founder – the Revd. J.L. Brereton. How should you say it? Because everybody connected with the school today says 'Breerton', one might conclude that it is the correct version. But 150 years ago it might have been 'Brairton' for all we know. It might have been 'Brurton', as in 'Brer' Rabbit. Conceivably it could have been 'Brerryton'.

We have one piece of luck with Brereton. Because the family was so huge, one or two members, almost by the law of averages, made it to the aristocracy, and so got their names into Debrett. That august publication declares that it is pronounced 'Breerton'. And who are we to argue with Debrett, particularly as it tallies with our own version?

But – with scholarly matters there is always a 'but' – according to a great-granddaughter of the man himself, the family used to say 'Brurton', as in 'Brer' Rabbit. Pick the bones out of that.

The chances are that the vast majority of us are not sufficiently interested to ponder the matter overmuch; we simply go with the flow. Even then, things could change, and, almost before we know it, another version will have emerged, which, with the water-drip persistence of time and habit, with force us to say it.

For instance, until not so very long ago, if you made yourself a bullying nuisance to somebody, you '*ha*rassed' them. Now you are supposed to 'har*ass*' them. No self-respecting commentator on television, whose obsession is to be seen (or heard) to be up to date, would be heard dead saying '*ha*rass'.

Who knows? One day we may have to make the acquaintance of the Revd. 'Breton'.

Foreign Legion

OVER THE YEARS, WEST Buckland has played host to pupils from over sixty foreign countries. These young people arrive at the school with little more than the clothes they stand up in. In the case of one Nigerian boy, quite literally; he was wearing nearly every item of clothing he had packed in his suitcase because he was so cold.

But they have to tackle a great deal more than the cold, and quickly – West Buckland horizontal rain and cross-country runs; scrambled egg and rhubarb crumble; cricket and the Royal Family; *Strictly Come Dancing*, *The 'X' Factor*, and *Coronation Street*.

Besides learning to cope with a foreign weather system, foreign diet, a foreign culture, and foreign TV, they have, of course, to learn a foreign language. After all, that is one of the reasons why their parents sent them here in the first place, possibly the main reason. How do they manage? Well, like any human group, they are a mixed bunch, and their levels of success and integration are bound to be mixed. As Damon Runyon said of his guys and dolls on Broadway, they 'do the best they can'.

But on the whole, by and large, and taking things all round, they don't do too badly. A Japanese boy has played cricket for the First XI. The Secretary or the Phoenix Society one year was Hungarian. Part of the school's website was designed by a Lithuanian. One scorer for the cricket team was Chinese. We have had head boys from Hong Kong, Thailand, and Uganda.

These young people do pretty well when they leave school too. By now integrated into West Buckland, and armed with some solid English, they have won entrance to, and distinction in, Oxford, Cambridge, London, and Manchester universities, and similar prestigious establishments, in both undergraduate and postgraduate courses. Some have gone on to represent England on the sports field.

Since education is a two-way business, the school has also had to learn. They have come to appreciate these students' impressive capacity for work, their sense of purpose, and (obviously) their talent, to say nothing of the evocative cultural colour that they can bring with them. It can also become a feat merely to read the register. Try these names for size: Lacava, Zaouk, Ongsaranakom, Yim, Chewprecha, Wing-Yiu, Gergely, Quaishi, Sayidzadeh, Wijesekeva, Tantisuvanichkul. Oh – and Karnasuta (I wonder what his nickname was).

A safe pair of hands

MANY VETERAN CRICKET FANS in England will declare without hesitation that the most celebrated batsman ever to play for Somerset was Harold Gimblett. Those with shorter memories will argue for Viv Richards or Ian Botham. The debate, in scores of Somerset cricket club bars, no doubt continues. And that is as it should be.

Be any of that as it may, it is a solid fact that Harold Gimblett attended West Buckland school in the late 1920's. He was playing for the First Eleven when he was thirteen, and was captain at fifteen. He was playing for Somerset when he was barely out of school. In his debut county match in 1935, he scored 123 – in eighty minutes, without giving a single chance. He played for the county 329 times. It is therefore safe to say, without any fear of partisan contradiction, that he was the greatest cricketer the school ever produced – by miles.

In 1975, the county authorities decided, understandably, to mark their centenary with a celebrity cricket match, and Harold was invited to play. At the age of 61.

The whole of Somerset respected and was proud of his distinguished record, and wanted him therefore to make a passable score. He had also been one of the most rapid run-scorers in the country, and so was a highly popular figure in every county ground. Everybody was also *willing* him to score – if only a token few.

He opened the batting, and even the fielding side was praying that he would score just *something*. A well-known cricketing journalist was fielding close to the wicket. The bowler kindly tossed up a gentle half-volley. Harold managed to spoon it up straight towards the journalist at short mid-off.

As the ball covered the intervening fifteen yards or so, this gentleman did a lot of thinking. When it reached him, he pretended to stumble, and to fumble, and with a huge effort managed to drop it.

He said afterwards, in his biography of Gimblett, 'I like to think it was the best thing I ever did on the cricket field.'

West Buckland? *West Buckland?*

IN THE EARLY DAYS of sixteen-plus public exams, there were only a few places where candidates could be tested – usually prominent cities of course. No doubt because of the prestigious association of these exams with the universities of Oxford and Cambridge, *The Times* used to print, every year, the names of the cities in which the exams had been set up – London, Manchester, Birmingham – places like that.

This presented problems for boys from the Devon County School, especially in the days before a railway network spanned the country. In 1862, no doubt as a result of energetic lobbying by the Revd. Brereton, special permission was given for DCS boys to take the exam in the school itself. DCS was the very first school to be allowed this privilege.

Accordingly, just before the next round of exams, in December, 1862, *The Times* printed the list of exam centres, thus: 'Bath, Birmingham, Cheltenham, Exeter, Leeds, Liverpool, London, Manchester, Oxford, Southampton, and West Buckland.'

This provoked some mystification in the leather armchairs of London clubland and Old Codger Country. Richard Chope, a regular contributor to the *Register* and the school's most relentless benefactor, recorded that one puzzled reader wrote to the *Times* Editor, asking, 'Where is West Buckland?' Chope commented drily that long after 1862 it would have been a query 'somewhat difficult to answer with any great degree of accuracy'.

Those codgers should have taken more notice. The DCS was the prophet of the new gospel of middle-class education, and it had the indefatigable Revd. Brereton to lobby for it – to say nothing of exam results which for three consecutive years put it at the top of the national league, ahead of places like Manchester Grammar School. It soon put itself on the education map, if not on the geographical one,

The first Headmaster, Revd. Joseph Thompson, was reported as saying in a speech to an Old Boys' Dinner in 1905:

'The school began with three boys, viz. James Waldron, Henry Dendle, and Henry Tyte. Soon afterwards they had 150 boys to teach. . . In the early days the Daily News sent a special commissioner to describe the school to the world, and there was a description of three or four columns in that paper. He had the pleasure of receiving at different times four Archbishops, Mr. W.H. Smith, when he was Chancellor of the Exchequer, and Sir Stafford Northcote, when he was also Chancellor of the Exchequer.

'On a certain day he remembered seeing 16 reporters at West Buckland, and at Barnstaple they had a special staff of telegraph operators sent down in order that the speech might be reported in the London papers the next morning.'

So there.

A line on railways

LINE? RAILWAYS? OH, NEVER mind.

On the morning of Saturday, 14th May, 1881, something happened on the Devon and Somerset Line: it was closed for five days. Why? So that the line could be converted from broad gauge (7ft 0¼in.) to narrow gauge (4ft 8½ins.)

For those who don't know, our railways have not always run in the same way ever since they were built. The 'narrow' gauge had been begun in the north of England by George Stephenson. Shortly afterwards, Brunel began his gargantuan efforts in the south, with the 'broad' gauge. (Heaven knows where the quarter of an inch came from. As for Stephenson's half-inch, one theory is that he used the same distance between tracks as had been employed by the old Roman chariots – fanciful but attractive.)

As the lines spread north and south, there was obvious confusion and delay while passengers changed trains and luggage, and goods were transferred.

This could not go on. Something Would Have To Be Done. A challenge was set up in 1846. Both gauges (and their trains) were put through a series of trials to measure relative speed, comfort, and safety. The broad gauge won hands down in all three departments. So the country went over to a universal narrow gauge. (Work that one out.)

Broad gauge trains continued to run patchily for another forty years or so, and the very last ran down to Penzance in 1892. So it is quite likely that Sherlock Holmes came down to deal with the Hound of the Baskervilles on a broad gauge train.

On the Devon and Somerset line, it says that 'several hundred men' spent five days lifting the old rails and installing new ones at the new width. One wonders what happened to all that old rolling stock, locomotives, and general metal. Some enterprising scrap merchants somewhere must have made fortunes.

It was money. The gauges. Think about it.

Going the distance

WHEN I SET UP the Archive, obviously the first thing to do was to search for, dig out, scratch together, enquire, discover, and generally turn the place upside down, in an effort to find out just what the school did have which might qualify it to be described as potential archive material. Stuff came in from lofts, attics, and long-unused cupboards. To be fair, someone had come across an old ship's travelling trunk, and piled into it a random collection of memorabilia. Almost as if, whenever that 'someone' found something which looked 'old', it became trunk fodder. The value of its contents turned to be everything from rubbish to priceless.

Once the word was out, the Archive became a regular repository (or welcome dumping ground) for grandfather's school caps, reports, textbooks, prize books, and for unspeakable stuff cleared out when a head of department decided to have a blitz on his own storage space. I was even once given a clutch of grubby, screwed-up papers found under the floorboards when workmen did some alterations. Literally – under the floorboards. And I did actually use some of it. (See *The Natural History of a Country school*, Chapter 46 – A Legionary's Underwear.)

One of the real finds was an enormous leather-bound tome which held all the athletic records and results which diligent headmasters had thought fit to enter there. Most of it was in Harries' handwriting, but the record-keeping survived till well after the War.

Naturally, pride of place went to the *Exmoor*, which was first run in 1859. Not even Harries could find the names of the first four winners; his records begin in 1863. Once he is up and running (to coin a phrase), the details are spread thickly – the first three home, the times, the houses they were in; later, when they had a Colts Exmoor and a Junior Exmoor, they were even fuller. The records died well before the girls established their own races. They are in the *Register* (or, since 1997, *The 3 R's*), but not in the Great Book.

A study – even a casual reading – of these pages soon demonstrates the fact that whatever activity is engaged in for a substantial length of time, sooner or later some stars will emerge.

Take Arthur Pearce, who was at the school in the first decade of the twentieth century. He won 13 out of 14 cross-country races. (The *Exmoor* was by no means the only such run. In the end there were 15 – each with its own name. Each no doubt engraved indelibly on the memories of generations of inmates.)

Then came Cecil Farmer, during the First World War. He of the most splendiferous clutch of Christian names a schoolboy could carry – Cecil Stanley Redvers – each one a hero of the 'Empire' at that time. Young Cecil soon became a hero of the school cross-country community in his own right. He won 20 out of 21 races, and would have won the 21st if it had not been for an accident, which put him a mere second. (Incidentally, in 1917, he also won 8 out of 9 events in the school sports – in one afternoon, after a rainy morning.)

By the time Herbert Tully came along, there were three Exmoors each year – an under-13 *Exmoor*, an under-15 *Exmoor*, and the senior one. Between 1930 and 1936, he won the Junior *Exmoor* twice, the Colts *Exmoor* twice, and the 'Exmoor' *Exmoor* twice. Just for good measure, thirty years later his son won the *Exmoor*.

Finally, how about Johnny Jones? In the mid-1950's, he won four *Exmoors* – on the trot, as you might say.

It is an irony that, in all those years – nearly 160 of them – of effort, blood, toil, tears, and sweat – not to mention obvious genuine ability – the only pupil of West Buckland School to win national honours in cross-country – wait for it – is a girl. Isobel Stoate.

All that male effort and suffering – rugby, yes; cricket, yes; and, unbelievably, golf. And, to date, no boy has run over hill and dale for England. Odd.

It's almost enough to make you wonder whether it was all worth it.

Something to set you thinking

THE *REGISTER* OF THE Easter term, 1912, produced a delightful melange of an editorial, almost each item of which provokes a mental reaction.

'Physical' drill was introduced, as a 'pleasant change on alternate mornings to early school'. [Well, OK. But you would have to dislike 'early school' somewhat bitterly to look forward to the 'pleasant change' of 'drill'. One suspects the entry is a fine example of the wishful thinking of well-intentioned school authorities; it would look good to parents in the magazine.]

[Funny how names change. By what alchemy of linguistics? Today we have 'P.E.' Before that it was 'Gym' – which has a nice succinctness which somehow gives it greater impact. 'Physical Education' has a ring of ascetic scholarliness which does not tie up with stinking plimsoles and sweaty armpits.]

[And what about the teaching of religion? Take your pick from 'Religious Instruction', 'Religious Education', 'Bible Knowledge', plain 'Religion', and 'Divinity'.]

R.P. Chope [that indefatigable benefactor] gave a lecture on 'The March of Invention'. [It was printed in the magazine, and ran to nine pages. Every contribution Chope presented to the magazine was over-academic, over-written, and too long. It took much bravery on the part of the editors to prune it.]

The school football team played Taunton School, and were 7-1 down by half-time. [Quite a feat, that.]

The Museum had only one new addition: an Indian envelope. [Well, that's what it says. Perhaps everyone was talking about Indian envelopes in the early months of 1912. Rather like the crazes of Rubik cubes and skate boards and hula hoops. All inescapable in their day. Imagine a quadrangle conversation between two second-formers (year 8 today):

'I've got seven Indian envelopes.'

'That's nothing. I've got twelve. And two of those have the gum unlicked.']

The Editor remarked tartly about the disrespect shown to magazines in the school library. The illustrated weeklies were, apparently 'terribly abused'. [Ammunition for paper darts? Sarcastic marginal notes – or worse?]

To snap up and to hold

THE *REGISTER* OF EASTER, 1884, made the following announcement:

'MARRIAGE. – On Monday, March 31st, Mr. J.G. Shain, one of the Masters, and Miss M.A. Simons, the Matron, were married in East Buckland Church. The ceremony was performed by the Rev. J.H. Thompson, and all the masters and boys were present. The wedding breakfast took place in the Board Room, among the guests being the masters and several of the older boys. The health of the Bride and Bridegroom was proposed by the Head Master. There was a whole holiday, and in the evening a Magic Lantern Entertainment was given by A. Martin Esq. and Mr. George Kelly.'

One could comment on this almost endlessly.

The most obvious thing to remark on is that such a wedding should take place at all. Think of the school matrons you know, and ask yourself how many young teachers they would have been likely to marry, or, for that matter, how many young teachers would have married a matron.

But, in a remote country boarding school in late Victorian England, it was by no means an uncommon occurrence. Think. No buses. No cars. Most of the domestic staff would have walked in from West Buckland village, so they would have been chambermaids or cooks or kitchen skivvies, and they would normally have fraternised with their fellow-villagers. A scattering of teachers' wives. Not only did the boys rarely see an adult female; the young staff didn't either. Certainly not a very available one.

It is true that whatever ancillary staff there was would have mostly lived in, like the bachelor teachers. So teachers and such staff would have been thrown together much more than they are today. In fact, when you think about it, it is not really surprising at all that a teacher should marry a matron.

There wasn't much other opportunity. Not unless they had access to a horse and dogcart. Or a bicycle – and that would have taken up all their courting energy pedalling miles into a nearby village. Barnstaple was nearly ten miles away. Bicycles, moreover, would not, in the 1880's, have evolved very far beyond the penny-farthing. So our Mr. Shain snapped up what was available. You can hardly blame him.

It looks odd that a member of staff at a school in *West* Buckland should get married in a church in *East* Buckland. But that went back to Earl

Fortescue. The school was equidistant from both villages, but Fortescue had a bigger concentration of property around East Buckland, and had frequently, and very generously, endowed its church. And, I believe, the chaplaincy too. He had the power of nominating the next incumbent.

My guess is that the school was first named 'West Buckland' because Brereton was the rector there, and, naturally, lived there. So, when he pencilled in the plans for his new school, he used the name of his own village. Perhaps he was tempted, as most of us would be, by the prospect of a slice of immortality. If you lived in one village, and you had the chance to christen your own school, you wouldn't have called it by the name of another village, would you? Curiously, the school has always worshipped, as a body, in East Buckland church. Whenever somebody associated with the school has died, the grave appears at East Buckland. So Brereton must have had to compromise a bit, and Fortescue did have the greater clout (and the money).

Look at the magazine accounts of any public occasion at West Buckland. There is always a reference to a meal of some kind afterwards. When one reads about the number of guests who regularly turned up, one marvels at the catering capacity of such a modest establishment.

However, the school lost no opportunity to economise. Note that 'all the masters and boys were present' at the wedding ceremony. But at the wedding breakfast there appeared only 'the masters and several of the older boys'. Were they afraid that the 'younger boys' might engage in behaviour that would not dignify such an occasion, or were they concerned that the pangs of hunger that perpetually tortured the stomachs of boarding school boys would account for most of the pies and pasties before anybody had a chance to get near the table?

Note that the ceremony was conducted, and the toast proposed, by one and the same person. Thompson took holy orders round about 1870.

He too took advantage of the local talent. He developed a fondness for the Revd. Brereton's eldest daughter, Anna. But, when he proposed, Brereton would not give his blessing to the union. 'I need her for the work,' he said, and that was that. All his do-goodery required assistants, and who better, and cheaper, than the family?

Poor Thompson had to wait until he (Thompson) retired before he at last succeeded in prising Anna away from her father. Brereton was so demanding that only two of his seven daughters made it to the altar.

Nor did it end there. The Rev. Harries, who came to be HM in 1907, had under his guidance four sons of a Bristol family, one of whom became Head Boy. Miraculously, all four survived service in the First World War. They had two sisters. Harries married one of them, and his brother married the other. You see? Keeping it in the family. And as both brothers were priests, they 'married' each other. In the family again.

This practice did not stop with the advent of buses and motor cars, radio and television, although, to be fair, those novelties did slow it down a bit. I worked in a comprehensive school in Barnstaple for fifteen years in the 1970's and 1980's, and in that time three members of staff married, not matrons, but pupils (after they – the pupils – had left, I am relieved to say). Perhaps it was the Devon air.

This impetus was not confined to the staff. Ex-pupils marry, which is to be expected. But West Buckland has had more than its share of foreign pupils, and there have been marriages in that department too – one involving a Czech girl and one a Hungarian boy.

Finally, a rather endearing postscript. (We are back to the wedding celebrations of Mr. Shain and Miss Simons.) 'A. Martin, Esq.', it said, gave a Magic Lantern Entertainment. It encapsulates the almost embattled atmosphere of a tiny country boarding school in the back end of beyond in Victorian England. It was all so local and family and intimate. Bit like a medieval village, you might imagine.

Before we laugh in our superior, modern way at this lack of sophistication of 'simple' people, we should remember that there wasn't much else, and my guess is that the bride and groom were willing members of the audience because their whole lives tended that way. They would have seen nothing incongruous about it. It may not have crossed their minds to object. And I bet everybody enjoyed it.

I bet too that they let all the younger boys in for that.

Waste not, want not

WEST BUCKLAND HAS ALWAYS looked after the pennies. Remember the school was designed to appeal to 'the middle classes', so costs (and facilities) were kept, shall we say, modest. Hence the assertion by scores of old boys with firm memories of it (well certainly before the middle of the twentieth century), if you could survive West Buckland, you could survive anything.

It is possible to make a case to the effect that they economised even on the number of prizewinners, at any rate in the Speech Day of 1880. (All right, that is not strictly true, but it makes a good story, and the truth should never be allowed to get in the way of a good story.)

In the prizewinners list, **F.A Wells** won the following distinctions:

The Brereton Scholarship, worth £20 (well, I did say things were modest).

The prize for 'General Distinction' – Cowden Clarke's *Shakespeare*, vols. i and ii.

A prize for obtaining First Class Senior Honours in the Cambridge Local Examinations – for which he received Cowden Clarke's *Shakespeare*, vol.iii.

The prize for Mathematics – Cowden Clarke's *Shakespeare*, vol.ii. [Again?]

The prize for Cricket – a bat with a 'silver plate'. [So he wasn't just a swot.]

The prize for Fives – a 'Stationery Case'. [Fives continued to by played at the school till the 1960's.]

F.H. White secured a similar haul:

The Fortescue Scholarship, worth [again] £20.

A prize for 'Second Class Senior Honours' at both Oxford and Cambridge, for which he received Gibbon's *Decline and Fall of the Roman Empire*, vols. i and ii.

A prize for 'First and Second Classes – Gibbon's *Decline and Fall of the Roman Empire*, vols. iii and iv.

A prize for Religious Knowledge – Gibbon's *Decline and Fall of the Roman Empire*, vol. v.

A prize for English – Guess what – Gibbon's *Decline and Fall of the Roman Empire*, vol. vi.

A prize for Latin – Gibbon's *Decline and Fall*, vol. vii.

A prize for Drawing – Gibbon, vol viii.

Always on the look-out for bright lads, the Foreign Office recruited him. He may well have become a spy, dying in mysterious circumstances in Somaliland in 1901.

Not to be outdone – far from it – R.P. Chope picked up this little lot:

The Duke of Bedford's Scholarship, worth, again, £20. [The Duke had been a previous contributor to the school, no doubt talked into it by the Revd, Brereton, who had a knack for collecting celebrities, especially nobly-bred ones.]

The Royal Agricultural Society's Scholarship, worth £20.

A prize for 'First Class Senior Honours at the Cambridge Local Examinations, 1879' and 'First Class Senior Honours at the Oxford Local Examinations, 1880' – Froude's *History of England* – vols. i to iv.

A prize for the 'first and second classes' [the two top classes in the school then] – Froude's *History of England* – vols. v,vi, vii.

A prize for English – Froude's *History of England*, vol. viii.

A prize for French – Froude's *History of England*, vol. ix.

The prize for 'First Senior in England in Drawing at the Oxford Local Examinations, 1880' – Froude's *History of England*, vols. x and xi.

The prize for Drawing, 'awarded by Sir. T.D. Acland, Bart., M.P.' – Froude's *History of England*, vol. xii. [Acland was a prominent local benefactor, and very busy in the matter of education reform. He helped to set up the 'Locals'. And, incidentally, helped to map out the course of the very first *Exmoor*.]

The prize for English Composition – *Shakespeare's Works*. [Presumably they had run out of Froudes.]

With these three super-teens around, it's a wonder anybody else bothered to turn up.

Come to think of it, perhaps the DCS was not so economical after all. Just work out what these books would have cost. We have several such volumes in the Archive, donated over the years by surviving members of various prizewinners' families. And none of your cheap paperbacks. These were all leather-bound, and they were embossed with the school crest in gold letters.

To say nothing of the cricket bat (with a 'silver plate') and the 'Stationery Case'.

A guarantee for old age

IN MARCH, 2012, THE school received news that Dido Stephens had died.

Who is Dido Stephens? She was the widow of Leslie Stephens, who became Headmaster of West Buckland in 1952 – sixty years before. Leslie himself had lived to be 89.

The first Headmaster, Joseph Thompson, lived to be 85. Ernest Harries (Headmaster from 1907 to 1934) lived to be 86. Cordy Wheeler (caretaker Headmaster in 1952 for six months) made it to 88. George Ridding, appointed in 1968, is still, at the time of writing (2018), in full vigour.

Graham Burrell Smith (caretaker HM in 1940), who retired from two headships because of ill health, lived to be 95. He was playing bridge the night before he died.

The moral appears to be: if you want fresh, bracing air and a lively old age, become a headmaster of West Buckland School. It's much cheaper than Switzerland.

On the other hand

THE *REGISTER* ANNOUNCED, IN 1921:

'Arthur George Grinstead. . . 1917-1921, died, we much regret to say, on March 3rd, at "Elwell" [one of the properties on the school's estate], within one day of his fourteenth birthday. The cause of his death was a very severe attack of pneumonia.

'Although he had hardly reached, owing to his age, a position of prominence in the School, he had always proved himself a zealous member of his House and at the time of his death was the Senior Member of the Choir.

'He was a boy of a quiet but cheerful disposition, and his sudden end – he was ill for only four days – cast a general gloom over the School.'

I'm not surprised. A very sad, and mercifully very rare, event.

Dropping a line

OF ALL SAD WORDS of tongue or pen, the saddest are these: 'It might have been.'

This from the *Register* of Easter, 1885.

'FILLEIGH AND LYNTON RAILWAY. – A bill for making this railway line has been passing through Parliament this Session. When introduced it was called the Filleigh and Blackmoor Gate Railway. It seeks power to incorporate a company for the purpose of constructing a railway from Filleigh to Blackmoor Gate, passing through East Buckland, West Buckland, Stoke Rivers, Charles, Bratton Fleming, Kentisbury, Challacombe and Parracombe; to make working arrangements with the Great Western and the London and South-West Railway Companies, and running powers over a portion of the Devon and Somerset Railway, &c.'

To a non-Devonian, particularly an urban non-Devonian, these places sound like typical quaint, out-in-the-sticks, obscure settlements, where nothing much has happened since Alfred the Great. One has to admit that, for once, this dismissive verdict has some truth. They are all still there, and they now have their motor cars and their satellite television like everybody else. But you can't change geography. Many of the smaller roads have more twists than a corkscrew, and many of these villages still don't have a bus service.

They don't have a train service either; the bill was never passed by Parliament.

But just think: it would have been some railway, wouldn't it? It might have saved the school a lot of expenditure on pricy coaches to get the kids to school. Only a Devonian is able to appreciate what a huge 'near-miss' it was.

Sadly, even if it had come into being, it would not have survived the axe of Dr. Beeching in 1963. Look at the Lynton to Barnstaple Railway; that closed in 1935. It did not need the attentions of Dr. Beeching of immortal memory to preside over its demise. The motor car managed that by itself.

The very first Valentine

A RARE FIND, THIS, from the Stygian depths of previously unplumbed Archive records. A precious file labelled 'Prehistoric'.

Cell XCIX
Colosseum
Rome
XIII Februarius

Dear God,
Just to remind you that I'm up for martyrdom tomorrow, and to let you know that I think you're wonderful.
An unknown admirer.

V.

14. 2013

WAS THERE LIFE BEFORE the tabloids?

From the *Exeter Gazette*, June 18th, 1875:

'Situated as the Devon County School is – midway between the two little villages of East and West Buckland – and containing as it does, about 150 hearty, frolicsome, but withal studious youths, the monotonous lives of the villagers must be considerably relieved by the lively proximity of such a large number of boys. But Tuesday last was their half-yearly "breaking up" day; and for the next six weeks, East and West Buckland must resume their wonted quietness, minus the occasional sallies from the school boarders.'

The more you look at this, the more observations come to mind.

In fact, the piece was written to describe the events of the day, because the school had invited everybody from both villages to attend the end-of-term entertainments. The writer said that they were 'indebted to Mr. Thompson (the Headmaster) for many a good laugh'.
All sorts of observations come to mind when you read *that* too.

It would make a good English homework to ask the class to write this same piece in the style of a modern tabloid.

Before Olivier, of course

WEST BUCKLAND SCHOOL AMATEUR DRAMATIC SOCIETY

—— PRESENTS ——

"OTHELLO"

BY

WILLIAM SHAKESPEARE

Friday, 2nd December,

and

Saturday, 3rd December, 1960.

No Charge is made for admission, but your countribution towards the cost of the production and of badly needed equipment will be gratefully received at the doors at the end of the performance.

The Chronicle Press (Ilfracombe), Ltd., Northfield Rd.

Going back a bit

A DISTINGUISHED MEMBER OF the 'benefacting' Fortescue family, Lady Margaret Fortescue, served for thirty-eight years as a governor. All the Fortescue family heads have so served (now, six generations of them.)

A year before she died in 2014, I put up this titbit about her and about her grandfather, the fourth Earl:

'The fourth Earl Fortescue was born in 1854 and died in 1932. He it was who opened the Memorial Hall, shortly before his death. (It had been built to replace – and no doubt to improve upon – the buildings which had been destroyed by the school's famous fire in 1930.)

'In his speech he said that he was probably the only person present who had been there to witness the laying of the original foundation stone by the second Earl in 1860.

'Also present, in 1932, was the fourth Earl's granddaughter Margaret, then a small girl.

'So Lady Margaret, who is still alive [she was in 2013], once sat on the knee of a man who witnessed the laying of the original foundation stone in 1860 – 153 years ago.'

Quite a span.

At Her Majesty's pleasure

I SOMETIMES GET ASKED if any ex-pupil of the school has 'done time'. I have not come across any such person, but then such a fact is not normally the sort of thing a school archivist spends much of his time looking for.. So there may well be someone out there who qualifies for this distinction, but he (or she) has not, to my knowledge, appeared in the official record. And it seems highly unlikely that this person will go out of his (or her) way to publicise, and prove, that I am wrong.

However, I did come across what might be termed 'a near miss'.

Between 1870 and 1872 (boys as a rule did not stay much more than two or three years), a J.R. Barrington attended. He later joined the Old Boys' Association, and in 1906 gave as his address 'Princetown, Dartmoor'.

The *Register* of October, 1907, records that on 1st June, 1907, he got married. At Lydford, which is not a million miles away from Princetown.

It seems, again, unlikely that an ex-con (or, even less likely, a present con) would give such a place as his normal abode. If he were a 'present con', how did he get out to attend an Old Boys' gathering? Or his own wedding, for that matter. And if he had, why would he have wanted to advertise where he had been, and why would he have wanted to go back?

So, to paraphrase Holmes, 'When we have eliminated the [near-] impossible, whatever remains, however unlikely, will be the [apparent] truth.'

So we are left with an Old Boy who served in HM Prison as a warder, a gardener (if they have, or had, gardens at Dartmoor), a maintenance man, or a cook.

Whatever he was, it seems very plausible that, among WB alumni, he is unique.

They have worked sex even into computers

WITH THE INCREASING, AND unstoppable, pervasiveness of computers, it was only a matter of time before they came to the notice of a school archivist. It is common knowledge that archivists spend their waking hours (and some of their sleeping ones), secreted up in some remote eyrie, where they pass the time blowing the dust off books, files, albums, and sundry other moth-eaten record collections that nobody is ever going to read.

But, just now and again, something pops up among the parchments and the quill pens which yanks them into the twenty-first century. I can't remember how I came to be acquainted with this, but it is a good illustration of the fact that you never know what is going to drop on to an archivist's desk. Because of the age of an archivist's working material, it is easy to conclude that the prevailing atmosphere is one of boredom because it springs from dullness, predictability, and age.

Not so. A school archive can produce its share of surprises. I think the following piece qualifies for a book like this because it is academic, it is 'modern', and it is relevant.

As is well known, the English have dispensed with sex – at any rate in nouns.

However, it survives in the languages of the rest of Europe. However (again), new nouns, which are always being coined – always the sign of a healthy language – present a problem.

Take computers. (So here we are at last in the twenty-first century.) What is the gender of the Spanish word for 'computer'? Is it *'el computador'* or *'la computadora'*?

The 'Masculine' lobby say it is feminine for the following reasons:

1. No one but their creator understands their internal logic.
2. The native language they use to communicate with other computers is incomprehensible to everyone else.
3. Even the smallest mistakes are stored in long-term memory for possible retrieval later on.
4. As soon as you make a commitment to one, you find yourself spending half your salary buying accessories for it.

On the other hand, the 'Feminine' lobby insist that it should be masculine, because:
1. In order to do anything with them, you have to turn them on.
2. They have a lot of data but still can't think for themselves.
3. They are supposed to help you solve problems, but half the time they **ARE** the problem.
4. As soon as you commit yourself to one, you realise that if you had waited just a little longer you could have obtained a better model..

A good read

AS I HAVE OBSERVED elsewhere in these memoirs (or this scrapbook if you prefer), the figure 100 is mesmerising. It is beloved of any writer who seeks an excuse for a celebration.

Nobody has satisfactorily explained why the figures 99 and 101 don't seem to have this *cachet.*

Maybe it is the two noughts. The figure 1,000 is even more mesmerising. We can't go into four noughts, because no written records go back that far, with any hope of being able to pinpoint an event to the day. Nobody can set the ball rolling for parties to celebrate the end of the Bronze Age.

So let's go back to the hundred. It is not only writers who fall under the spell of this phenomenon; archivists are just as vulnerable. Over the years, when I have been stuck for a little squib to put up on the Common Room notice board, it is a safe bet that I can find something put-uppable from a school magazine, a Governors' minute, or a sepia photograph. Indeed, when I began the Archive, I was amazed not only to discover a large amount of old photographs, but to see in what remarkably good condition many of them were. Some could have been taken last week.

By the same token, the school Reading and Debating Society, which saw the light of day in 1903, has come to my rescue more than once. In 2013, I found this in the Society's Minutes from 6th October, 1913:

On this day, the Society debated the motion that 'the reading of novels is bad for the intellect'.

'Mr. Muncaster opened his speech by giving the House a short history of the novel. [Brave lad; nowadays he would have simply downloaded relevant paragraphs from the net.] . . . [he then] gave us various instances of the lurid type of modern novel and pointed out that for every good novelist there were 99 bad ones;. [So things have not changed very much.] Time spent on novel reading might be spent in athletics or art.'

[So that may explain the success of those two celebrity West Buckland *alumni* Jonathan Edwards and Damien Hirst, first of whom attended in the 1980's and second of whom sent his son to the school.]

Christmas cheer

IT CAN DO TWO things – make you pleased and grateful, and make you laugh. Whether these two items make you do either, now, it seems likely that they were expected to do just that in 1913, when the December number of the *Register* recorded them.

Firstly, the School Museum (which, according to the slender surviving evidence, was set up by the Revd. Harries – HM from 1907 to 1934), was the beneficiary of the following:

1. Mr. Inniss, a teacher from Trinidad (Maths), gave us 'the nest of a weaver bird, a stuffed flying fish;' [and] 'a piece of auriferous quartz from the famous mine of El Calao (El Dorado)'. [Just what we had always wanted.]
2. J.L. Ries 'gave two stuffed birds from Africa'.
3. W.J. Wheale offered 'an alligator's head'. [Now you never know when you might need things like that.]

Secondly, the indefatigable Mr. Chope (the school's most merciless benefactor) inserted into the *Register* [the hapless editors always found it difficult to resist him] some gems he had culled from the answers to the General Knowledge Test, which he set, remorselessly, every year.

Candidates were invited to explain the meanings of 'common' terms. [Were they 'common' even in 1913?]

1. *Man in the street* – a person who has gone to the dogs; the working man who votes as he is bribed to; one who has no fixed abode [well, logical at least].
2. *Carte blanche* – point blank; a clean sheet; a free pass; to show the 'white feather'. [Not, alas, as has been suggested since – 'will someone please get Blanche out of here'].
3. *Kismet* – the Mahometan Bible, an instrument shaped something like a dagger; a person of wealth in India', a key-word to a puzzle; an Egyptian charm.
4. *Kumiss* – a preparation of oil from a whale; a sort of herb obtainable only in India or Africa.
5. *Sang-froid* – to express contempt; not caring a bit. [Can one imagine Rhett Butler saying to Scarlett, 'Frankly, my dear, I don't give a sang-froid'?]

Still on Record

Conspicuous by its absence

UNDER THE HEADING OF 'I thought-this-was-worth-sharing', I put up, on 28th November, 2013, this extract quoted by John Julius Norwich in his *Illustrated Christmas Crackers* [Atlantic Books, 2013, with the drawings by Quentin Blake].

In the tradition of Mr. Bowdler, political correctness, and the diplomatic corps general code of practice, JJN offered this:

'Although written many years ago, *Lady Chatterley's Lover* has just been re-issued by Grove Press, and this fictional account of the day-to-day life of an English game-keeper is still of considerable interest to outdoor-minded readers, as it contains many passages on pheasant-raising, the apprehending of poachers, ways to control vermin, and other chores and duties of the professional game-keeper.

'Unfortunately, one is obliged to wade through many pages of extraneous material in order to discover and savour these sidelights on the management of a Midland shooting estate, and in this reviewer's opinion the book cannot take the place of J.R. Miller's *Practical Gamekeeper*.'

[I'm not surprised.]

Now what on earth was I going, or was unable, or forgot, to put here?

Remember, remember, the fifth of November

IT IS NOT ALWAYS easy, or practicable, to produce little notice-board squibs to keep pace with the anniversaries of well-known events, but this one deserves the comment 'tried hard'.

'I have not yet discovered any item from the school's history which might be considered strictly relevant to today's anniversary [5th November], but, under the heading of 'Flames and Drama', I have come close.

'As will be readily appreciated, in the single-sex days before girls were discovered, school dramatic productions laboured under the burden of casting young juniors in the female parts.

'One old boy remembered being put on the stage as a fairy. There must have been some candles among the scenery [fairy-tale 'atmosphere' no doubt], because his fairy get-up caught fire – wings, wand, tutu, and all. What you might call the *'tutu ensemble'*.

'Being a resourceful lad, he wrapped himself in the front curtain, but, in his excitement (understandable under the circumstances) he overbalanced. He fell on to the piano at the foot of the stage, creating a rare chord of truly post-modern originality.

'But he was still partly alight, it seemed. "Up rushed the French master," he recalled. "He lifted me up, put his arms round me, kissed me on both cheeks, said 'Oh, pouf!', and extinguished the flames."'

There's no business like. . . .

At Her Majesty's further pleasure

FIVE OR SIX PAGES before this one, I told the tale of a former pupil of the school (name of Barrington) who, at an Old Boys' Dinner in 1906, had given his address as 'Princetown, Dartmoor', and I speculated on the obvious possibilities.

It often happens that when you come across something unusual, another instance of it turns up very quickly afterwards. And here it is.

In the course of building a database of all pupils (still not complete – bit like the Forth Bridge), I found a Dr. R.S. Dyer, who attended between 1877 and 1879. Seven years after Barrington.

This time there appears to be no doubt about his status. He was a doctor. And he too gave his address as 'Princetown, Dartmoor'. So it looks as if he was the official prison medicine man.

One hopes that he looked on the bright side; his rounds would not have been very extensive. Bearing in mind the supposed chief activity of the inmates, and the high level of their supervision, it seems safe to assume that all his patients were no more than a stone's throw away, as you might say. And nobody would have been out when he called.

As there were only a few years between them, had they known each other?

Was it possible that these two gentlemen met in Dartmoor? Did J.R. Barrington ever visit Mr. Dyer with complaints about a bad back, in an attempt to get a few days off from stone-crushing? If he did, did they exchange fond reminiscences about the jolly old school?

Or – a bit of a long shot, this – had they in fact been partners? In crime. Had J.R. Barrington been careless and got caught, while Dr. Dyer had eluded the long arm of the law for several years more? Had Dr. Dyer shopped Mr. Barrington?

Whatever had happened, it seems that, by 1906, they had both paid their debt to society, both attended the same Old Boys' Dinner in 1906. What would they have said to each other?

15. 2014

Archive culture session

NEVER LET IT BE said that the Archive neglected an opportunity to enhance the education of the establishment it was set up to serve. I forget now where I saw this gem , but it seemed such a pity to leave it out. How on earth a document like this found its way into the dust of a country school archive I can not imagine. Chances are that the person who found this couldn't think of anywhere else to send it. One doesn't like to be shown up as the ignorant philistine who carelessly jettisoned a document which others might find valuable. There is no time to ask all and sundry if they are interested. So send it to the Archive. Over the years I have been supplied with a near-medieval office hole-punch, hundred-year-old glass slides, a pair of racing-enthusiast (or shooting range) binoculars, and the leopardskin apron worn on parades and marches by the bass drummer in the long-expired cadet band.

Things don't always get sent or delivered; I have sometimes found interesting things for myself. Even under the floorboards. (Literally, under the floorboards, when the builders came to create new classrooms out of the old dormitories. One of the workmen gave some scraps to me. And I know I've said this before somewhere.)

Anyway, this will do by way of example.

It is an extract from a synopsis of Bizet's opera *Carmen*, which the Paris Opera thoughtfully provided for the benefits of its English and American patrons:

'ACT 1.

'Carmen is a cigar-makeress from the tabago factory who loves with Don Jose of the mounting guard. Carmen takes a flower from her corsets and lances it to Don Jose (Duet: "Talk to me of my mother"). There is a noise inside the tabago factory and the revolting cigar-makeresses bursts in to the stage. Carmen is arrested and Don Jose is ordered to mounting guard her but Carmen subduces him and he lets her escape.'

'ACT 2.

'The Tavern. Carmen, Frasquita, Mercedes, Zuniga, Morales. Carmen's aria ("the sistrums are tinkling"). Enter Escamillio, a balls-fighter. Enter two smuglers [sic] (Duet: " We have in mind a business") but Carmen refuses to penetrate because Don Jose has liberated from

Still on Record

prison. He just now arrives (Aria: "Slop, here who comes!") but here are the bugles singing his retreat. Don Jose will leave and draws his sword. Called by Carmen shrieks the two smugglers interfere with her but Don Jose is bound to dessert, he will follow into them (final Chorus: "Opening sky wandering life"). . . . '

[We never found out what happened to 'ACT 3'.]

'AXT 4 [sic], a place in Seville. Procession of balls-fighters, the roaring of the balls heard in the arena. Escamillio enters. (Aria and chorus: "Toreador, toreador, All hail the balls of a Toreador.") but Carmen repels him wants to join with Escamillio now chaired by the crowd. Don Jose stabs her (Aria: "Oh rupture, rupture, you may arrest me, I did kill her") he sings "Oh, my beautiful Carmen, my subductive Carmen . . . '

Gustav Kobbé's *Complete Opera Book* , the standard work of reference on the subject, tells us that the premiere of *Carmen* at the Opéra-Comique in 1875 was a failure.

One dares to wonder whether, if members of that audience in 1875 had had access to this masterly synopsis, things might have been different.

I don't know the full provenance of this piece, but I am eternally grateful that it reached me. It is enough to brighten any day.

Touché, touché, touché

IF YOU WANT TO get your name in the paper, do the most of something. There is no end to the fertility of imagination that people will give evidence of in order to achieve this. Makes you wonder sometimes. The longest non-stop dance, the greatest number of ascents of Scottish Highland peaks called 'Munros'. And so on. Even the largest number of people who could get into a Mini at the same time. (This was the event that probably gave rise, or contributed to, the rash of 'elephant' jokes that abounded at the time. 'How do you get thirteen elephants into a Mini?' 'Easy: six in the front and seven in the back.')

The *Western Morning News* came up with one in March, 1989. All about fencing. Beats even Errol Flynn and Basil Rathbone. Two sixth-formers from the school embarked on what was billed as the longest-ever marathon of this most energetic and explosive activity.

They did it properly. Only five minutes' rest every hour. Ten 'experts', judges, adjudicators, or what you will on hand to ascertain that no rules were broken, no corners cut (sorry about the pun). They did it too. Only one serious hiccup, when one of the contestants became sick near the end. He recovered enough to continue, but for a while the attempt had been in jeopardy. The casualty said afterwards that he 'couldn't remember much about that part'. I'm not surprised.

They recorded 3,596 hits during 226 fights.

[I didn't know they were called 'fights'. Not very romantic for such a dashing activity. One would have expected something like 'encounters', or 'clashes', or 'challenges', or 'thrusts'.

At the very least 'bouts' or 'contests' or even 'meetings'. But no – 'fights'. Perhaps there is a proper name, and the journalist recording the event didn't know what it was.]

Be that as it may, they beat the previous record, held by two members of the RAF, who had managed a paltry 13 hours, 26 minutes. The breathless West Buckland pair were able to look back, through the pain and the sweat, at more than 15 hours of endeavour.

They were able to raise £650 towards the North Devon Scanner Appeal and the school's development appeal.

So it was not a frivolous teenage jape. There had been some point to it all (ho-ho!).

Being aware

BY 1914, THE SCHOOL was basking in its new name. In 1912, the old share company, which had started the Devon County School, went into voluntary liquidation (long story), and re-emerged as West Buckland School, henceforth dependent on fees and council grants. On Thursday, 2nd July, it laid on its annual Speech Day. The *Register*, naturally, gave it full coverage. Very full.

'But for a temporary shower, the weather was very favourable.' [That was a change.]

'Luncheon was served from 12 o'clock, and at 2 o'clock the prize distribution was held in the Karslake Hall.' [If half the reports in the *Register* are to be believed, the school never missed an opportunity to lay on a substantial meal. No common, stand-up midday snack either. It was never a lunch; it was always a 'luncheon'. Sounded so much bigger and better. It always reminds me of Toad Hall. They had luncheon – 'which of course was excellent, as everything at Toad Hall always was'. And look at the time they took – two hours. It must have been a bit like the sacred French *déjeuner*.]

'The CHAIRMAN, before calling upon Canon Pryke {ex-Headmaster of Lancaster Grammar School] to distribute the prizes, said that on behalf of the Governors he should like to congratulate the Head Master and his staff, and the matron and her staff, upon the great success which the School had attained. (Applause.) They had heard from the Head Master that the School was full. [Only nineteen years before, William Knight had taken on the headship when the pupil numbers were down to 31.] Yes, and full to overflowing – (applause) – and the Governors had been considering a scheme for enlarging the School.'. . .

'Canon Pryke said that he should like to say a few words about books.' [Which he did – for a full page of the *Register*.] . . .

Typical among the prizewinners was M. F. Kidwell, whose awards included *De Quincy's Essays*, *The Works* of Byron, Drummond's *Commentaries*, and Tennyson's *Works* [which should have taught him].

Apparently, the School Museum had been the beneficiary of two gifts: one was 'a collection of hand-carved calabashes and a collection of beetles, sent from Trinidad'. [You never know when you may need some calabashes and beetles from Trinidad. But it was meant well; I should guess with some confidence that this was the work of Mr. Innis, a maths teacher at the school, who came from Trinidad, and who had only recently left.]

The other gift was 'a piece of the bark of the tree at Glenelg under which was read the proclamation which made South Australia part of the British Empire'. [South Australia, as we all know, had a coastline on the Great Australian Bight. Was this a case of the bark being worse than the Bight?]

What is remarkable about this exhaustive report is not what it recorded, but what it did not. Only five days before this event, Archduke Franz Ferdinand had been assassinated on the streets of Sarajevo, the capital of Bosnia, in the Hapsburg Empire. Within six weeks of that tragedy, the whole of Europe was at war – well, nearly all of it.

People then must have been aware of the system of alliances and treaties which involved England, France, Prussia, Austria, Italy, Belgium, Serbia, and Russia. It had woven a net which, when crisis came, was to drag them all into Armageddon. And they certainly had their prejudices. There had been no world war for 99 years; people talked glibly about it because they had no idea what it would bring about.

Yet not a flicker of consciousness is shown in any of the reports and speeches, or in the *Register* reports. The world is simply not there (apart from calabashes and beetles from Trinidad). It is almost a law of historical physics: the greater the storm that came afterwards, the more idyllic the calm that survivors later perceived before it. Many people said for years afterwards that the world before the 'Great' War had something – charm, light, magic, sun, softness, what you will – which disappeared in 1914, never to return.

During the proceedings, the school cricket team was mentioned, if only to report that they had won a mere four games (but they had beaten the great rival, Barnstaple Grammar School). There is in the Archive an evocative photograph of the First XI of that year – blazers, caps, gleaming white everywhere. Not a trace of what was coming.

Yet, by the end of that year, ten of them had joined up. The last one joined up later. Two won the MC. One was mentioned in despatches. One was wounded twice. Another four times. One died three days before that first Christmas. Look at their faces.

Still on Record

Answering another call

WHEN WAR CAME IN 1914, it was not merely senior schoolboys who felt the urge to 'do' something. (By the time of the Second World War, it was called 'doing your bit'.)

At one end of the scale, there are countless instances of large boys lying about their age, and getting away with it, and getting in – and getting killed. At the other, there were plenty of cases of men doing the same in their middle years, who were technically over military age – who, for all I know, also lied about it.

It is difficult for us now to understand the strength, sharpness, and unanswerability of the spur to the pride that the situation produced. In every country – not just England. Records show that young men – in Britain, France, Germany, Russia, and America (and no doubt in Italy, Serbia, the Commonwealth, and lots of other places too) –. queued up, in their hundreds and thousands, to join the colours.

The worst letter a young man could receive was not his call-up papers, but a plain, anonymous envelope which contained one small white feather.

This overwhelming pressure reached, and enveloped, an assistant teacher in an obscure, unknown, remote boarding school on the edge of Exmoor.

Michael Watson had come to the school in 1896. He had already notched up 18 years by the time war broke out. One wonders what he thought when he saw all those ex-pupils rushing to the recruiting offices. When *he* joined up, the war had been running for nearly four years. He could not stand it any longer. He was forty-five years old.

Perhaps luckily for him, by the time he had finished his basic training, the war was coming to an end. He duly returned to his music-teaching at West Buckland, and for years was the backbone and bastion of the musical accompaniment to the school's productions of Gilbert and Sullivan operas. He stayed till 1938, the eve of the Second World War. One wonders whether, in his more fanciful moments, he felt any temptation to join that.

Incidentally, he is the longest-serving member of the school's academic staff.

16. 2015

If you think you are hard done by

ACCORDING TO THE REPORT of the School Inspectors in 1905, the Headmaster (William Arthur Knight) spent, each week, twenty-seven hours in the classroom.

How many headmasters today spend twenty-seven hours a week in the classroom? Come to think of it, how many *teachers* spend twenty-seven hours a week in the classroom? Indeed, today, what with games sessions, PE periods, laboratory experiments, outdoor art work, cadet parades, lunchtime clubs, play rehearsals, choir practice, religious gatherings of one kind or another, one might be hard pushed to it to find a *pupil* who spent twenty-seven hours a week in the classroom.

To be fair to the inspectors, they did remark, with customary British understatement, that they thought twenty-seven hours was 'a little excessive'.

But not because of any concern for his health. It was because of concern that he could 'not keep so careful a supervision over the work of his assistants as would be desirable to ensure that satisfactory methods of teaching and a high standard of work are maintained throughout the school'. When Knight became Headmaster, the pupil numbers had dropped to 31 (another long story), so one wonders how many 'assistants' there were whose behaviour needed constant supervision in order to maintain 'a high standard of work'.

In my own school, in the 'old days', I was told by an elderly surviving teacher, the Headmaster, after morning break and lunch, used to stand at the foot of the stairs leading from the common room to the corridor of classrooms, with a significant turnip watch in his hand, and a significant expression on his face – just to keep them up to the mark.

As a matter of fact, Mr. Knight had energy to spare. He found the wherewithal to be a keen cricketer and footballer, and to father three children during his six-year tenure of office.

He found energy to beat boys too. Quite frequently, apparently. Perhaps, if you had to spend twenty-seven hours a week in the classroom, as well as running a school and getting the total number of pupils up from 31, you too might feel a little short-tempered from time to time.

Justified or not, during his reign, the school was known as 'The City of Dreadful Knight'.

Man of few words

THE TEACHER IN CHARGE of the *Exmoor* for many years in the 1950's and 1960's was Ian McLintock. Nickname 'Ticktock'. My impression is that more teachers in the 'old days' had nicknames than they do now.

This could easily be the cue for old pupils with long, rose-tinted memories to start a monologue about 'characters', and how thin they are on the ground today. Well, possibly. It could also be that the 'old' teachers got more nicknames then because they had more quirks, fads, and eccentricities than they do now. There was more for pupils to notice and fasten on to. It could be, once again, that there is less now for pupils to fasten on to because modern teachers do not exhibit as many of these odd behaviourisms because they are too busy doing their job. It could even be that they are better, and concentrate on work rather than 'being a character'. Ordinary, but more efficient. The debate can easily continue at any gathering of old survivors and their modern successors in the classroom.

Anyway, Ticktock was clearly a character. Bachelor. Most of them were. (Food for discussion there too.) Bachelors had few household ties and no family responsibilities, so they had *time* to be characters.

Ticktock certainly gave unstintingly of his time to the school. He served for thirty years or thereabouts. He taught Latin and French. He organised the *Exmoor*, as I said. He also ran the cadet force. During the War, he was responsible for a universal nocturnal activity known as 'Fire-Watching'. The name is pretty self-explanatory, but it is further evidence of yet more hours spent in the service of the school. Very unsociable hours too. It has to be admitted that the likelihood of squadrons of Junkers and Heinkels and Dorniers regularly filling the night sky over Exmoor and raining high-explosive and incendiary bombs on Challacombe and Brendon Two Gates was somewhat small – as Jeeves would have remarked, 'The contingency was remote' – but the time had to be put in, and even doing nothing and being in constant readiness could be taxing. Boredom can be a great enervator.

'Mac' (another, and obvious nickname) was a great traveller. In the Archive are several index-card boxes chock full of picture postcards he sent home – to the school, to colleagues, rather touchingly to his parents – from countless British and foreign tourist attractions. (It makes one drool to see old postage stamps for a penny and a ha'penny.) I don't know if he took school parties, but, from his record and his personality, the 'contingency' seems anything but 'remote'. Also among the index-card boxes are dozens of cards written *to* him by friends, colleagues, and family. So he was clearly well liked.

Stories stuck to him of course. Especially one-liners, snap rhymes, instant cartoons. We must be content here with just one, from May/June, 1940, when the danger of losing our entire Army in France and subsequent invasion was at its height:

One of the school cross-country runs was known as 'The Beeches'. A worried junior, who, like everybody else then, was glued to the wireless every evening to hear the news, came up to Mac and said, 'Sir, why did Mr. Churchill say that we're going to fight Hitler on the Beeches?'

Which brings us full circle back to the *Exmoor*. This is a good point to highlight how much less paper work there was then than there is now. Cue this time for complaints about forms, bumf, useless admin, pettifogging rules about health and safety. Well, yes, OK, we all know that. We are stuck with it, just as we are stuck with computers and motorways and washing-up machines.

I simply want to illustrate this point. I should like to mention a piece of the old quarto-sized paper (about three-quarters the modern A4) which had found its way into the Archive. It was posted on the common room notice board in 1969 to explain the arrangements for the coming cross-country race. For those who have not bothered to read the rest of this book, the *Exmoor* was, and still is, the oldest tradition in the school. On one day at the end of every Easter term, the school in effect shut down, and still does, for an event which involved a six-mile walk to Five Barrows up on the Moor, and a nine-mile run back. Over the years there evolved, inevitably, a junior Exmoor, and, later, with remorseless logic, a dozen more such races, each with its own name – the Crossbury, the Bray, the Railway, the Westacott, the Long (I bet that was murder – longer than the *Exmoor* itself, apparently; they didn't call it 'the Long' for nothing), and so on.

Think for a moment of what these races, especially the long ones, involved – maps, course markers, whippers-in, guardians of sackfuls of outer clothing shed just before the race, requests to local farmers to permit scores, even hundreds, of boys galumphing across their fields. To say nothing of special arrangements for malingerers, drop-outs, accidents, sandwiches before, traditional pea soup after, extra showers and baths, and a hundred other things that only an organiser would know about.

The teacher who organised the 2002 *Exmoor* needed 82 pages of closely-typed and printed A4 to make his meaning clear to all concerned.

Ticktock got all this, handwritten, on to one piece of quarto paper, thus:

JUNIOR EXMOOR 17 Nov 1969. [Note the total absence of punctuation.]

Normal till 1210
1215 All boys in Hall
1245 Lunch
130 Runners leave
135 Markers leave
315 START from New Cross
350 Soup and baths
615 Tea and cups [not for drinking, but for presentation]
715 Film
815 Normal routine.   ISML
[34 words, against 82 pages.]

I was once told that, when Mac died, they didn't find him for a fortnight.

Still on Record

A point of view

REACTIONS TO THIS COULD be a good example of people's views being the product of their interests, their tastes, their cultural awareness, and their knowledge (or lack of it).

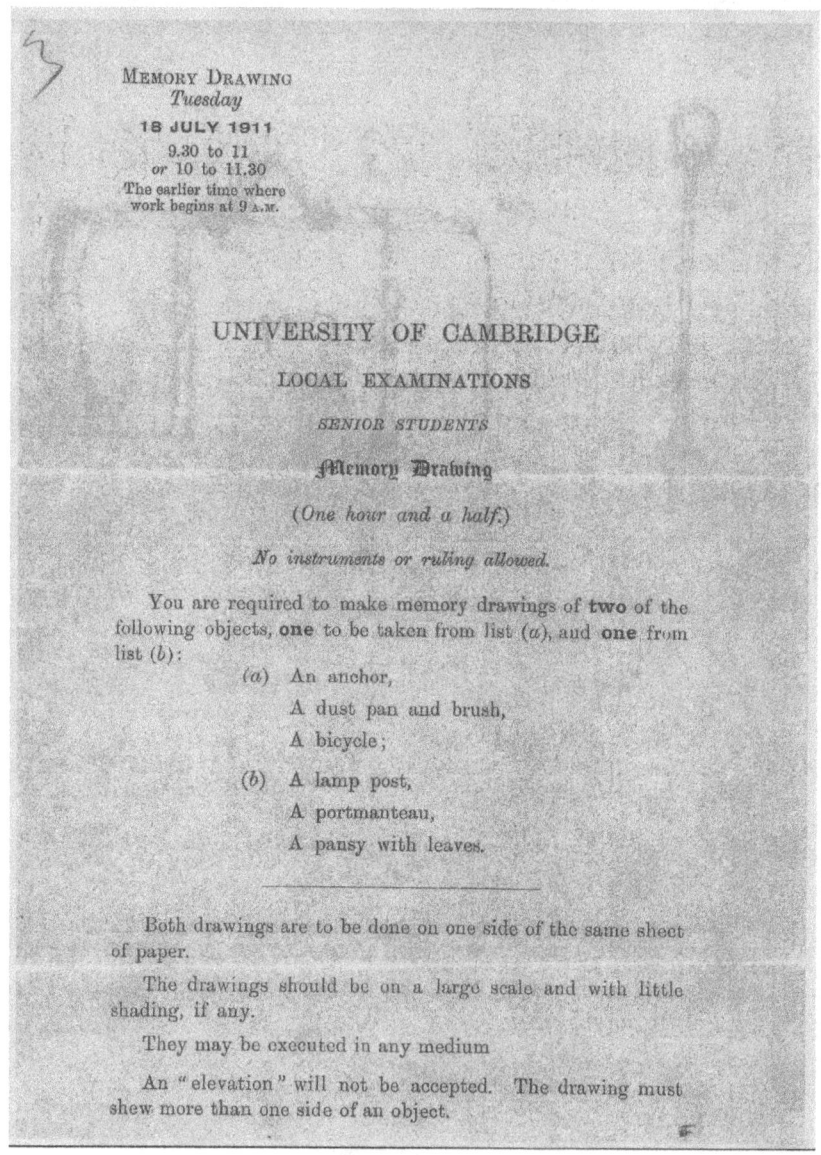

MEMORY DRAWING
Tuesday
18 JULY 1911
9.30 to 11
or 10 to 11.30
The earlier time where work begins at 9 A.M.

UNIVERSITY OF CAMBRIDGE

LOCAL EXAMINATIONS

SENIOR STUDENTS

𝔐𝔢𝔪𝔬𝔯𝔶 𝔇𝔯𝔞𝔴𝔦𝔫𝔤

(*One hour and a half.*)

No instruments or ruling allowed.

You are required to make memory drawings of **two** of the following objects, **one** to be taken from list (*a*), and **one** from list (*b*):

(*a*) An anchor,
A dust pan and brush,
A bicycle;

(*b*) A lamp post,
A portmanteau,
A pansy with leaves.

Both drawings are to be done on one side of the same sheet of paper.

The drawings should be on a large scale and with little shading, if any.

They may be executed in any medium

An "elevation" will not be accepted. The drawing must shew more than one side of an object.

Plus ça change, plus c'est la même chose
OR, if you prefer, politics never gives us any surprises

THE FOLLOWING ARE EXTRACTS from the Minutes of the school Reading and Debating Society (founded in 1903), on the topic of the General Election of 1906.

'The motion was that "this House views with apprehension the [election to] power of a Liberal-cum-Labour Government".' [A fate worse than death.]

'The same member dwelt on "the possibility of the reduction of the Army and Navy, and went on to deal with the Education question. . . and Chinese Labour.' [For 'Chinese Labour' read ' immigrants' today.]

'Mr. _____, opposing, said that he was unable to find a single correct statement of any importance in Mr. ____'s speech. . . He claimed that the political morality of all parties at election times is very low.'

'Mr. ____ gave a list of the beneficial acts of the previous Liberal governments, and of the harmful acts of the Tory governments.'

'Mr. ____, summing up, said that the Government which had just resigned was chiefly famed for its incompetency, mismanagement, and strict disregard for the truth.'

But it wasn't all the traditional sniping.

In the Minutes of October, 1908, the Society was ahead of its time:

'Mr. Bagshawe moved "that nationalisation of railways would be of benefit to this country".

In 1939, the year the Second World War started, the Society was still on the ball:

1. The Phoenix Society (the new name of the Reading and Debating Society, bestowed in 1926 [we still don't know why]) debated the motion: 'In the opinion of this House, Gas will play an important part in Modern Warfare.' Only 27 days after war broken out.
2. The following week, on 6th October, the Phoenix Society went one better: they debated the motion that 'in the present emergency, the flowers in front of the School should be replaced by vegetables'. The motion was lost.

Crumbs at the bottom of the bag

Size does matter

On Monday, 14th February, 1916, the Reading and Debating Society turned their attention to the motion that 'short people are better off than those of greater height'. The motion was carried.   [Very useful for shallow trenches.]

Breaking bowlers' hearts

In the very hot summer of 1913, the wickets were so hard and unhelpful to the bowlers that, in only five senior house matches, the total runs scored came to 2451.

Letting the youngsters have a go

In mid-1860's, the Headmaster, the Second Master, and the Third Master had an average age of about 25.

Still ahead of his time

On 16th May, 1904, in the Reading and Debating Society, S.E. Passmore proposed a motion in favour of a Channel Tunnel.

Next to godliness

In 1903, in their drive to replace 'the Old Bathing Pond', the school sought expert advice, and was told that 'with the sum of about one hundred and fifty pounds, a really first-class bath may be built'.

Must be the bracing air

Twins have been born to the Headmaster, in the original Headmaster's house – twice. But not the same headmaster.

Brave girl

The school may have not admitted female pupils on a regular basis till the 1970's, but the academic staff received (and I hope welcomed) its first female member in 1914. Head of department too – English. And, later, Head of the Brereton House.

The place to be

When the school was only ten years old – in 1868, that is – Prize Day numbered among the guests: the Earl of Devon, Lord Taunton (Chairman of a landmark Government education commission, and very much in the news at that time), the Revd. J.L. Brereton (along with Lord Fortescue, the founder of the school), the Revd. W.H. Karslake (who later was the driving force behind the building of the school dining hall – still known as 'the Karslake'), Thomas Hughes (author of *Tom Brown's Schooldays*), and the Revd. Jack Russell (he of the dogs – who was the incumbent at Swimbridge only a few miles away).

And there was no railway in North Devon then. The line up from Exeter had been opened only four or five years before.

Double take

The two portraits of the Revd. Brereton and his wife Frances, in the Memorial Hall, painted by George Richmond (a prominent portrait painter of his day) and exhibited at the Royal Academy in 1868, were sold to Lord Fortescue for £200 – the pair. (Which I understand was a substantial sum of money then – for paintings.)

The England team could do with players like this

T.H. Watts, playing for the First XI against North Devon on 29th June, 1903, scored 145, which is still the highest known individual score by a pupil of the school. He also set a record for throwing the cricket ball – 105 yards, 3 inches. (I shouldn't think that has been beaten either.)

He also went on to play football for Notts County.

He was killed in the First World War.

Likely lad

F.A. Wells, between 1876 and 1880, won 23 prizes and received 34 leather-bound volumes. He also won scholarships to the value of £75, which represented about half the cost of his education at the school during that period.

[From Jon Edmonds, *A History of West Buckland School*. p. 21.]

Look after the pennies

In 1871, the total salaries for the entire academic staff came to 881 pounds, 4 shillings, and 11 pence.

Well qualified

After a candidate for the post of School Nurse had presented herself for interview, the Headmaster scribbled on a note in her personal file:

'The only snag is her youth and attractiveness.' [Source confidential.]

Allowing for any eventuality

From the Articles of Association of the Devon County School: 'The office of Governor shall be vacated... if he become lunatic.'

Privileges of office

There still blows about the Archive the faintest whiff of suspicion, the merest wisp of rumour, that a tradition once existed which allowed the Head Prefect to keep a dog – and to wear a beard. (Not necessarily at the same time.)

Not a scrap of documentation or evidence for these claims or assertions exists; it just emanates from the woodwork.

Though some figures with moustaches in the photographs of the 1880's could well be pupils. They were certainly fond of bowler hats and watch chains.

Maintaining a sense of family

Talking of bizarre assertions, an old boy, in reminiscent mood, once claimed that one of his contemporaries was expelled for 'sleeping with the Matron'. [Names withheld – thank God.]

Brief encounter

In his Headmaster's Report for the year 1900-1901, Mr. Knight, who had clearly been doing some homework, deplored the fact that 'the average length of stay at the School does not exceed 5 terms'.

This must have been all the more worrying, as the total number of pupils when he took over was 31.

What is remarkable is that the school was able to make such an impression on its pupils in such a short time; legions of old boys used to make the effort regularly to attend Old Boys' Dinners.

Run rate

In 1898, the *Register* reported that, in a cricket match between 'Mr. Challen's XI' (Challen was HM in the late 1890's, and a gifted batsman) and the Hampshire Nondescripts – admittedly in a two-day match – the total number of runs scored was 833.

Sport on a shoestring

In the very first number of the *Register* in the twentieth century, the Editor noted that 'The First Xi have at last a decent set of goal-posts and nets'. [What did they have before? Piled-up jackets?]

Otherwise known as

On the back of the Prize Day programme for 1880 was printed the news that, with effect from 1st January, 1881, the name of the local railway station would be changed from 'Castle Hill' to 'Filleigh'. [Make what you like of that.]

A menu to die for – or to die after

The first-ever Old Boys' Dinner was held in the Prince of Wales' Salon at the Holborn Restaurant on Monday, 20th December, 1886. On the menu were Calf's Tail Soup, Cod and Shrimp Sauce, Whitebait, Lamb Cutlets and Peas, Pigeons Sauté and Mushrooms, Ribs of Beef and Horseradish, Boiled Turkey and Celery Sauce, Ham and Madeira, Plain and Sauté Potatoes, Brussels Sprouts, Mince Pies, Plum Pudding, Macédoine Jelly, Ice Pudding, Cheese, Celery, and 'Dessert'.

The original menu survives. [Would a purist have put 's' after '*sauté*'?]

Good blood stock

The *Register* of Christmas, 1882, reported that on the previous 8th November, the Revd. J. Hallifax, Rector of Breane, Somerset, died. He had sent eight sons to the school – boarders of course. He was described as 'a warm friend of the School'. [Very warm.]

More blood stock

The Board of Education Report on the school in October, 1938, remarked that 'the general Physical Education is producing a virile set of boys'.

A little knowledge
From a General Knowledge Examination of 1929:

Q. Explain the reference to 'Somer is i-cumin in'.
A. 'It is the first line of a poem by a man with a cold.'

And from 1914: 'Tennyson was the greatest writer of Roman prose, he wrote the 'Iliad' and 'Paradise Lost'.

Olympian training – Ancient or Modern?
The school athletic sports in 1876 included the Standing Long Jump and Throwing the Hammer.

The *Register* added that the 'Sports were commenced on July 28th . . . and, as they were not quite finished on that day, they were completed on September 7th. [Long time to keep your plimsoles on.]

Field marshals' batons
The school cadet force, known then, naturally, as the 'Officers' Training Corps', was set up by letter from the War Office in 1909. This letter survives.

The first commanding officer was the Headmaster, a clergyman.

Strictly formal
Junior boys wore Eton collars until after the First World War.

Dress regulations between the wars provided for a regular change of pants – every fortnight.

Being prepared
In the summer of 1917, the Headmaster, the Revd. Harries, attended a course at Gosport in physical training and bayonet fighting, and obtained a satisfactory certificate.

The mind boggles
In a copy of *Health and Strength* for April, 1907, found in the Archive, there appeared the following advert:

'Friction Strap. For use wet or dry in or after a Turkish Bath or ordinary water bath. Made from the fibre of the Gourd. Cleanses and invigorates the skin and stimulates and promotes health.'

[Now, what sort of shop would you go to to buy something like that?]

The philosophy of the *Exmoor*

The *Exmoor* has been there for ages, and it doesn't look set to decline.
It's something we've all had to live with since 1859.
It's as permanent as the whole planet; it's as sure as the sea and the sky.
Yet have you ever considered the simple question: 'Why?'
The answer is simple as well, and it's obvious – look at the map.
Stuck out in the back end of nowhere – all those wide open spaces on tap.
They had very few sporting opponents to keep the testosterone down.
They had nowhere to go to be tempted; they never got into town.
A run was the perfect solution; it worked like a conjuror's spell.
The more you could wear out their muscles, the less likely they'd be to raise Hell.
The school became cross-county crazy. The *Exmoor* soon wasn't unique.
They cooked up fourteen more races. It felt that they had one each week.
Today we enjoy every comfort; in games we are spoilt for choice.
But one thing remains from the old days; the past retains one still, small voice.
The *Exmoor*'s our oldest tradition, and traditions are precious and rare.
You don't have to be soppy about it; just respect it because it is there.
It can still provide us with challenge, and challenge is good for the soul.
The Cleave and the Bray and the mudslide; the cowpat, the hedge, and the hole.
Don't forget, it's *supposed* to be daunting; it's *supposed* to be make or break.
Where's the pride in getting house colours if you know it's a piece of cake?
And perhaps there is this satisfaction: when other schools ask 'Who are you?'
You can say, 'We do something that you can't. The *Exmoor*, that's what we do.'
You're not sure as you stand on the start line. The most you can do is your best.
Don't think about falling or failing; take a very good look at the rest.
They're just as uncertain as you are. So say to yourself – on the sly,
'If some of these wimps here can do it, then, sure as Hell, so can I.'

The truth about the *Exmoor*

THERE IS A STORY that a recent survey has come up with the following replies to this question:

'Why did the school set up the *Exmoor*, and why, in these modern times, do they continue with it?'

'Search me.'
'In those days they were building an empire and had to find people to run it.'
'I presume it must have seemed a good idea at the time. Can't think why.'
'It only survives because the Child Abuse Brigade have not got around to it yet.'
'I sometimes wonder.'
'You wait till Brussels hears about it.'
'It illustrates, if further illustration were needed, that the teaching profession is riddled with sadists.'
'Only a nation like the English would have even thought of it, never mind set it up.'
'I understand that Mr. Putin is showing an interest in it as a means of getting to the bottom of the English character, so that he can hack into it. As far as I am concerned, he can hack away.'
'Would you like to see my blisters?'
'God knows what our foreign pupils must think of us.'
'At least it has nothing to do with the English worship of the ball.'
'It homes in on the idea that kids enjoy getting dirty.'
'If they knew what really went on out there, they'd stop it tomorrow.'
'I tell you, the Minister of Education should see this.'
'We ought to demonstrate about it.'
'Nobody can remember why, and they haven't thought of a good enough excuse yet to stop it.'
'It's going to make England great again.'
'If they left it out of the prospectus, it would do wonders.'
'Well, I like it. Must go. Here come the little men in white to take me away.'

Summing it up

WEST BUCKLAND COULD BE defined by a lot of things: education for ordinary people, remoteness, fresh air, rain, space, sport, sixty nationalities, respect for each other, the idea that everybody has something to offer. And more. But it is also defined, however sharedly, by the *Exmoor*. The school admits that it is not famous, rich, or fashionable, and nobody knows where it is, but it likes to cosset itself with the idea that no other school has a run quite like the *Exmoor*. (Not that anybody would be likely to want it.)

A few years ago I was in a Christmas-time conversation with a boy who had left in the July to go to university, and he came back to visit at the end of his first term. He had had the usual encounters and experiences you would expect for an eighteen-year-old newly away from home: meeting scores of new faces, tackling a specialist timetable for the first time – that he had chosen for himself, being responsible for organising his own life – morn to night.

So his responses were also what you would expect. He had no doubt foreseen most of them himself.

But one unexpected thing had stuck in his mind. Naturally, he had attended many freshmen meetings, and they had exchanged the usual questions, and in replies he was careful in his dealings with people who might be cleverer, richer, odder, or smarter than he was. He was concerned to be respectful to others, but to keep his own end up while he was doing it.

Inevitably, one boy said to him, 'What school do you come from?'

Now this is a bit of a googly to take first ball, because the average eighteen-year-old has barely heard of Barnstaple, never mind West Buckland.

Anyway, Joe bravely met the enemy head on, swallowed hard, and said, 'West Buckland'.

To his surprise, he was met not with raised eyebrows or glazed eyes or vacant expressions, but by a knowing tilt of the head.

'Oh, yes,' said his interlocutor. 'You're the school that has that run.'

THE END

Acknowledgements

As with the other four West Buckland books, I am once again grateful that the school has given me complete freedom in the handling, selection, editing, and presentation of the material herein, and has made no attempt to intervene in its composition. So the book is in no way, and is not intended to be, a reflection of school thought or policy.

Again, as with the other four books, I owe a great debt to Yvonne Reed, who has brought her sharp eye, common sense, and instinct for language to the supervision of the text. To regard what she does as merely putting in the missing letters is rather like thinking that teaching consists only of saying, 'Get out your text-books and do the next chapter.'

Mark Webb at Paragon Publishing has, as before, been interested, willing, prompt, and efficient.

I feel like a member of a good team.

www.ingramcontent.com/pod-product-compliance
Lightning Source LLC
Chambersburg PA
CBHW050555170426
43201CB00011B/1696